Nation, State and the Coexistence of Different Communities

Nation, State and the Coexistence of Different Communities

Theo van Willigenburg
Robert Heeger
Wibren van der Burg (eds.)

Proceedings of the 1994 Conference of the Societas Ethica – the European Society for Research in Ethics

Berekfürdö, Hungary, August 1994

Kok Pharos Publishing House – Kampen

CIP-GEGEVENS KONINKLIJKE BIBLIOTHEEK, DEN HAAG

© 1995, Kok Pharos Publishing House,
P.O. Box 5016, 8260 GA Kampen, The Netherlands
Cover Design by Rob Lucas
ISBN 90 390 0421 8
NUGI 631/619

Introduction

What is a nation? What makes a nation a relevant community in distinction to e.g. an ethnic group on the one hand, and the state on the other hand? Nations are to be distinguished from states for the obvious reason that a state may include more than one national group, and people sharing a common national identity may be found to be living under the auspices of two ore more states. But what does this common national identity involve? Why would the Sami who live in Norway, Sweden, Finland and Russia be considered a nation? Obviously, nationality is constituted by a set of shared beliefs about belonging and loyalty, common history and distinctive characteristics. But many of these beliefs are clearly mythical and based on an attempt to reconstruct some fictional common heritage. How could it be that individuals derive part of their identity from their belonging to a highly fictional community?

These are some of the questions which are addressed in the contributions to this volume. The rise of nationalism in Europe and the revival of patriotism in the United States has evoked a new interest in the meaning of national belonging. At the same time, the growing awareness of the identity of national, ethnic or cultural groups and the call for recognition of the distinctiveness of these groups, has raised questions about the duties of states to respect the integrity of minority cultures, which might involve the assignment of special rights to ethnic or cultural minorities. However, respecting the uniqueness and relative autonomy of a cultural group might involve a weakened immunity for individuals in that group. Fundamental human rights define a range of immunities and presumptions of uniform treatment. An ethnic/cultural group or nation may, however, define a conception of the individual or common good which conflicts with some of these personal immunities. How to respect, then, both group rights and individual rights? Are there collective rights which might be morally justifiable?

5

In addressing these questions, the papers in this volume are collected around two major themes: 'Identity and Belonging' and 'Collective Rights and the State'.

The issue of *identity and belonging* calls upon some major discussions between liberals and communitarians. In this volume there is an intriguing contribution to this discussion from an English scholar who reports on his participant observation and historical and social study of Scottish identity. And there is a colorful defense of the 'cosmopolitan' perspective by an American scholar, who reflects on the experiences of a migrant *par excellence* (Salman Rushdie), and argues that personal identity is not defined by one's location or ancestry or citizenship or language, because the allegiances and commitments of the modern individual are much more multiple and diverse. Personal identity, says the cosmopolitan, is in need of a variety of cultural frameworks, be they global or local. Obviously, this hardly leaves any special room for the nation as a substantive and sensible identity-conferring framework.

The issue of *collective rights and the state* touches on the complex discussion whether vulnerable cultural identities should be protected by assigning group rights to cultural communities (including the guarantee of an exit option for individuals in a group), or whether such an enterprise will show to be a hopeless wandering around in muddy waters. German and Dutch scholars in this volume are engaged in a fierce discussion on the meaning and implication of a right to cultural identity, and on the question how political theory should deal with the fact of multiculturalism. It is argued that the central position in political theory of the concept of the culturally homogeneous nation-state is one of the main obstacles for an adequate theoretical and practical approach of multiculturalism. In this volume, there is a Swiss plea to base political theories and practices not upon the nation-state as a homogeneous cultural/ethnic entity, but upon the state as a functional organization with a limited task (thus relinquishing the relation between nation and state). This accords with a more global or even cosmopolitan approach, which takes the world community as such as the political point of reference, and which considers states as having a mandate 'from mankind'.

The contributions to this volume form a selection of original papers discussed during the 1994 Conference of the *Societas Ethica*, the European Society for Research in Ethics. This conference was held in August 1994, in Berekfürdö, Hungary – a topical place for a conference on this theme. The editors are happy to be able to include in this volume also the resourceful essay of Jeremy Waldron on cosmopolitanism which originally appeared in the *University of Michigan Journal of Law Reform*, and which was deliberately added to the set of papers discussed during the conference. The two concluding articles were specially written for this volume.

Special thanks are due to Reint Sekhuis, philosophy student at Utrecht University, for his editorial assistance.

Utrecht, June 1995

Theo van Willigenburg
Robert Heeger
Wibren van der Burg

Contents

Culture, Nation, State

Robert Heeger

1. The Problem

'National' and 'nationalistic' are loaded words for many people. Nevertheless they are emerging again, and tend to appear quite frequently in news bulletins, for instance. This is not merely related to the dissolution of the Iron Curtain, nor does it concern Central and Southeastern Europe only. We learn that some national states are oppressing ethnic minorities. We have to take note that there are radical nationalistic currents, which can ignite conflicts of unimagined proportions. We hear that in many places people are becoming conscious of their national identities, fearing to lose their own achievements as a result of European or global integration, etc. Attempts to assess such phenomena morally are frequently thwarted by a conceptual problem: when something is called 'national' or 'nationalistic', what exactly is meant by that, and what exactly is the point?

It is certainly possible to pass spontaneous moral judgements without addressing this problem. For example, a person may spontaneously disapprove of oppression of an ethnic minority. Such disapproval does not require profound study into the sense or significance of the term 'nation' or other, related terms. For a well-considered moral judgement, however, a different approach may be required. Such moral judgements differ from spontaneous ones by the fact that they can stand up to criticism; criticism based on relevant facts. If one's view of the way in which a nation should treat an ethnic minority (to continue with our example) is to be well-considered rather than spontaneous, the question arises what 'nation' and an 'ethnic minority' ('nationality', 'ethnic group') exactly mean, and whether their definitions have any consequences for our view of the relationship between these entities and between them and the state.

Obviously, there is a point in addressing this conceptual problem. We shall do so briefly by considering the following question: to what extent can the term 'nation' be understood to refer to a community that can be distinguished not only from the state but also from an ethnic group?

2. Nation and State

Unfortunately, there is no simple answer to our conceptual question that would solve all the related problems. The main reason is that no definition is available that would enable us to state unambiguously and objectively whether we are dealing with a nation or not. All sorts of objective criteria have been advanced – political, cultural, ethnic, etc. – but none is universally applicable. This is not surprising, for the current picture associated with a 'nation' contains contradicting elements and can be traced to very different sources.[1]

If we are to find an acceptable solution to our problem, we will have to take the main contrastive tenets into account, which are evident from a widely accepted distinction between two nation concepts. We are to distinguish between a 'state nation' (Staatsnation) and a 'cultural nation' (Kulturnation), between a 'West-European, subjective' and a 'Central and East-European, objective' nation concept or between a 'revolutionary' and a 'romantic' nation concept. Although the names are different, the distinction is more or less the same. Since this distinction emphasizes the contrasts between the various nation concepts, it also helps to clarify the connotation and denotation of the concept of nation and will therefore be used in the formulation of proposals towards solving our problem. It is important to realize that this problem consists of three constituent problems, namely whether or not a 'nation' is meant to refer to a community, whether or not a 'nation' can be distinguished from the state and whether or not it can be distinguished from an ethnic group. For the sake of simplicity we shall start with the second question and use the terms 'state nation' and 'cultural nation', which can be traced back to Meinecke.[2]

12

The following simple outline may help to answer our question.

The concept of 'state nation' focuses on the internationally recognized organization of a sovereign state. The state is equal to the nation, the state's people (Staatsvolk). Within the state there can be various nationalities or ethnic groups, yet these collectively constitute the state nation. For decades this has been the way in which the political behaviour of West-European nations, e.g. of the French, English and Dutch, has been described. Nowadays, in English and international usage, 'nation' and 'state' often mean the same. Think, for instance, of the 'United Nations'.

The concept of 'cultural nation', in contrast, concerns nationalities, peoples and ethnic groups, which are bound together in the first place by a common culture and which lack the internationally recognized organization of a sovereign state. Here 'nationality' is not defined by citizenship, but by ethnic belonging, ethnic descent, language, religion and common history. 'Cultural nation' was the term used to describe the political behaviour of the peoples of Central Europe, e.g. the Germans, Italians, Poles and Austrians. A cultural nation can reach beyond the borders of a single state. It is also possible that various cultural nations live together in one state.[3]

It is evident that we are dealing with two different nation concepts. We think about the nation either in terms of a state or of a particular culture. In the case of the latter, it can be distinguished from the state; in the case of the former, it cannot. Here we have our first answer. If a nation is to be distinguished from a state, the concept of the cultural nation can do good service. However, this in itself does not sufficiently clarify the relation between cultural nation and state. We need further arguments, some of which are presented below.

3. Nation as a Community

Can a nation be understood to be a community? This depends first and foremost on the extent to which we are prepared to regard a social entity as a community at all. The term community is sometimes subject to such narrow definitions that it cannot possibly coincide with the term nation. A social entity is a community, for example, only if its members are a face-to-face group based on personal acquaintance and direct practices of mutual aid, or if they are linked in some sort of fraternity. If 'community' is defined as narrowly as this, only entities such as the traditional family or village can be communities. It can be argued, however, that 'community' can also have a wider meaning, in which case the question whether a nation can be a community does not necessarily have to be answered in the negative.[4] It has, then, still to be established how broad the term 'community' is to be taken.

If one concedes this, it is worthwhile to investigate the differences between a state nation and a cultural nation a bit more closely. Above we pointed out that the concept of the state nation focuses on the sovereign state, whereas the state plays no role in the cultural nation. This becomes vivid if we have a look at the contexts in which these nation concepts evolved in the 18th century. The concept of the state nation developed within the context of the already existing state. The French autocrats had brought about a process of modernization and rationalization. The concept of the state nation was put forward for the sake of emancipation and democratization and was directed against the sovereigns and the social order of absolutism. It was introduced to legitimize the claim for collective self-determination by free and equal citizens. To this end, the 'nation' was defined as the 'union of those who are subject to the same law and are represented by the same legislative assembly'.[5]

The concept of the cultural nation did not originate within the context of the already existing state, but in spiritual currents which directed their attention to the authentic lifestyle and culture of a people or of an ethnic group. It was put forward mainly in Germany, but also elsewhere, in order to lend weight to claims for separate nation states. Aspects such as common culture, language and history were used to support these claims.

If one pays attention to the context in which these nation concepts

14

evolved, it becomes clear that 'state nation' is a political and 'cultural nation' a pre-political concept. If one, moreover, is aware of the fact that 'state nation' has to be understood in terms of a social contract, then some differences between the two concepts become visible which are relevant to the question whether or not a nation is a community.

Firstly there is the difference between self-determination and predetermination. From the political perspective, an individual's membership of a nation is a matter of self-determination: it is the will, the consent, the free choice of living together, as well as mutual respect, which turn a group of individuals into a nation. Belonging, however, which is central to the pre-political concept, is governed by predetermination: an individual simply finds himself part of a nation, being born into it. It is to be accepted, whether he likes it or not.

Secondly there is the difference between universalism and particularism. From the political perspective, a nation is a free union of individuals, that is of all who sign the conditions in the social contract, who agree to the constitution, to the universal principles of the democratic constitutional state. From the pre-political perspective, a nation is not an artificial union but an all-encompassing spiritual bond which unites its members through language, culture and history, and which constitutes the basis for all contracts and unions.

Thirdly there is the difference between openness and limitation. From the political perspective, a nation cannot have a natural border. The borders of a nation reach as far as the principles of the social contract are subscribed to. Not only the individual who speaks our language, is born here or descends from us is admitted to the nation, but everyone who subscribes to its principles. The nation is an open society. If they reject the agreements of the social contract, individuals can also lose or give up their nationality. From the pre-political perspective, however, a nation is credited with natural boundaries. There are objective criteria such as language, descent and culture which define the borders of a nation. Losing or rejecting one's nationality is as impossible as rejecting the membership of one's family.

Fourthly there is the difference between the abstract and the concrete interpretations of the individual. From the political perspective, 'I' and the others within the nation are abstract, rational and anonymous individuals who have signed a contract. They do not have any strong links with a specific tradition or culture, but are mere representatives of the human race. They are abstract beings, unmarked by any individual factuality, contingency or finiteness. From the pre-political perspective, the individual is a social being which cannot be imagined without its factuality, contingency or finiteness, as his identity is fully determined by the particularity of his culture and by his belonging to the nation as a social environment which concerns him in all his being.

If we accept this contrastive approach[6], we can answer the question whether or not a nation is a community. From the *political* perspective, a nation is a living together which is the result of *free self-determination* of *abstract* and rational individuals, which is characterized by conformity to the *universal* principles of the democratic constitutional state, and which is open in the sense that, while it does recognize political-moral borders, it lacks natural borders such as those defined by language and descent. Can such an entity be seen as a community? On the one hand it can, in that all its members live voluntarily by the universal principles of the democratic constitutional state, and are represented by the same legislative assembly. If we regard mutual acceptance of obligations as a condition for a group to call itself a community, we see that this at least is a condition which the political interpretation of the nation can meet.

On the other hand it cannot, on account of its degree of abstraction. It lacks every reference to such natural facts as a common history, a specific way of life or the awareness of a bond. If these factors are regarded as prerequisite ingredients in the definition of 'community', a political nation cannot be a community.

In the *pre-political* perspective, a nation is the all-encompassing spiritual bond, which keeps all individuals of the same language, culture and history together, which *determines* their individuality, whether they like it or not, and which provides the *concrete* individuals within this system with their identity through a sense of togetherness. This bond is *particular* because of the individuality of the language, culture and history of the group, and has a natural *border*. Can such an entity be called a 'community'?

On the one hand it can, in that its members are linked to each other by language, culture and history, even if most of them do not even know each other by face. This broad interpretation of the concept of community seems justifiable.

The pre-political nation cannot, however, be seen as a community in the light of the assumed total determination of the individual by the nation. This objection does not concern the fact that the pre-political view of a nation postulates constitutive attachments which are not voluntarily acquired. It emphasizes something else. A community requires mutual acceptance of obligations, and should therefore include the freedom of the individual to critically consider the natural facts of his particular environment: to admit them, to regard them as meaningful, to refuse them or to withdraw from them. The assumed total determination of the individual by the nation deprives him of this freedom. This means that there can be no mutual acceptance of obligations either. We therefore propose to leave out the notion of *total* determination of the individual by his social environment. On this condition, a pre-political nation be considered a community.

4. Nation and Ethnic Group

Can one distinguish a nation from an ethnic group? This question seems to be important especially in the context of the cultural nation. Above we proposed that a cultural nation can be considered a community. However, this in itself does not distinguish it from an ethnic group, since an ethnic group, too, can be a community. We can speak of an 'ethnic community', for example, as a 'particular people sharing a heritage of custom, ritual, and way of life that is in some real or imagined sense immemorial, being referred back to a shared history and shared provenance or homeland'.[7] Are we then to assume that a cultural nation is the same as an ethnic community? In many recent attempts to define the nation concept, the answer is no. A specific consciousness and political claims have been presented as distinguishing features of a nation, as in the following quote: 'Essential features of the nation are the consciousness of a social group (people) of being a nation or wishing to be one, and the claim for political self-determination'.[8]

What these claims exactly comprise, however, varies from author to author. For us it is important to distinguish between the more modest and the stronger claims. We emphasize this difference since it points to an important aspect in the concept of the 'cultural nation'.
Let us first state some examples of the rather modest demands. National minorities are to be distinguished from ethnic ones because they have a 'collective consciousness and furthermore (...) the will to collectively exert those rights that enable them to participate in the political decision-making process, either on a national or a regional level'.[9] The members of a nation typically have 'shared beliefs' – about belonging together, about their long history of living together, about special characteristics shared by all members which make the group different from others, about the loyalty of every individual towards the community – as well as the conviction that the group enjoys 'some degree of political autonomy'; because 'a social group that had no political aspirations at all would surely be counted as an ethnic group rather than as a nation'.[10] National minorities are nations in the sense of 'historical communities' – with a common language and culture – which, while falling within the boundaries of a larger political whole, 'claim the right to govern themselves in certain key matters'. What they want is the transfer of power and legislative jurisdictions from the central government to their own communities'.[11]

But there are also stronger demands, which the following examples serve to illustrate. A nation is an entity that has become conscious of 'its mutual ties and its particular interests (...). It presents a claim for political self-determination or has already realized this claim within a nation state'.[12] A nation is 'a society which, by virtue of its common historic descent, forms a community of collective political will' and sees itself 'as a community of solidarity'. It is dependent on a basic

18

consensus in its political culture (...). Its most important goal is to gain full responsibility for the formation of its own living conditions and to achieve political self-government (sovereignty) within its territory, a nation state of its own.[13]

In these 'stronger demands', political consciousness and political claims are aimed at the realization of an independent state. The group does not need to have realized such a state in order to call itself a nation, but it must be its goal. This collective formation of will is what transforms a population into a nation. The more modest claims, too, presuppose the presence of political aspirations for a community to call itself a 'nation'. However, this community can resign itself to 'some degree of political autonomy' and does not need to be focused on a state of its own.

These diverging answers to the question of what distinguishes a nation from an ethnic group point to an important aspect in the concept of the cultural nation, concerning the relationship between cultural nation and state. The concept of the cultural nation was once put forward to lend weight to the claim for an independent nation state. The 'cultural nation' was mostly understood as such: as a pre-political community, whose growing insight into its individual nature and collective formation of will call for the foundation of an independent nation state. The borders of this state coincide with the borders of the nation, and the nation is the basis of the state. We are dealing here with a 'nationalistic' concept.[14] From this perspective, a 'political' unity develops from the 'pre-political' community. However, we can now conclude that this is not the only possible relationship between the cultural nation and the state. The term 'cultural nation' can also be meaningful in cases where there has been no claim for the formation of an independent nation state. It is important to note that the term 'nation' thereby has not been reduced to an ethnic group which only keeps itself busy with 'care for culture' (Kulturpflege), since the pre-political community of a cultural nation – according to the above-mentioned modest claims – asserts at least 'some degree of political autonomy'.

We hope to have made clear that a cultural nation can be distinguished from an ethnic group. The discrepancy between the strong and modest claims is related to the subquestion *by what* a nation distinguishes itself more specifically from an ethnic group.

As for the state nation, the question whether this entity can be distinguished from an ethnic group does not appear to be very interesting. If the state nation is interpreted in terms of the social contract, the answer is yes without any need for further details. One does not *belong* to a nation, for example because one has French parents or because one speaks French, but one *becomes* Frenchman by one's free consent to the universal principles of the constitution. However, this is not all there is to say about the state nation. If the obstinate reality of a society is to be disciplined, the basic and abstract concept of the state nation must be made more concrete. To give two significant examples: what keeps the residents of a country together as citizens of a state? Is it their agreement concerning the principles of justice, or is it more than that?[15] What generates the indispensable loyalty to the government among citizens in a democratic state, and what makes them regard this government as legitimate?[16] Such prerequisites for stability and exertion of power call for more than the universal and abstract principles of the social contract.

The concept of the state nation, too, calls for attempts to form a 'political community', a 'common identity', the collective convictions which characterize a cultural nation.[17] The strength of these calls is probably dependent on the extent of centralism of the state, on the degree of state interference in the life of the people, on the need for citizens' loyalty and homogeneity and on the pluriformity of the population. We know that national states strive to transform residents in a state into citizens of a nation, by applying a 'pedagogy of nationalities'.[18] This is illustrated, for example, by the behaviour of European states in the second half of the previous century. Sometimes existing convictions of one or more ethnic groups are used in the formation of a nation. Conversely, attempts can be made to transform a population into one ethnic group, an ethnically unified people of a

20

state. This is a 'nationalistic' concept of the state nation. Such a 'manufactured nation' primarily distinguishes itself from an ethnic group by the fact that this nation is created with state instruments.

5. Summary and Prospect

Considered moral judgements about phenomena which carry the labels 'national' or 'nationalistic' often present a conceptual problem: what is the term 'nation' understood to mean? We specified this problem into a three-part question: is a 'nation' a community? Can it be distinguished from the state? Can it be distinguished from a single ethnic group? We attempted to answer this question by means of a contrastive discussion of nation concepts such as state nation (Staatsnation) versus cultural nation (Kulturnation). We have found that a nation *can* be a community. The pre-political cultural nation can be seen as community, provided that the notion of total determination of the individual by the nation is not included. The members of a cultural nation are linked by language, culture and history and collectively claim 'some degree of political autonomy'. By this claim such a community can be distinguished from an ethnic group. The cultural nation can also be distinguished from the state, since the community of a cultural nation does not need to be defined as a state people, nor does it need to be directed by a collective formation of will towards the construction of a nation state of its own, of a state whose borders coincide with the borders of the cultural nation.

Should we now think of the term 'nation' in the same light? It seems justified to regard the cultural nation as a relevant entity. But should we reserve the term 'nation' for this community, or should we also use it to refer to the concept of the state nation? This is not merely a question of terminology. In our view, the choice of the right term above all depends on whether another term can be found for the most important features of the state nation concept: the collective self-determination of free and equal citizens, the universal principles of the democratic constitutional state and the common political culture of its citizens, which holds the citizens together and makes them loyal

21

towards the state. We might consider using the term 'active citizenship' for this.[19] If we do, we should be able to account for the abovementioned features of the state nation within a theory of active citizenship, because 'we cannot go back beyond' the achievements of the democratic constitutional state. They are too important for us from a moral point of view, and sometimes call for an adjustment of our view of the cultural nation. Within a single state there can be several communities which merit the term 'cultural nation'.

While the individual can feel 'at home' in his own community and the community can have some degree of independence, this should not lead the community to develop into a prison for the individual, or to set itself apart from other communities or prevent smaller communities from asserting their rights. At this point the state should be a guardian of openness and of pluralism. Moreover, many major problems in a modern society pose tasks in the fields of education, economy, science and technology, security or the environment which can only be solved on a higher level. If these tasks are to be dealt with successfully by the entire society and the state, a common political culture and a certain degree of 'homogenization' of its citizens are indispensable. But the communality of active citizens can also be an important feature of society in its own right. It can create a net of valuable social relations. It can even be advisable, for the sake of this communality, to sacrifice part of one's own 'culture-related national' identity – in a well-balanced accommodation.[20]

Notes

1. See for the history of the term RITTER, J. & GRÜNDER, K. (ed.), *Historisches Wörterbuch der Philosophie*, vol. 6, Basel und Stuttgart 1984, pp. 406-414
2. MEINECKE, F., *Weltbürgertum und Nationalstaat. Studien zur Genesis des deutschen Nationalstaates*, München und Berlin 1908
3. SCHWARZ, J., *Die nationale Frage in der internationalen Politik und die Sicht des Völkerrechts*, in: GABRIEL, I. (ed.), *Minderheiten und nationale Frage*, Wien 1993, pp. 109-131, 115-118
4. This is put forward in the confrontation between communitarians and liberals by MILLER, D., *The Ethical Significance of Nationality*, in: *Ethics* 98 (1988), pp. 647-662, 654, and idem, *Community and Citizenship*, in: AVINERI, S. and A. DE-SHALIT (eds.), *Communitarianism and Individualism*, Oxford 1992, pp. 85-100, 100
5. Thus SIEYES, E., *Qu'est-ce que le Tiers état?* Edition critique avec une introduction et des notes par R. ZAPPERI, Genève 1970, p. 126
6. It relies above all on expositions in MEINECKE, R., *Weltbürgertum und Nationalstaat*, München 1969, and PUTTE, A. VAN DE, *Nationalisme en naties*, in: *Tijdschrift voor Filosofie* 55 (1993), pp. 13-47
7. WALDRON, J., *Minority Cultures and the Cosmopolitan Alternative*, in: *University of Michigan Journal of Law Reform* 25 (1992), pp. 751-793, reprinted in this volume, Ch. 1
8. ALTER, P., *Nationalismus*, Frankfurt a. M. 1985, p. 23
9. ERMACORA, F., *Der Minderheitenschutz im Rahmen der Vereinten Nationen*, Wien 1988, cited and reviewed by RÖPER, M., *Das Problem der Definition des Begriffes Minderheit*, in: GABRIEL, pp. 81-88
10. MILLER 1988, p. 648
11. KYMLICKA, W. & NORMAN, W., *Return of the Citizen: A Survey of Recent Work on Citizenship Theory*, in: *Ethics* 104 (1994), pp. 352-381, 372
12. ALTER, op.cit.
13. DANN, O., *Nation und Nationalismus in Deutschland 1770-1990*, München 1993, p. 12
14. GELLNER, E., *Nations and Nationalism*, Oxford 1984, p. 1
15. See e.g. KYMLICKA & NORMAN, pp. 376-377
16. See e.g. PUTTE, VAN DE, p. 37
17. See e.g. MILLER 1988, p. 654, 657
18. See e.g. RODE, F., *Kirche, Nationalitäten und nationale Minderheiten*, in: GABRIEL, pp. 37-47, 37
19. See for that e.g. KYMLICKA & NORMAN, pp. 352-353

20. With regard to the morally well-balanced accommodation, see WONG, D. B., *Coping with Moral Conflict and Ambiguity*, in: *Ethics* 102 (1992), pp. 763-784, 777-779

Identity and Belonging:
National Resurgence as Ethical Problem

Richard Roberts

1. Introduction: the Problematics of Identity

Nationality and nationalism (Anderson 1983, 1991; Brah 1994; Brass 1991; Gellner 1983, 1987; Hobsbawm 1991; Mews 1982; Smith 1991b) are important components in the analysis of the ethical problems involved in the co-existence of different communities, not least because many individuals derive part of their identity from the national group to which they belong. However, this relation between identity and national belonging is not easy to understand. Identity as manifested in modernity (Beck 1992; Berman 1982; Giddens 1989, 1990, 1990; Lash and Friedman 1992; Luhmann 1990, 1992; Touraine 1994) seems to be predominantly a personal or individualized identity, and not identity as determined by a predetermined role within a given social order.[1] In modernity, when as Karl Marx observed, all that is solid tends to melt, social groups are determined by the division of labour and stratification. In postmodernity (Bauman 1992; Charles 1990; Gellner 1992; Harvey 1989; Lyotard 1984), these latter, functional sureties may also enter into a state of flux. Under the conditions of the globalization of culture and values (Featherstone 1990; Robertson), human identity tends – paradoxically – to become more individualized (Ester, Halman and de Moor 1994; Harding, Phillips and Fogerty 1986; Inglehart 1977, 1990; Klages 1985; Reich and Adcock 1976; Rokeach 1968). After the "end of ideology" (Bell 1960) and the "End of History" (Fukuyama, 1989) the striving of each after an ideal of originality or authenticity, an original way of being human, is further stimulated. Individuals and communities are trapped between contradictory and conflicting forces driving towards uniformity and differentiation.

In an era which succeeds both the security of the pre-modern ancestral hierarchy, which disappears with modernization, and the relative stability derived from the modern solidarities of class and function, personal identity becomes highly vulnerable (Giddens, 1991). Extraordinary burdens are placed on the individual and identity is at least in part formed through interaction with others who matter to us, indeed we seek out what Janina Bauman has aptly termed "pockets of identity" (Bauman, J. 1988). However, human identity needs, and is vulnerable to, the recognition of our authenticity and dignity and this may be given or withheld by those significant others. In the intimate sphere, and in the sphere of ethnic, religious, and/or cultural groups, personal identity seems to be closely connected to *belonging*. How, in what sense, and to what degree does belonging to a national group meet these needs for identity through recognition? Again, in what sense and to what extent may our personal identity depend on our belonging to a nation group? Comprehension of such identity formation demands an understanding of the nature of contemporary resurgent nationalism and its impact upon social and cultural identity.

It is our contention that this process of recognition is more problematic and risk-fraught than might appear at first to be the case. Our contention is that the dynamics of "recognition" and "belonging" thus understood constitute an inherently dangerous circumstance, which involves dialectical conceptions of culture that are both unstable and absolutist in tendency. Moreover, we maintain that such cultural processes are profoundly inimical to universalist liberalism. In order to illustrate these difficulties, in this paper we explore them through a case study of the cultural roots of the twentieth century Scottish attempt to re-emphasize difference and transform cultural identity into effective political agency and ultimately full national autonomy (Beveridge and Turnbull 1889; Crisk 1991; Foster 1989; Gallagher 1991; Harvie 1977, 1989/91, 1992; Lynch 1991; McCrone 1989, 1992; Smout 1969, 1977; Storrar 1990, Underwood 1970).

Central to this case study is the twentieth century "Scottish renaissance" in poetry, literature and cultural specificity. This is a movement largely inspired and motivated by the poet Hugh MacDiarmid (born Christopher Murray Grieve, 1892-1978), whose efforts (Bold 1990; Scott and Daiches 1980; Glen 1972) were directed at nothing less than the re-creation of a culture which could both serve the requirements of national identity and energize the drive towards national independence. MacDiarmid's dialectical Promethean idea of culture draws ambiguously upon religious roots, thus also illustrating the contention that nationalism itself may exercise a quasi-religious role in the modern world.

Moreover, this representative example shows that "identity as belonging" inevitably involves *difference* and *not belonging*. Indeed, the idea of a "culture" as the basis of identity (De Levita 1965; Hobsbawm 1991; Mol 1976, 1978; Krober and Kluckhohn 1963; MacDonald 1993; Robbins 1982; Wheelis 1958) may present itself in terms of an ultimacy that transcends attempts to ground intercommunal ethics and the co-existence of communities in universal principles of mutual recognition. Such ethics would imply a conditioning, a limitation of the claims of cultural identity. Yet our example will show that the definitions of "culture" exploited in the resurgence of national identity imply a potent engagement with absolutes. An adequate response to the latter may involve recourse not merely to abstract universalist principles, but also imply the need for a comprehensive sense of human commonality. The latter implies the actualization of means of societal binding together; perhaps only forms of *religion* grounded in transcendental principles may prove in principle capable of relativising the absolutes involved in nationalist cultural revivalism. In other words, this would imply a contrast between an in-part religiously-derived national cultural identity and a civil religion committed to universal human values. This tension is now apparent in present-day Scottish experience. Indeed, in terms of our genealogical example, we find that another Scottish (but also Orcadian) poet Edwin Muir (1887-1959) also represents the universalist (and in his case a religious) response to national cultural absolutism. Edwin Muir and his wife Willa rejected the extremity of MacDiarmid and his immediate circle (Muir, E. 1954; Muir, W. 1968). The Muirs grounded their identity, and indeed their highly self-conscious sense of "belonging", not only in place, but also in Christianity and a cosmic personalism, respectively. On this basis we shall contend apparent that both the ethics of the co-existence of different communities and the co-existence of individuals and different groups within communities demands the redefinition of the distinction between the ethical *ultimate* and the cultural *penultimate*, a distinction which cannot, paradoxically, be sustained by liberalism alone.[2]

In attempting to come to terms with the theme of the co-existence of different communities we do not merely confront issues of painful immediacy but also a problematic of great intrinsic complexity. In effect, we are working simultaneously at the leading edge of events and the cutting edge of social theory – this is an uncomfortable position to be in, even if as ethicists we operate from, as it were, the proverbial armchair or as *Kathederphilosophen* (McBride 1994). For many of us, and this writer included, the issues raised are not merely academic, they are self-involving and existential, and thus the more difficult to confront with unsparing rigor and objectivity.

Some of us may also, I suspect, know what it is like to experience the testing that comes about when an individual's identity is judged – and perhaps found wanting – for reasons which lie way beyond the particularities of his or her own self-image and self-understanding. This societal response may involve reactions that occasion resonance and dissonance at the most fundamental level between the identity of the individual and that of the wider community, thus rupturing that mutual recognition, which Charles Taylor rightly regards as the foundation of healthy selfhood and identity. We might well take Taylor's understanding of this mutual dialogic selfhood as the basis of an ethical *ideal*, in relation to which the selfhoods of national and cultural identity may be judged. Human life is not, according to Taylor, monological (what we might call the equivalent of a private language), and in order to understand the close connection between identity and recognition, we must take into account his view that:

This crucial feature of human life is its fundamentally *dialogical* character. We become full human agents, capable of understanding ourselves, and hence of defining our identity, through our acquisition of rich human languages of expression. For my purposes here, I want to take *language* in a broad sense, covering not only the words we speak, but also other modes of expression whereby we define ourselves, including the 'languages' of art, of gesture, of love, and the like. But we learn these modes of expression through exchanges with others. People do not acquire the languages of self-definition on their own. Rather, we are introduced to them through interaction with others who matter to us – what George Herbert Mead called "significant others". The genesis of the human mind is in this sense not monological, not something each person accomplishes on his or her own, but dialogical (Taylor 1992: p. 32).

As a humane optimist, Charles Taylor assumes the acceptance of the dialogic mode in the formation of community. When, however, identity *dissonance* becomes too marked, then individual torment may become societal disruption, failure of community – and violence; this happens when exclusion of the *Other* is perceived as the *condition* of the integrity of one identity at the expense of that other. In such contexts, half-latent folk memories, ideologies, and prejudices deeply embedded – even seemingly buried – in the societal unconscious may undergo resurgence and release forces which may well overwhelm both mind and feelings, not least of those trained in liberal thought and encouraged to trust in the capacities of human reason, the *sensus communis* and the potency of the common good.

Cultural Identity and the transvaluation of particulars
In approaching the topic of "identity as belonging" we shall regard the following proposition as an axiom: that at the root of the contemporary identity problematic there is the transvaluation of the contextual *particular* from the status of relative contingency to its assimilation into a *cultural transcendental*, which may in turn conflict with the drive towards the *ethical universal*. In other words, if we radicalize David Miller's (1988) observations concerning the ethical significance of

nationality, then we can conceive of situations in which the formulation of ethics and the conduct of human relations becomes secondary to the prioritisation of cultural factors that determine the nature and limits of ethical and humane response (Almond 1983; Avineri and de-Shalit 1992; Gellner 1987; Gibbins 1989; Hanf 1994). The topic of "identity as belonging" obliges us to confront the dynamics of identity formation which appear at the same time to make the *inclusion* of the one in *recognition* and thus *belonging* the inevitable *exclusion* and failure of recognition and the explicit *not belonging* of the other (Jones 1978). Taylor recognizes this ambiguity between recognition and non-recognition and belonging and non-belonging when he argues that, "We define our identity always in dialogue with, sometimes in struggle against, the things our significant others want to see in us" (Taylor, 1992: 32-3). Thus the very act of subsuming the particularities of any resurgent identity under the rubric of the universal of nation or ethnic collectivity may block both dialogue and analysis from the outset. Taylor weakens his treatment of the ambiguity by retreating from the Hegelian image of a dialectically related Lord and Bondsman. Because of his relatively gentle approach we therefore have to devise a procedure which comprises both the recognition implicit in dialogue and the means of approaching the *denial* of recognition and belonging in identity formation. This is in addition to allowing for the irreducible and dialectical complexity of any given context in which conflict is latent and endemic.

One of the most striking features of the new problematic that arises after the "end of ideology" – and even more recently beyond the so-called "End of History" – is the resurgence of cultural particularity. Ester, Halman and de Moor (1994) have tried to explain this resurgence as a response to the alienation and anomie associated with the cultural homogenization of globalization. Others have related the renewal of cultural differentiation to economic crisis and to postmodernisation. Whatever the precise aetiology may be, cultural factors can no longer be regarded as having an epiphenomenal status.

Given the reality of the renewed importance of cultural particularity (for whatever reasons), the most effective ways of rendering this visible is to begin each analysis with a case study. The recognition through which the underlying features of identity are expressed is not merely to be reduced to myths of origin grounded in often wayward interpretations of history, but in continuing and ever renewed stories or narratives of identity (Banton 1988; Hobsbawm and Ranger 1983; MacIntyre 1990; Maffesoli 1994; Miller 1988; Pye 1973; Roosens 1989; Smith, A. 1976; Smith A.D. 1991a, 1991b; Solles 1989; Zwerblowsky 1976). Seen in this way, examination of narratives of identity may permit us to use tools of socio-cultural analysis apposite to a new era. Those who struggle with the post-Marxian deficit of good theory, that is of *meta-theory* capable of serving as the basis of social ethics, will be aware that the problem of co-existence of communities in an era of the crisis of national and cultural identity involves a wide array of factors. These do not fit the theoretical parameters which many of us, I dare to suggest, were originally equipped.

On the basis of the assumption that the cultural particular tends to overwhelm the ethical universal and through reification may itself strive for the status of transcendental principle of inclusion and exclusion, we begin with the meta-narrative expressed most powerfully in twentieth century Scottish poetics. In order, however, to make conflict visible, I implicitly propose to go where Taylor points, but does not himself venture, that is in the direction of an admission of a dialectical and conflictual conception of identity-formation.[3] Such a strategy does involve, of course, the theorization of what in terms of both sources is relatively undeveloped. Our thesis is, however, as follows: the cultural/national identity problematic involves conflict as embedded in narratives of identity, and as what Taylor terms "rich human languages of expression" it invites dialogic and dialectical interpretation. Such an approach implies, but does not necessarily articulate, other dimensions which we relegate to subtext status.

2. Recognition, Belonging and Identity: the Case of Scotland

Scotland has a population of under six million and thus this comprises less than one tenth of that of the United Kingdom. In constitutional terms, the Union of the Crowns in 1603 and the Act of Union of 1707 that conveyed political sovereignty from Edinburgh to Westminster eventually brought to an end centuries of warfare and political strife. Whilst the historical interpretation of these events is not surprisingly a matter of dispute, the partial integration of Scotland was not a matter of straightforward conquest, but to a considerable degree a self-imposed act (McCrone 1989; Lynch 1991; Smout 1969, 1977). Distinct legal and educational systems were retained and likewise the Scottish Church guarded its autonomy. Deep internal differences within Scotland over the nature of Scottish identity and the best future of a country in need of "improvement" and the benefits of "polite society" were resolved in the direction of anglicization, above all in the late eighteenth century and the Scottish Enlightenment (Broadie 1990; Chitnis 1976; Davie 1991; Grave 1960; Lynch 1991; MacIntyre 1981, 1988; Rendell 1978; Smith, Adam 1723/1790/1976; Smith, Adam 1776/1976; Smout 1969). The direction that Scottish identity should take remains a deeply contentious issue.

It is evident that there are acute dissonances within the contemporary resurgence of national consciousness in Scotland. These stem from a variety of sources: historical, political, cultural and religious. The singular and composite identities of Scotland (preserved, certainly at the level of social representations, in a remarkable way) embody a history of waves of migration, the decisive elimination of the Picts by Irish Scots, a primordial split between the Highland Gaeldom and the Lowland Scots, intense internal dynastic and clan wars, the conflict with England, an extremely violent and divisive Reformation (the long term consequences of which still persist), the Highland Clearances, and mass emigration on a very considerable relative scale. The highly effective nineteenth and early twentieth participation of Scotland with England in British imperialism has not prevented an sense of self-questioning, provoked by what contemporary cultural nationalists (applying the ideas of Paulo Freire to Scotland) regard as an imputed "inferiorism", a failure of national self-confidence. Scotland is now perceived, in the words of the distinguished Scottish sociologist David

McCrone, as a "stateless nation" (McCrone 1992). In an era of the continuing economic and political decline of Britain, the attractions of integration correspondingly decrease and the possible gains that might accrue from separation become more tempting. This said, the question of independence has been politically embodied since the founding of the Scottish Nationalist Party in 1928. The basis for this eventuality is, however, grounded in an enhanced sense of Scottish cultural "recognition" and "belonging" which was driven forward throughout the mid-century above all by such figures as the poet MacDiarmid. The Scottish cultural revival continues in a new generation of writers (Beverdieg and Turnbull, 1989).

The crisis in contemporary Scottish cultural identity is intimately associated with the crisis of modernity/ism and rise of Scottish nationalism in course of the twentieth century. The self-conscious development of "synthetic Scots" and the cultural re-functioning of "the infinite" by the poet Hugh MacDiarmid as a means of meeting this crisis is a prime example of the "invention of tradition", comparable with other attempts to emphasize cultural difference and ethnic identity in the history of nationalism, defined here following Anthony Smith, as:

> an ideological movement for attaining and maintaining autonomy, unity and identity on behalf of a population deemed by some of its members to constitute an actual or potential "nation" (A.D. Smith 1991: p. 73).

The prime indicators of cultural identity, most notably of those operating on the level of language and an elite literary revival, have undergone a process of revitalization.[4]

3. MacDiarmid and Muir: the Poetics of Identity

Thus, as we shall see, the prime architect of the renewal of twentieth century Scottish cultural identity, the poet Hugh MacDiarmid, urged an encounter with the societal – even the racial unconscious. His declamatory dialogue with language, history and a social particularity simultaneously involved the repeated rejection of an at the same time potent yet impotent Other, *Englishness* in all its forms. Indeed, such a writer understood in his context provokes the question: can there ever be real cultural identity without a primal negative and destructive *difference*? Thus MacDiarmid believed in a personal and universal destiny which involved remaking the distinction between Scottish and "British" (that is to say a falsely generalized *English*) cultural identity:

The British are a frustrated people
Victims of arrested development.
Withered into cynics
And spiritual valetudinarians,
Their frustration due
To a social environment
Which has given them no general sense
Of the facts of life,
And no sense whatever
Of its possibilities;
Their English culture a mere simulacrum,
Too partial and too provincial
To fulfil the true function of culture
The illumination of the particular
In terms of the universal;
Beside the strong vigour of daily life
It is but an empty shadow.
(CP II, p. 938)

It is in two figures, the poets Hugh MacDiarmid and Edwin Muir, that we may find contrasting and fascinating renditions of Scottish identity in the present century. MacDiarmid, as we shall see, sought to reassert Scottish identity in the most fundamental way possible, that is through the recreation of Lowland Scots, so-called Lallans: Muir, a man born in Orkney of farming stock, was a poet who, even as an Orcadian Scot, felt an alien in the homecountry. Alternative possibilities of identity and non-identity emerge in their writings; MacDiarmid and Muir

34

present us with compelling yet contrasting narratives and images of recognition and belonging.

MacDiarmid: Epic, Infinity and the "Bigger Christ"

Hugh MacDiarmid understood the need for a new common Scottish metanarrative which might supplant both the (from his standpoint both problematic and exhausted) inheritance of Christianity in its conflictual manifestations and the threat of a mindless, mechanical modernity. His strategy involved three basic elements. The first was the re-establishment of a distinct linguistic identity for Scotland through the re-creation of Scots (Lallans) as modern and powerful literary language and the use of Gaelic as a linguistic unconscious firmly closed to Anglo-Saxon sensibility (Bourdieu 1991; Chapman 1978, 1992; Edwards 1985). The second was the provision of epic narratives of Scottish self-identity in the extraordinary *A Drunk Man Looks at the Thistle*, and then on a high metaphysical level in *On a Raised Beach* where narrative and geographical identities give way to a primal geological identity.[5] The third aspect of his strategy was political, and in this he can be said to have been least successful.

A *Drunk Man* is an epic poem in which an inebriated Scot makes his way home, falls down on a hillside and falls into stupor and dreams the constituent fragments of his identity. This work was written as a direct challenge to the modernism of T.S. Eliot's *Wasteland*. Whereas Eliot eventually propounded a cultural strategy which involved the central role of a Christian clerisy charged (despite a brutish populist secularity in the masses) with the mission of safeguarding the essential core of English culture (Eliot 1939, 1948), MacDiarmid risked a new mythologisation, a cultural refunctioning of an encounter with "the infinite" on behalf of the whole people[6] and a concern with the nature of Scottish metaphysical and cultural contradiction expressed above all in the notion of "Caledonian Antizyzygy" (Kreitzer 1992; Laing 1965). Whilst this preoccupation with the "infinite" can be traced back at least to the present writer's St Andrean predecessor John Mair's (1469-1550) *Propositum de infinito*, MacDiarmid also simultaneously succeeded in bridging the contemporary divisions within the then identity of

Scotland by proposing a strategy which stressed the cosmic destiny of the Scot (Kolakowski 1983). Indeed,

He canna Scotland see wha yet
Canna see the Infinite,
And Scotland in true scale to it.

This prime example of the "re-invention(s) of tradition" (Hobsbawm and Ranger 1983) is comparable with other attempts to emphasize cultural difference and stress cultural identity to be found in the history of nationalism. The "refunctioning" of tradition (Ernst Bloch) is perhaps a more apt term. This is indicative of a situation in which the interpretation of cultures in the Geertzian sense challenges the schemata of abstract systems. Thus Clifford Geertz in a well-worn but still useful definition argues that:

> Interpretative explanation trains its attention on what institutions, actions, images, utterance, events, customs, all the usual objects of social-scientific interest, mean to those whose institutions, actions, customs, and so on they are. As a result, it issues not in laws like Boyle's, or forces like Volta's, or mechanisms like Darwin's, but in constructions like Burckhardt's, Weber's, or Freud's: systematic unpacking of the conceptual world in which condottière, Calvinists, or paranoids live. Culture is the fabric of meaning in terms of which human beings interpret their experience and guide their action; social structure is the form that action takes, the actually existing network of social relations (Geertz 1966).

MacDiarmid confronts the political union of Scotland with England likening its unthinking justification to the call of a parrot and striving to open a *cultural* chasm:

The Parrot Cry

Tell me the auld, auld story
O'hoo the Union brocht

Puir Scotland into being
As a country worth a thocht.
England, frae whom a'blessings flow
What could we dae withoot ye?
Then dinna threip it doon oor throats
As gin we e'er could doot ye!
My feelings lang wi'gratitude
Ha'e been sae sairly harrowed
That dod! I think it's time
The claith was owre the parrot!
(CP I, p. 192)

I ken the stars that seem sae far awa'
Ha'e that appearance juist because my thocht
Canna yet bridge the spiritual gulf atween's
And the time when it will still seems remote
As interstellar space itsel'
Yet no 'sae faur as 'gainst my will I am
Frae nearly a'body else in Scotland here.
But a less distance than I'll drive betwixt
England and Scotland yet
(To Circumjack Cencrastus, CP I, 205-6)

Language is fundamental to this assertion of cultural difference, but this disjunction is imperfect, hobbled by the involution of Scots and English:

Curse on my dooble life and dooble tongue,
- Guid Scots wi' English a'hamstrung -

Speakin' o' Scotland in English words
As it were Beethoven chirpt by birds;
Or as if a Board school teacher
Tried to teach Rimbaud and Nietzsche.
(To Circumjack Cencrastus, CP I, p. 236)

Furthermore MacDiarmid not only had to fight off the corruption of English influence, but also drive his campaign forward against a Scottish popular culture that thrived in "Kailyard" (or "cabbage patch") sentimentality. Thus the masses are relativized not merely by the thought of philosophy, but by *geology*, it is this latter that provides not merely the figurative, but the literal bedrock of Scottish cultural identity. Thus MacDiarmid could exploit his sense of extraordinary cultural mission that transcended mere common humanity:

The relation o' John Davidson's thocht
To Nietzsche's is mair important
Than a' the drivel aboot 'Hame sweet Hame'
Fower million cretins mant.

And gin we canna thraw aff the warld
Let's hear o' nae 'Auld grey Mither' ava,
But o' the Middle Torridonian Arkose

Wi' local breccias,
Or the pillow lavas at Loch Awe....
(To Circumjack Cencrastus, CP I, p. 261)

Even more pointedly in his later masterpiece, *On a Raised Beach*, MacDiarmid develops an identity which repudiates all recognition, other than that through which we realize our ultimate identity; for being enamored of the desert at least,

I lift a stone; it is the meaning of life I clasp
Which is death, for that is the meaning of death.

"Belonging" in this context is strictly delimited, for true cultural identity involves actual geographical presence. Thus returnees from the Scottish diaspora seeking (as many still do) to rediscover their Scottish roots come in for withering contempt and (to borrow Erving Garfinkel's term) ritual "status degradation" at the quayside:

38

The Lion Rampant

Damn a country whaur turnin' a corner
You could lippen on nocht but a sheep!
Thank God for a lion on Greenock quay
Its vigil aince more to keep,
And when the American clansmen land
No' bash them wi' a paw
But by the gangway tak' its stand
And gently off them draw
As they come trippin' doon't
Their imitation kilts and gar
The blighters look for a' the warld
Precisely as they are!...
(To Circumjack Cencrastus, CP I, p. 274)

Identity can only be gained by heroic and Promethean endeavour. For
MacDiarmid, Lenin is the equivalent of John Milton's heroic Satan in
Paradise Lost. Thus MacDiarmid admires to the point of idolatry the
achievements of an adamantine and utterly ruthless Lenin, represented
once more in the imagery of stone:

(Second Hymn to Lenin)

Unremittin', relentless,
Organized to the last degree
Ah, Lenin, politics is bairns' play
To what this maun be!
(CP I, p. 328)

The Skeleton of the Future
At Lenin's Tomb

Red granite and black diorite, with the blue
Of the labradorite crystals gleaming like precious stones
In the light reflected from the snow; and behind them

The eternal lightning of Lenin's bones.
(CP I, p. 386)

The achievement of a true culture, the illumination of the particular in terms of the universal, is only possible if the individual consciousness itself attains to proximity with divinity:

Vestigia Nulla Retrorsum
In Memoriam: Rainer Maria Rilke 1875-1926

No more is interposed between God and us
But the last difference between human and divine,
And yet we have not yet chosen between Heaven and Hell,
Too alive to both. When but the last films of flesh fell,
When we were in the world and yet not in it,
And the spirit seemed to waver its eyas wings
Into the divine obscurity, it could not win it.
We would not, if we could, the difference resign
Between God and us – the God of our imaginings.
(CP I, pp. 417-8)

The consciousness which identifies with the divine *is* the people, such an individual transcends mere politics, even nationalist party politics. Thus MacDiarmid's conception of identity, and his own role as the embodiment of the nation, leads him into an exultant political impossibilism:

The Difference

The difference between MacCormick and his friends and I
    Is this – that they
Constitute the National Party of Scotland,
    I am Scotland itself to-day,
They have dared to stake less than the highest
    In Scotland's name.
Scotland will shine like the sun in my song

40

While they vanish, like mists, whence they come.
(CP II, p. 1277)

All the while, the counterfeit culture of England has to be deconstructed on every level in Scottish consciousness. This alien culture is understood not as a partner or neighbor, but as a false consciousness, base and corrupt – in reality it is a *non-culture* – for:

The Battle Continues

A man of genius must take life as he finds it;
The material of his art is the existence of his contemporaries;
English life presents him with nothing but money and sex
And with them he must do his best, for he will get no other.

Impossible with such impure material; the imagination
Becomes critical, finds nothing to criticise
Sees the humour of the situation, and finds its material
Admirably suited for satire.
(CP II, p. 935-6)

and,

England is Our Enemy

Who among English writers is thus axiomatic?
Accepted thus by either the Anglo-Saxon
Or the foreigner of some culture?
Yours will say in your haste:
'But there are *hundreds*!'
After cursory reflection you will say:
'But... there are none.'
(CP, II, p. 860)

In short,

North and South

The plagues that waste the North at times
Are always born in Southern climes.
(CP, p. 1271)

Hugh MacDiarmid represents a charismatic (Lindblom 1990) – albeit a profoundly problematic – inheritance. His celebration of the internally contradictory character of the Scottish intellect and sensibility and extravagant implied self-presentation in *A Drunk Man* (Watson 1972) of himself as "a greater Christ, a greater Burns may come" reveals a Nietzschian glorification of the will-to-power that inspires as many as it repels. A cultural refunctioning of the will-to-power may not be adequate (or indeed desirable) as the best means of giving to Scots that self-confidence that will carry them into devolution within the United Kingdom (the moderate political goal) or independence in Europe (the aim of the Scottish National Party).

Muir and the Gentle Christ
Edwin Muir is the obvious counterpoint to MacDiarmid, but, unlike the latter, he repudiated the revival of Scottish identity through the rebirthing of Lallans or Lowland Scots. Instead, his poetry reflects the ineradicable nostalgia for the lost integrity of an ideal Orcadian childhood desecrated by the move of his family to Glasgow. In a way extraordinarily different from twentieth century England, the transition from rural to urban life is fundamental to Scottish sensibility in the present century, as is an ongoing sense of the importance of a serious and always dangerous spiritual and moral reality that interposes in the life of mortals whose lives are but playthings in the face of natural forces.[7] In his poem *Scotland 1941*, Muir wrote notoriously of the "sham bards of a sham nation". A loss of confidence was apparent to Edwin Muir before the Second World War, when he saw that,

> Though Scotland has not been a nation for some time, it has possessed a distinctly marked style of life; and that is now falling to pieces, for there is no visible and effective power to hold it

together. There is such a visible and effective power to conserve the life of England; and though in English life, too, a similar change of national characteristics is going on, though the old England is disappearing, there is no danger that England should cease to be itself. But all that Scotland possesses is its style of life; once it loses that it loses everything, and is nothing more than a name on a map (Muir, 1935, p. 26).

Ironically, after over a half century, the reverse is now the case. English post-imperial social and cultural identity is now fractured and problematic (Anderson 1992), whereas Scottish identity is resurgent and stridently self-assertive. In terms of Scotland, MacDiarmid and Muir may be understood as analogous to the pointed opposition of Prometheus and Christ of which Karl Löwith wrote after the Second World War in *Weltgeschichte und Heilsgeschehen*. The influence of MacDiarmid upon the contemporary revival of Scottish cultural identity can scarcely be overestimated; yet his is a problematic inheritance illustrating all too clearly the power of a culture that places the particular on the level of the universal and relatives all human relations in the light of an absolute commitment to a local identity which seeks its finality in the individuality of the stone, which is itself the representation of an impersonal infinite.

4. Conclusion: Identity as the Will-to-Become

As the noted commentator Tom Nairn remarked in *The Scotsman* (13.1.92), what faced Scotland in the coming General Election of 1992 was the necessity of overcoming three centuries of depoliticisation through "the unfreezing of the Scottish will" that is through a distinctive recovery of the *will-to-power*. The crisis in contemporary Scottish cultural identity is intimately associated both with the crisis of modernity/ism and with rise of Scottish nationalism in its modern form in the course of the twentieth century. Central to this resurgence has been the question of identity. As regards this, *pre-modernity* provided Scotland with the conflictual identities of the Reformation (and a suppressed pre-Catholic Celtic unconscious). *Modernity* (intellectual, agrarian and industrial) disrupted local and regional identities and was characterized by Irish Roman Catholic immigration and massive outward migration. *Postmodernity* would seem to afford the Scottish intellectual with sufficient cultural capital the option of a return to roots; but the mass of the population wallow in indecision and unwilling to become "little Christs" to the self-proclaimed "Bigger Christ" of MacDiarmid.

De-industrialization has stripped out both the working class Tory vote and destabilized its socialist counterpart. Underlying the nationalist slogan of 1992: "Rise Now and Be a Nation Again!" is a veritable mare's nest of issues, transcended perhaps, by a single, potential (but not yet fully actualized) axiom: a primordial negative definition of Scottish identity as "hatred of Englishness". The departure from politics after the Election of Jim Sillars (one time Labour MP who had earlier shifted over to the Scottish National Party) with the bitter words that the Scots had "not got the bottle" to grasp independence was indicative: there is, and there remains, a crisis of self-confidence. If poetry alone could have recreated such a will-to-become, then it would be difficult to conceive of a body of work more suited to this destiny than that of Hugh MacDiarmid.

The General Election of 1992 brought about an as-yet unresolved crisis in the evolution and political expression of this identity. The problem of Scottish identity is, however, fraught with a wide array of historical, political and religious factors. Despite acute secularization, a growing loss of religious observance and declining church membership, the religious and quasi-religious re-definition of Scottish cultural identities continues to play a remarkable role in a frustrated political process. The recent history of Scottish cultural identity raises important theoretical and practical issues concerning "re-traditionalization" and the re-functioning of myth, as opposed to "de-traditionalization" in late industrial societies, besides the definition and cultural construction of racism and ethnic identity.

The active involvement of religious leaders, notably Church of Scotland

(Presbyterian) and Episcopal Church (Anglican) ministers has been a remarkable feature of recent constitutional and cultural debate. Thus such figures as William Storrar and Canon Kenyon Wright were leading architects of the Constitutional Convention (which re-activated a pre-modern, and indeed highly traditional conception of the Claim of Right, traceable in form through the Covenanters of the seventeenth century to the Declaration of Arbroath of 1320) and promoted the re-examination of the religious factors in Scottish identity. Scottish political sovereignty resides in the people whereas English sovereignty is seen as grounded in monarchical and parliamentary absolutism. Indeed in terms of "post-political" era the question of cultural identity as the basis of nationhood remains central to the debate.

William Storrar in his book *Scottish Identity: A Scottish Vision* (much read in, but little known beyond Scotland) has produced a typology of Scottish culture as Catholic, Reformed and secular, the latter now characterized by a "second Disruption", a very recent (and from his point of view catastrophic) departure of the bulk of the population from the churches, in particular from the Church of Scotland. Interestingly, religious and theological elements are admitted into the mainstream discussion of Scottish identity represented by (for example) *Common Cause*, a cross-party alliance of leading cultural figures.

The Scottish example challenges in a variety of ways the assumptions of the problem of the co-existence of different communities, inasmuch as Scottish social and cultural identity has always involved acute conflict and extreme forms of reflexivity alien, by and large to English experience (Anderson 1992; Jenkins 1975; Jowell, Prior and Taylor 1992; Nairn 1977, 1981, 1988; Porter 1992; Thomas 1988), but present, I would venture to suggest, in full measure in the problematic of identity as recognition and belonging in the wider context of Europe. This example shows that "identity as belonging" inevitably involves *difference* and *not belonging*. The ethics of co-existence of communities and existence within communities would imply a conditioning of cultural identity: the *ultimate* and the *penultimate* need to be distinguished anew. The ethics of universalism relies upon the operation of reason and moderation for its successful implementation. The dynamics of cultural identity in the context of contemporary nationalistic resurgence may involve the quasi-theological fusion of the absolute with the relative. When this happens, then the powers of myth and of mythopoesis are released and the rational and compassionate recognition of the humanity and rights of the "Other" may be low on the agenda. Whether, as was argued earlier, ethical reflection alone can restrain or condition the drive towards cultural specificity is doubtful. Perhaps, in a strategy of greater risk but perhaps more promise, beneficent myth embodied in a civil religion (modelled, perhaps, on North American experience) grounded in trans-cultural ultimacy would have to confront the negative and malevolent aspects of the cultural transcendentals of a given society. Here perhaps, ethics and religion must once more meet on the grounds of a common intention: the promotion of the co-existence of different communities.

Notes

1. Notwithstanding, it is important to note that some theorists argue the contrary, as in the case of the French sociologist Michel Maffesoli (1994) who argues that "tribalisation" is the main phenomenon of our time, see *The Time of the Tribes: The Decline of Individualism in Mass Societies*, London: Sage Publications.
2. The allusion to Bonhoeffer's *Ethics* is intended; and a parallel between explicit and latent forms of fascism is not ruled out.
3. In the parable of Lord and Bondsman in the *Phenomenology of Mind* of 1807, Hegel provided us with an extraordinary text that prefigures and exceeds in potential not only the Marxian dialectic, but virtually all significant narratives of power in the modern/postmodern struggle for identity of the last two centuries. See R.H. Roberts (1988 and 1989).
4. Neither Muir nor MacDiarmid had much time for the commercialized "tartanry" of what has now become a globalized Scottish "culture" as ubiquitous in its own way as the commercialized mythology of Christmas. Thus, for example, in locations as far flung as (e.g.) Cape Town in South Africa, there are shops successfully marketing products that embody a globalized Scottish cultural identity.
5. This tradition continues. As part of his duties in St Andrews the present writer assessed a prize essay ostensibly concerned with the geological evolution of Ben Nevis, the major point of which was to show that cultural differentiation was related to the fact that Scotland and England were only joined through the migration of landmasses after the break-up of Gondwanaland. And so, given the different origins of the geological structures underlying the geography (and thus the cultures of both countries), their differences are quite literally pre-prehistoric.
6. In certain respects MacDiarmid's thought as expressed in some of his poetry is "völkisch" in tone. Despite the present writer's reservations on these grounds, he nevertheless regards MacDiarmid at his best as one of the greatest poets of the twentieth century writing in "English". His courage with regard to linguistic innovation and freedom to re-create is exemplary – to experience MacDiarmid's work in Scotland under the influence of that country's culture, society, geology and landscape is an intoxication understood in the fullest meanings of the word.
7. The trilogy of Lewis Grassic Gibbon 1932-4/1986), *A Scots Quair*, London: Penguin, is essential reading in this respect.

Ethics of Identity Bibliography

ABRAMS, M.D. GERARD, and N. TIMMS (eds), *Values and Change in Britain*, London: Macmillan, 1985

AJZEN, I. and M. FISHBEIN, *Understanding Attitudes and Predicting Social Behaviour*, Englewood-Cliffs, N.J.: Prentice-Hall, 1980

ALMOND, G.A., *The intellectual history of the civic culture concept*, in: G.A. ALMOND and S. VERBA (eds), *The Civic Culture Revisited*, Boston/Toronto: Little, Brown and Company, 1980

ALMOND, G.A., *Communism and political culture theory*, in: *Comparative Politics*, 1983, 16, pp. 127-138

ALMOND, G.A. and S. VERBA, *The Civic Culture. Political Attitudes and Democracy in Five Nations*, Princeton: Princeton University Press, 1963

ANDERSON, B., *Imagined Communities, Reflections on the Origins and Spread of Nationalism*, London: Verso, 1983

ANDERSON, P., *English Questions*, London: Verso, 1992

ANDERSON, P., *Nation-States and National Identity*, in: *London Review of Books*, 9, May 1991, pp. 3-8

ANDERSON, P., *Ferdinand Braudel and National Identity*, in: *A Zone of Engagement*, London: Verso, 1992, pp. 251-78

ASHFORT, S. and N. TIMMS, *What Europe Thinks. A Study of Western European Values*, Aldershot: Dartmouth, 1992

AVINERI, S. and A. DE-SHALIT (eds.), *Communitarianism and Individualism*, Oxford: Oxford University Press, 1992

BANTON, M., *Racial Consciousness*, London: Longman, 1988

BARKER, D., L. HALMAN and S. VLOET, *The European Values Study 1981-1990. Summary Report*, London: Gordon Cook Foundation on behalf of the European Values Group, 1992

BAUMAN, J., *A dream of belonging: my years in postwar Poland*, London: Virago, 1988

BAUMAN, Z., *Intimations of Postmodernity*, London: Routledge, 1992

BECK, U., *Risk Society: Towards a New Modernity*, London: Sage Publications, 1992

BELL, D., *The End of Ideology: On the Exhaustion of Political Ideas in the Fifties*, New York: Free Press, 1960

BELLAH, R.N., *The Broken Covenant: American Civic Religion in Times of Trial*, Chicago: Chicago of Chicago Press, 1975

BELLAH, R.N. et al., *Habits of the Heart: Individualism and Commitment in American Life*, New York: Harper Row, 1986

BELLAH, R.N., *Between Religion and Social Science*, in: *Beyond Belief Essays on Religion in a Post-Traditional World*, New York: Harper and

Row, 1970, ch.15, pp.237-259

BERMAN, M., *All That Is Solid Melts Into Air: The Experience of Modernity*, London: Verso, 1982

BEVERIDGE, C. and R. TURNBULL, *The Eclipse of Scottish Culture Inferiorism and the Intellectuals*, Edinburgh: Polygon, 1989

BOLD, A., *MacDiarmid*, London: Paladin Grafton Books, 1990

BOURDIEU, P., *Language and Symbolic Power*, Cambridge: Polity, 1991

BRADLEY, I., *The Celtic Way*, London: Darton, Longman and Todd, 1993

BRAH, A., *Time, Place, and Others: Discurses of Race, Nation, and Ethnicity*, in: *Sociology*, 1994, vol. 28/3, pp. 804-13

BRASS, P.R., *Ethnicity and Nationalism: Theory and Comparison*, New Delhi, 1991

BROADIE, A., *The Tradition of Scottish Philosophy: A New Perspective on the Enlightenment*, Edinburgh: Polygon, 1990

BROWN, G. and R. COOK (eds), *Scotland. The Real Divide. Poverty and Deprivation in Scotland*, Edinburgh: Mainstream Publishing, 1983

CAMERON, D, *The Field of Sighing*, London: Longmans, Green and Co, 1966

CHAMBERS, I., *Border Dialogues. Journeys in Postmodernity*, London: Routledge, 1990

CHAPMAN, M, *The Celts – The Construction of a Myth*, London: Macmillan, 1992

CHAPMAN, M., *The Gaelic Vision in Scottish Culture*, London: Croom Helm, 1978

CHITNIS, A.C., *The Scottish Enlightenment: A Social History*, London: Croom Helm, 1976

COLEMAN, J.S., *Foundations of Social Theory*, Cambridge, Mass.: Harvard University Press, 1990

CRICK, B., *National Identities. The Constitution of the United Kingdom*, Oxford: Blackwell, 1991

DAICHES, D. (ed.), *The New Companion to Scottish Culture*, Edinburgh: Polygon, 1983/1991

DAVIE, G.E., *The Crisis of the Democratic Intellect: The Problem of Generalism and Specialisation in Twentieth-Century Scotland*, Edinburgh: Polygon, 1986

DAVIE, G.E., *The Democratic Intellect: Scotland and her Universities in the Nineteenth Century*, Edinburgh: Edinburgh University Press, 1961 (reprinted 1986)

DAVIE, G.E., *The Scottish Enlightenment and Other Essays*, Edinburgh: Polygon, 1991

DE LEVITA, D.J., *The Concept of Identity*, Noew York: Basic Books, 1965

DOBBELAIRE, K., *Church involvement and secularization: Making sense of the European case*, in: E. BARKER, J.A. BECKFORD and K. DOBBELAIRE (eds), *Secularization, Rationalism and Sectarianism*, Oxford: Clarendon Press, 1993

EDWARDS, J., *Language, Society and Identity*, Oxford: Blackwell in association with Andre Deutsch, 1985

EISENSTADT, S. (ed.), *Patterns of Modernity*, New York: New York University Press, 1987, vol. 1, *The West*

ELIOT, T.S., *The Idea of a Christian Society*, London: Faber and Faber, 1939

ELIOT, T.S., *Notes towards the Definition of Culture*, London: Faber and Faber, 1948

ELTON, G., *The English*, Oxford: Blackwell, 1992

ERIKSEN, T.H., *Ethnicity and Nationalism: Anthropological Perspectives*, London: Pluto Press, 1993

ESTER, P., L. HALMAN and R. DE MOOR, *The Individualizing Society: Value change in Europe and North America*, Tilburg: Tilburg University Press, 1994

FEATHERSTONE, M. (ed.), *Global Culture: Nationalism, Globalization and Modernity*, London: Sage Publications, 1990

FERGUSON, A., *Essay on the History of Civil Society*, Edinburgh: Edinburgh University Press, 1776/1966

FOSTER, J., *Nationality, Social Change and Class: Transformations of National Identity in Scotland*, in: McCRONE, D., S. KENDRICK and P. SHAW (eds.), *The Making of Scotland: Nation, Culture and Social Change*, Edinburgh: Edinburgh University Press and The British Sociological Association, 1989

FUKUYAMA, F., *The End of History and the Last Man*, London: Hamish Hamilton, 1989

GALLAGHER,T. (ed.), *Nationalism in the Nineties*, Edinburgh: Polygon, 1991

GEERTZ, C.J., *Religion as a Cultural System*, in: M. BANTON (ed.), *Anthropological Approaches to the Study of Religion*, London: Tavistock, 1966, pp.1-46

GELLNER, E., *Nationalism and two forms of cohesion in complex societies*, pp. 6-28 and *The Rubber Cage: Disenchantment with Disenchantment*, pp. 152-165, in: *Culture, Identity, and Politics*, Cambridge: Cambridge University Press, 1987

GELLNER, E., *Nations and Nationalism*, Oxford: Blackwell, 1983

GELLNER, E., *Postmodernism, Reason and Religion*, London: Routledge, 1992

GIBBINS, J.R., *Contemporary political culture: An introduction*, in: J.R. GIBBINS (ed.), *Contemporary Political Culture: An Introduction: Politics in a Postmodern Age*, London/Newbury Park/New Delhi: Sage Publications, 1989

GIBBON, L.G., *A Scots Quair*, London: Penguin, 1932, 1933, 1934, 1986

GIDDENS, A., *Sociology*, Cambridge: Polity Press, 1989

GIDDENS, A., *The Consequences of Modernity*, Cambridge: Polity, 1990

GIDDENS, A., *Modernity and the Self-Identity: Self and Society in the Late Modern Age*, Cambridge: Polity, 1991

GOFFMAN, E., *The Presentation of the Self in Everyday Life*, Garden City, New York: Doubleday, 1959

GRAVE, S.A., *The Scottish Philosophy of Common Sense*, Oxford: Clarendon, 1960

GREENFIELD, L., *Nationalism: Five Roads to Modernity*, Cambridge, Mass: Harvard University Press, 1992

HABERMAS, J. and P. LAURENCE (tr.), *The Philosophical Discourse of Modernity: Twelve Lectures*. Cambridge, Mass.: Polity & Blackwell, 1987

HABGOOD, J., *Church and Nation in a Secular Age*, London, 1983

HALMAN, L., F. HEUNKS, R. DE MOOR and H. ZANDERS, *Traditie, secularisatie en individualisering. Een studie naar de waarden van de Nederlanders in een Europese context*, Tilburg: Tilburg University Press, 1987

HANF, T., *The Sacred Marker: Religion. Communalism and Nationalism*, in: *Social Compass*, 41/1, 1994, pp. 9-20

HARDING, S., D. PHILIPS and M. FOGERTY, *Contrasting Values in Western Europe: Unity, Diversity and Change*, London: Macmillan, 1986

HARVEY, D., *The Condition of Postmodernity: An Enquiry into the Origins of Cultural Change*, Cambridge: Blackwell, 1989

HARVIE, C., *Cultural Weapons Scotland and Survival in a New Europe*, Edinburgh: Polygon, 1992

HARVIE, C., *Europe and the Scottish Nation*, Scottish Centre for Economic and Social Research, 1989/1991

HARVIE, C., *No Gods and Precious Few Heroes: Scotland since 1914*, Edinburgh: Edinburgh University Press, 1981

HARVIE, C., *Scotland and Nationalism: Scottish Society and Politics 1707-1977*, London: Allen and Unwin, 1977

HAYS, D., *Europe: The Emergence of an Idea in History*, Edinburgh: Edinburgh University Press, 1968

HEATH, S. and D. McMAHON, *Consensus and Dissensus*, in: JOWELL, R.,L. BROOK, B. TAYLOR and G. PRIOR (eds.), *British Social Attitudes. The 8th Report*, Aldershot: Dartmouth, 1991, pp. 1-22

HOBSBAWN, E.J., *Nations and Nationalism since 1780: Programme, Myth, Reality*, Cambridge: Cambridge University Press, 1991

HOBSBAWN, E.J. and RANGER, T., *The Invention of Tradition*, Cambridge: Cambridge University Press, 1983

HOGG, J., *The Private Menoirs and Confessions of a Justified Sinner*, London: Harmondsworth: Penguin, 1824/1983

INGLEHART, R., *The Silent Revolution: Changing Values and Political Styles among Western Publics*, Princeton: Princeton University Press, 1977

INGLEHART, R., *Culture Shift in Advanced Industrial Society*, Princeton: Princeton University Press, 1990

JENKINS, D., *The British Their Identity and their Religion*, London: SCM, 1975

JONES, R.K., *Paradigm Shifts and Identity Theory: Alternation as a Form of Identity Management*, in: MOL, H. (ed.), *Identity and Religion International, Cross-Cultural Approaches*, London: Sage, 1978, pp. 59-82

JOWELL, K.G., G. PRIOR and B. TAYLOR (eds.), *British Social Attitudes: The 9th Report*, Aldershot: Dartmouth, 1992

KAA, D. VAN DE, *Europe's second demographic transition*, in: *Population Bulletin*, 1997, 42, pp. 1-57

KLAGES, H., *Wertorientierung im Wandel: Rückblick, Gegenwartsanalyse, Prognosen*, Frankfurt/New York: Campus Verlag, 1985

KNOX, J., *John Knox's History of the Reformation in Scotland*, W.C. Dickinson (ed.), vols. I and II, London, 1949

KOLAKOWSKI, L., *Totalitarianism and the virtue of the lie*, in: HOWE, I. (ed.), *1984 Revisited. Totalitarianism in our Century*, New York: Harper and Row, 1983

KREITZER, L., *R.L. Stevenson's Strange Case of Dr. Jekyll and Mr Hyde and Romans 7: 14-25: Images of the Moral Duality of Human Nature*, in: *Journal of Literature and Theology*, vol. 6, 1992, pp. 125-144

KROBER, A.L. and KLUCKHOHN, *Culture, A Critical review of Concepts and Definitions*, New York: Vintage Books, 1963

KUNDERA, M., *Un occident kidnappe*, in: *Le debat*, November 1983: pp. 3-22

KUNG, H., *Global Responsibility: In Search of a New World Ethic*, London: SCM, 1990

LAING, R.D., *The Divided Self: an Existential Study in Society and Madness*, Harmondsworth: Penguin, 1965

LASCH, C., *Haven in a Heartless World*, New York: Basic Books, 1977

LASCH, C., *The Culture of Narcissism. American Life in an Age of Diminishing Expectations*, New York: Norton and Company, 1979

LASH, S. and J. FRIEDMAN, *Modernity and Identity*, Oxford: Blackwell, 1992

LINDBLOM, C., *Charisma*, Oxford: Blackwell, 1990

LUHMANN, N., *The paradox of system differentiation and the evolution of society*, in: ALEXANDER, J. and P. COLOMY (eds.), *Differentiation Theory and Social Change. Comparative and Historical Perspectives*, New York: Colombia University Press, 1990, pp. 409-440

LUHMANN, N., *Beobachtungen der Moderne*, Opladen: Westdeutscher Verlag, 1992

LYNCH, M., *Scotland A New History*, London: Pimlico, 1991

LYOTARD, J.-F., *The Postmodern Condition: A Report on Knowledge*, Manchester: Manchester University Press, 1984

McBRIDE, W.L. et al, *Global Order, National identity, and the Responsibility of Philosophers*, in: *Proceedings and Addresses of the American Philosophical Association*, 1994, 67/6, pp. 67-80

MACDIARMID, H., *A Drunk Man Looks at the Thistle*, K. Buthlay (ed.), Edinburgh: Scottish Academic Press, 1925/1987

MACDIARMID, H., *Hugh MacDiarmid Complete Poems 1920-1976*, Michael Grieve and W.R. Aitken (eds.), 2 vols., London: Brian & O'Keefe, 1978

MACDONALD, S., *Identity Complexes in Western Europe: Social Anthropological Perspectives*, in: MACDONALD, S. (ed.), *Inside European Identities Ethnography in Western Europe*, Providence/Oxford: Berg, 1993, pp. 1-26

MACINTYRE, A., *After Virtue: A Study in Moral Theory*, London: Duckworth, 1981

MACINTYRE, A., *Three Rival Versions of Moral Enquiry: Encyclopaedia, Genealogy and Tradition*, London: Duckworth, 1990

MACINTYRE, A., *Whose Justice? Which Rationality?*, London: Duckworth, 1988

McCRONE, D., S. KENDRICK and P. SHAW (eds.), *The Making of Scotland: Nation, Culture and Social Change*, Edinburgh: Edinburgh University Press and The British Sociological Association, 1989

McCRONE, D., *Understanding Scotland: The Sociology of a Stateless Nation*, London: Routledge, 1992

MAFFESOLI, M., *The Time of the Tribes: The Decline of Individualism in Mass Societies*, London: Sage Publications, 1994

MEWS, S. (ed.), *Religion and National Identity*, Oxford: Blackwell, 1982

MILLER, D., *The Ethical Significance of Nationality*, in: *Ethics*, 1988, 98, pp. 647-662

MOL, H., *Identity and Religion International, Cross-Cultural Approaches*. London: Sage, 1978

MOL, H., *Identity and the Sacred*, Agincourt: Book Society of Canada, 1976

MUIR, E., *An Autobiography*, London: The Hogarth Press, 1954

MUIR, E., *The Complete Poems of Edwin Muir: An Annotated Edition*,

BUTTER, P. (ed.), Aberdeen: The Association for Scottish Literary Studies, 1991

MUIR, E., *Scottish Journey*, London: William Heinemann, 1935

MUIR, W., *Belonging A Memoir*, London: Hogarth Press, 1968

NAIRN, T., *The Break-Up of Britain*, London, 1977/1981

NAIRN, T., *The Enchanted Glass: Britain and Its Monarchy*, London: Radius, 1988

PORTER, R., *Myths of the English*, Cambridge: Polity, 1992

PRZEWORRSKI, A. and H. TEUNE, *The Logic of Comparative Social Inquiry*, New York: John Wiley and Sons, 1970

PYE, L.W., *Culture and political science: problems in the evaluation of the concept of political culture*, in: SCHNEIDER, L. and C.M. BONJEAN (eds.), *The Idea of Culture in the Social Sciences*, Cambridge: Cambridge University Press, 1973, pp. 65-76

REICH, B. and C. ADCOCK, *Values, Attitudes and Behaviour Change*, London: Methuen, 1976

RENDELL, J., *The Origins of the Scottish Enlightenment*, 1978

ROBBINS, K., *Religion and identity in modern British history*, in: MEWS, S. (ed.), *Religion and National Identity*, Oxford: Blackwell, 1982, pp. 465-88

ROBERTS, R.H., *The Reception of Hegel's parable of the Lord and Bondsman*, in : *New Comparison*, 1988, 5, pp. 23-29

ROBERTS, R.H., *Lord, Bondsman, and Churchman: Integrity, Identity and Power in Anglicanism*, in: GUNTON, C.E. and D.W. HARDY (eds.), *On Being the Church*, Edinburgh: T. & T. Clark, 1989, pp. 156-224

ROBERTSON, R., *Globalization; Social Theory and Global Culture*, London: Sage, 1992

ROKEACH, M., *Beliefs, Attitudes and Values*, San Francisco: Jossey-Bass Inc Publishers, 1968

ROOSENS, E., *Creating Ethnicity: The Process of Ethnogenesis*, London: Sage, 1989

ROSIE, G., *The Englishing of Scotland*, Fourth Lecture, Scottish National Party Annual Conference, 1989

ROUTLEDGE and THOEMMES, *Scottish Enlightenment I*, 8 vols, 1989 and II, 12 vols, 1991

RUPNIK, J., *Totalitarianism revisited*, in: KEANE, J. (ed.), *Civil Society and the State. New European Perspectives*, London/New York: Verso, 1988

SCOTT, P.H. and A.C. DAVIES (eds), *The Age of MacDiarmid*, Edinburgh: Mainstream, 1980

SEFTON, H., *The Church of Scotland and Scottish nationhood*, in: MEWS, S. (ed.), *Religion and National Identity*, Oxford: Blackwell, 1982, pp. 549-556

SLATTERLY, M., *Key Ideas in Sociology*, London: Macmillan, 1991

SMITH, A., *Social Change: Social Theory and Historical Processes*, London: Longman, 1976

SMITH, A.D., *Towards global culture?*, in: FEATHERSTONE, M. (ed.), *Global Culture. Nationalism, Globalization and Modernity*, London: Sage Publications, 1990

SMITH, A., *The Theory of the Moral Sentiments*, RAPHAEL and A.L. MACFIE (eds.), Oxford: Clarendon, 1723/1790/1976

SMITH, A., *The Wealth of Nations*, Oxford: Clarendon, 1776/1976

SMITH, A.D., *The Ethnic Revival*, Cambridge: Cambridge University Press, 1991a

SMITH, A.D., *National Identity*, London: Penguin, 1991b

SMOUT, T.C., *A History of the Scottish People 1560-1830*, London: Fontana, 1969

SMOUT, T.C. (ed.), *Scotland and Europe: 1200-1850*, Edinburgh: John Donald, 1986

SMOUT, T.C., *The Scottish Identity*, in: UNDERWOOT, R. (ed.), *The Future of Scotland*, London: Croom Helm, 1977

SOLLORS, W., *The Invention of Ethnicity*, Oxford, Oxford University Press, 1989

STEINER, G., *In Bluebeard's Castle: Some Notes Towards the Re-definition of Culture*, T.S. Eliot Memorial Lectures, London: Faber, 1971

STOETZEL, J., *Les valeurs du temps present: une enquete européenne*, Paris: Presses Universitaires de France, 1983

STORRAR, W., *Scottish Identity: A Christian Vision*, Edinburgh: The Handsel Press, 1990

SZUCS, J., *Three historical regions of Europe. An outline*, in: KENEA, J. (ed.), *Civil Society and the State, New European Perspectives*, London/New York: Verso, 1988, pp. 291-332

The European Identity, 14 December 1973, in: *Bulletin of the European Communities*, 12-1973, pp. 118-22

TAYLOR, C., *The Ethics of Authenticity*, Cambridge, Mass.: Harvard University Press, 1991

TAYLOR, C., *Multiculturalism and the Politics of Recognition*, Princeton: Princeton University Press, 1992

THOMAS, T., *The British: Their Religious Beliefs and Practices 1800-1986*, London: Routledge, 1988

THUNE, W., *Die Heimat als soziologische und geopolitische Kategorie*, Neue Würzburger Studien zur Soziologie, Würzburg: Creator Verlag, 1986

TIMMS, N., *Family and Citizenship, Values in Contemporary Britain*, Dartmouth, 1992

TURNER, B.S., *Religion and Social Theory*, London: Sage, 1983/1991

UNDERWOOD, R. (ed.), *The Future of Scotland*, London: Croom Helm, 1977

WALZER, M., *Zwei Arten des Universalismus*, in: *Babylon*, 1990, 5, pp. 7-25

WATSON, R., *The Symbolism of A Drunk Man Looks at the Thistle*, in: GLEN, D., *Hugh MacDiarmid A Critical Survey*, Edinburgh: Scottish Academic Press, 1972, pp. 94-116

WHEELIS, A., *The Quest for Identity*, New York: Norton, 1958

WIENER, M., *English Culture and the Decline of the Industrial Spirit 1850-1980*, Cambridge: Cambridge University Press, 1981

WILLIAMS, R., *Culture and Society 1750-1980*, London: Chatto and Windus, 1958

WILTERDINK, N., *Europa als ideaal*, in: ZWAAN, T. et al (eds.), *Het Europees labyrint. Nationalisme en natievorming in Nederland*, Meppel: Boom, 1991, pp. 129-48

YANKELOVICH, D., *New Rules*, New York: Random House, 1981

YANKELOVICH, D, H. ZETTERBERG, B. STRUMPEL, M. SHANKS a.o., *The World at Work. An International Report on Jobs, Productivity and Human Values*, New York: Octogon Books, 1985

ZWI WERBLOWSKY, R.J., *Beyond Tradition and Modernity: Changing Religions in a Changing World*, London: Athlone Press, 1976

Franglais
On Liberalism, Nationalism, and Multiculturalism

C.W. Maris[1]

1. Two Concepts of Liberty

In "Two concepts of liberty" Isaiah Berlin draws a famous distinction between negative and positive freedom. His aim is to clarify the conceptual confusion that results from the unhappy marriage between such conflicting values as individual freedom and collective solidarity under the common denominator of 'liberty'. Since the aim of this article is to look at recent attempts to create a synthesis between liberal individual rights and communitarian collective liberties, I will begin with Berlin's analytical divorce of the two, using the analytic-synthetic method (section 1). Section 2 illustrates the contrast between individual and collective liberties with a discussion of the claim to universality of the liberal "Universal Declaration of Human Rights". Section 3 discusses Charles Taylor's communitarian synthesis, while section 4 deals with John Rawls' liberal synthesis. Section 5 argues that Rawls' political liberalism is preferable. Section 6 contains a conceptual finale.

According to Berlin, *negative freedom* defines the area within which the subject may do what he likes, without interference by others or the state. This is the liberal concept of freedom: individual liberty may legally be limited in the name of justice, but an area of private life should remain that is free *from* public authority. In particular liberty of religion, opinion and property are to be respected. According to Mill's harm principle, the only reason why the state may restrict the freedom of the individual to pursue his own good as he wishes is the prevention of harm to others.

Whereas negative freedom concerns the question how far the government (and other persons) may interfere in the private life of the individual[2], *positive freedom* has to do with the source of interference that regulates your behaviour, in other words with the question of whom you are governed by. One has positive freedom as long as one is one's own master. 'Self-government' in this positive sense involves more than just an absence of coercion. It presupposes a concept of human identity that one is free to live up to. Berlin discusses different variants of the concept of positive freedom, including the rationalist and the nationalist ones. I will concentrate on the latter (which Berlin – in my view, incorrectly – considers atypical).[3] According to the nationalist, communitarian form of positive freedom, one's identity is determined by one's community:

> For am I not what I am, to some degree, in virtue of what others think and feel me to be? When I ask myself what I am, and answer: an Englishman, a Chinese, a merchant, a man of no importance, a millionaire, a convict – I find upon analysis that to possess these attributes entails being recognized as belonging to a particular group or class by other persons in my society, and that this recognition is part of the meaning of most of the terms that denote some of my most personal and permanent characteristics. (p. 155)

Mill therefore states that 'the lack of freedom about which individual people or groups complain amounts, as often as not, to the lack of proper recognition' (p. 155). Moreover, he says, because of the social origin of one's identity

> the only persons who can so recognize me, and thereby give me the sense of being someone, are the members of the society to which, historically, morally, economically, and perhaps ethnically, I feel that I belong. (p. 156)

The communitarian kind of positive freedom also presupposes negative freedom, but in a collective sense: one's social group or nation must be free *from* alien domination. However, collective positive freedom is not the sum of the negative freedoms of the individual group members. It requires that they interpret freedom in a specific way – they are free, that is, to live according to the way of life of their community. Communitarianism therefore can take the form of nationalism. This ideal of self-rule does not require any individual negative freedom or democratic political participation at all. It is sufficient to be governed by an authority that one can identify with. Even a dictator like Hitler will do, provided he 'is one of us'. (During the Gulf War many non-Iraqi Arabs admired Saddam Hussein in the same breath as they acknowledged that he was a cruel dictator, because he voiced Arab pride against what was experienced as Western neo-colonial arrogance.) Positive freedom therefore can lead to a complete abolition of the negative freedom of the individual members of a social group or nation: 'Dein Volk is alles, du bist nichts!' (The people are everything, you as an individual are nothing).

Berlin's conceptual analysis of these two concepts of liberty results in an unmasking of the term 'positive liberty' as used in this nationalist sense: on closer inspection, it is not *liberty* at all. Communitarians falsely attach the predicate liberty to the desire for status or recognition, which in fact is more similar to solidarity or fraternity. To use the word 'liberty' to define this desire for 'union, closer understanding, integration of interests, a life of common dependence and common sacrifice' is to confuse alien, and even contrary values. Speaking more generally, Berlin suggests that the classical positive concept of liberty as such wrongly claims the title of freedom:

> Can it be that Socrates and the creators of the central Western tradition in ethics and politics who followed him have been mistaken, for more than two millenia, that virtue is not knowledge, nor freedom identical with either? (p. 154)

However this may be, negative and positive liberty are 'not two different interpretations of a single concept, but two profoundly divergent and irreconcilable attitudes to the end of life' (p. 166). Negative freedom is almost at the opposite pole from the purposes of those who believe in liberty in the 'positive' – self-directive – sense. The former want to curb authority as such. The latter want it placed in their own hands. (p. 166)

The opposition between those two concepts of liberty becomes apparent when we look at the charges they level at each other. Mill cautions that absolutist positive liberty could easily turn into a tyranny of the majority (or of an elite that claims to represent the people and the nation). Communitarians counter with the objection that Mill's liberal ideal of individual negative freedom is based upon a false view of man. There is no such thing as a private individual in the sense of Robinson Crusoe. 'I form not an isolable atom, but an ingredient in a social pattern' (p. 157). Since one does not live on an island, Mill's attempt to posit a private realm with its own boundaries does not work. His harm principle does not produce the individual liberty that liberals expect: every individual action might harm others. Individual liberties are in fact immoral because they tend to isolate the individual, alienating him from his social environment.

The confusing fusion of these two concepts under the common label of 'liberty' stems from the ancient human longing for cosmic harmony. In a harmonious universe, the basic unity of all values would dissolve every conflict between solidarity and negative freedom, between the 'we' and the 'I'. This ancient monistic faith however is in Berlin's view no more than a metaphysical chimera. Mankind has a variety of conflicting ends. Values therefore like negative liberty, justice and equality cannot not make any absolute claim, but must be weighed against each other. Berlin views both the longing for individual freedom and the longing for social recognition in one's community as ultimate values which have 'an equal right to be classed among the deepest interests of mankind' (p. 166).[4] He recommends that we look for a compromise between them, instead of hiding the conflict behind the mask of liberty.

2. Antithesis: Individual Versus Collective Freedom

Traditionally however, far from showing any preparedness to compromise, both ideals of freedom make absolute, mutually exclusive claims. The debate on the "Universal Declaration of Human Rights" of 1948 offers a clear example. In 1947, a number of cultural anthropologists protested in a "Statement on human rights" that the liberal freedoms proclaimed in the Universal Declaration are not universal at all, but only represent an individualism that is typical of Western culture. The Declaration, they argued, wrongly neglected the anthropological fact 'that the personality of the individual can develop only in terms of the culture of his society' (p. 540). Its universal application would lead to frustration, because non-western people 'will thus be excluded from the freedom of full participation in the only right and proper way of life that can be known to them, the institutions, sanctions and goals that make up the culture of their particular society' (p. 543).

According to the "Statement on human rights", anthropological science demonstrates that there are no universal moral standards, because morals are always dependent of particular cultural traditions. On the basis of this epistemological cultural relativism the Statement concludes by arguing for a normative cultural relativism: all cultures deserve equal respect. It formulates an alternative Bill of Rights, based on the principle 'that man is free only when he lives as his society defines freedom, that his rights are those he recognizes as a member of his society' (p. 543). Its first proposition states:

The individual realizes his personality through his culture, hence respect for individual freedom entails a respect for cultural differences. There can be no individual freedom, that is, when the group with which the individual identifies himself is not free. There can be no full development of the individual personality as long as the individual is told, by men who have the power to enforce their commands, that the way of life of his group is inferior to that of those who wield the power. (p. 541)

Other anthropologists however have pointed out that the notion of collective cultural freedom runs up against the problems that Mill mentioned: it implies the acceptation of repressive or totalitarian cultures like the caste system in India or Nazism in Nazi Germany that completely ignore individual liberties.[5]

Moreover, normative cultural relativism offers no solution to the problems of multicultural societies. Respect for all cultures might be possible if they dwell in separate areas. But when there are no transcultural standards, how can one deal with intercultural conflicts within one society?

3. Taylor's Synthesis: Civic Humanism

More recently, both liberals and communitarians have tended to take these criticisms of their own approaches into account. In keeping with Berlin's recommendation, this has led to attempts from both sides to find compromises between the concepts of collective positive freedom and individual negative freedom. Liberals like John Rawls recognize that the willingness to respect each other's liberal rights presupposes some identification and solidarity with one's community. Aristotelian communitarians like Charles Taylor agree that community values should include basic individual liberty rights. However, the respective compromises they have come to still put a greater emphasis on one or the other – on collective or on individual existence.

In "The Politics of Recognition" Taylor develops a synthesis between the need for social belonging and recognition on the one hand and the need for individual freedom on the other. Although Taylor presents his synthesis as an alternative variety of liberalism, it entails a communitarian emphasis on the need for recognition. Like Berlin's communitarian positive freedom, Taylor's 'politics of recognition' is based on the assumption that there is a link between social recognition and identity:

The thesis is that our identity is partly shaped by recognition or its absence, often by the misrecognition of others, and so a person or group of people can suffer real damage, real distortion, if the people or society around them mirror back to them a confining or demeaning or contemptible picture of themselves. (p. 25)

This need for recognition is a driving force behind nationalism and the 'politics of multiculturalism' that promotes the interests of cultural minorities. According to Taylor, national identity is usually based on a specific language and culture. Inherent in it is the history of a cultural group, an often fictitious history that enables this group to develop a sense of its common origins and destiny (Taylor 1992/3, p. 14-5). In practice nationalism means the demand of groups of this sort for the positive freedom to organize their lives around their cultural traditions.

According to Taylor, traditional liberalism cannot meet the demand for the recognition of a distinct collective cultural identity; all it has to offer is a universal charter of equal rights. The liberal state adopts a principled neutral stand towards different substantive commitments to individual or collective ideals of the good life. It does not commit itself to what is good, but to what is right – that is, to the restricted procedural task of guaranteeing the equal treatment of all members of society. The underlying idea behind the neutrality of liberalism towards any ideal of the good life is the view that personal autonomy is essential to human dignity: each individual should have the right to determine his own way of life in full autonomy. According to Kant all human beings as rational agents have an equal right to respect. This abstraction of cultural differences, Taylor maintains, results in 'forcing people into a homogeneous mold that is untrue to them' (p. 43).

As an example Taylor refers to the conflict between the local laws of Quebec that are designed to guarantee the right of the people of Quebec to a distinct cultural identity and the liberal Canadian Charter of Rights that guarantees individual freedoms and the right of all Canadians not to suffer discrimination. The laws of Quebec protect the French language: they forbid francophone parents to send their children to English-language schools; French is obligatory in commercial signage; it is also required usage in companies with more than 50 employees. A constitutional amendment was proposed to recognize Quebec as a 'distinct society', thus making way for a particular interpretation of the constitution in Quebec. Cultural provisos like this obviously run counter to the liberal principles of individual freedom and equality contained in the Canadian Charter: they restrict freedom in the choice of schooling and favour the culture of one specific group.

To a certain extent, liberalism would permit special protection for a minority culture. It might consider the French culture and language as a collective resource for the well-being of a group of citizens who are unable to attain it by themselves. Federal bilingualism could then be made obligatory in order to offer equal opportunities to all citizens: the French language would be available to all who want to speak or write it. But from the point of view of the minority group, Taylor argues, this is not sufficient. Cultural minorities do not just want the facilities that are available to the majority; their aim is to ensure the survival of their cultural community in the future. Cultural survival requires the creation of new community members, and a guarantee of the ongoing identity of future generations as French speakers. Instead of a neutral state, it requires that the state be organized around the idea of the good life of their culture. This entails a lasting inequality of treatment between those who belong to the favoured cultural group and those who don't – something that clearly conflicts with traditional liberalism.

Taylor's synthesis recognizes this communitarian claim to cultural identity: the state may favour the ideal of the good life of a particular culture. Up to this point Taylor agrees with the claim to positive collective freedom of the "Statement on human rights". He does however acknowledge the objection that collectivism may violate fundamental individual rights. National traditions can clash radically with the principles of liberal democracy. He therefore confines the collective right to cultural identity to the classical liberal rights, such as the rights to life, liberty, justice, free speech and religion. Contrary to traditional liberalism however, collective cultural ends can overrule less fundamental individual rights, such as the rights to commercial

64

signage and education in one's own language. Since his synthesis recognizes fundamental individual liberties, Taylor nevertheless presents it as a non-procedural and non-homogenizing version of liberalism, that is particularly suited to multicultural communities.

Taylor is however effectively much closer to Berlin's notion of positive freedom that implies collective self-government, than he is to the concept of negative freedom. He subscribes to the concept of freedom associated with the 'civic humanist tradition' that 'was not defined mainly in terms of what we would call negative liberty. Freedom was thought of as citizen liberty, that of the active participant in public affairs' (Taylor 1989, p. 170). Taylor even views this kind of positive freedom as a necessary condition for negative freedom. According to his 'republican thesis', the voluntary self-discipline required for the respect of fundamental liberal rights in a non-despotic state, is possible only if the citizens are motivated by a strong feeling of patriotic solidarity and by an identification with a common good. Respect of the law, a willingness to pay taxes and to serve in the army cannot be explained in terms of the rational self-interest of the individual citizens, amongst other things because of the problem of 'free riders'. In a stable society one has in many respects to put the public interest before one's own self-interest. Moreover an identification with universal liberal values as such is not in itself a sufficient basis for community life. It presupposes *patriotism*, or 'a common identification with an historical community founded on certain values' (id., p. 178):

> (...) patriotism is based on an identification with others in a particular common enterprise. I am not dedicated to defending the liberty of just anyone, but I feel the bond of solidarity with my compatriots in our common enterprise, the common expression of our respective dignity. (Id., p. 166)

Although Taylor is also inspired by Aristotelian republican communitarianism, he is not nostalgic for the safe homogeneity of pre-modern hierarchical and authoritarian societies; he accepts the diversity of the modern world. In "The Politics of Recognition" he opposes modern liberalism with a modern counter-movement – that of late 18th century romanticism – as a source for his concept of collective positive freedoms. Both movements were responses to the collapse of the pre-modern feudal order. This collapse led to people losing their self-evident but unequal positions in the social hierarchy. Recognition of one's identity became problematic, something that clamoured for an effective solution. Liberalism reacted by putting a rationalist emphasis on universal equal rights, guaranteeing dignity to all citizens as autonomous, rational persons (Kant). This egalitarian 'politics of equal rights' concentrates on what people have in common. Contrary to rationalism, romanticism leads to a 'politics of difference' that recognizes that all individuals and cultures are unique. Rousseau emphasized individual authenticity (that he allowed to be swallowed up however in the collective unity of the *volonté générale*); Herder on the other hand gave priority to the collective cultural authenticity of different peoples. It is from the latter that Taylor derives his notion of the collective positive freedom to enjoy cultural integrity and collective self-rule – a position that justifies the differential treatment of the members of a particular group as a separate nation, or as a distinct cultural entity within a multicultural society. He takes the position of civic humanism however in acknowledging that cultures are not homogeneous, but can have internal conflicts. He therefore stresses the need of procedures for participatory debate and for fundamental individual rights as a bulwark against totalitarian collective claims. The most stable democracies are those where national identity coincides with the institutions of liberal self-government: where the evolution of democratic institutions forms the central theme of national history, true or mythical.

4. Rawls' Synthesis: Political Liberalism

While the communitarian Taylor takes liberal criticism into account, Rawls in his turn accommodates liberalism to the communitarian objections to it.[6] He opposes his 'political liberalism' to the classical 'metaphysical' version of liberalism, in order to meet the objection that liberalism is based upon an atomistic anthropology. This objection has an ontological and a normative aspect (see also Taylor 1989; 1985 p. 233). Critics of classical liberalism point to the social nature of man to prove that individualistic atomism is ontologically false, and cannot account for the emergence of social cohesion. Moreover, communitarians argue, classical liberalism is normatively biased. It is not neutral as it pretends to be in its attitude towards different conceptions of the good life, because it depends on a notion that individual autonomy is a good thing.

In later publications, Rawls emphasizes the modest *political* character of his liberalism more than he did in "A Theory of Justice" (1971). In the introduction to "Political Liberalism" of 1993, he rejects the comprehensive moral claims of his earlier liberal theory of justice as unrealistic. Modern democratic society with its characteristic freedom of opinion will give rise to a whole range of reasonable, but incompatible comprehensive doctrines of the good life. Consensus on a single comprehensive moral or religious ideal is not to be expected. Political philosophy should therefore avoid making controversial moral statements concerning life as a whole and fall back instead on the central question of political liberalism: 'How is it possible that there may exist over time a stable and just society of free and equal citizens profoundly divided by reasonable though incompatible religious, philosophical, and moral doctrines?' (xviii). In other words: 'What are the fair terms of social cooperation between citizens characterized as free and equal yet divided by profound doctrinal conflict?' (xxv). As a result Rawls' political liberalism does not try to replace comprehensive views, but concentrates on the basic political structures. Its aim is to develop a political concept of a just constitutional regime that is acceptable to all these conflicting but reasonable moral doctrines, so that it can serve as a shared neutral basis for public discussion. For this reason political justice entails a 'thin theory of the good': it is restricted to a fair distribution of *primary goods*, goods that are a prerequisite before any comprehensive ideal of life, such as liberties, opportunities and income.

Rawls argues that an *overlapping consensus* can be reached on the following principles of justice: (1) Each person has an equal right to an adequate framework of equal fundamental rights and liberties, a framework for the individual that is compatible with a similar framework for all. Rawls assumes that everyone will agree to this principle, because it gives one the greatest scope for following whatever ideal of the good life one might happen to have – always with the proviso that one does not interfere with the freedom of others to do the same. (2) Social and economic inequalities are possible provided two conditions are satisfied: (a) they must relate to offices and positions that are open to all under conditions of equality of opportunity; (b) they must be of most benefit to the least privileged members of society.

The first principle guarantees Berlin's negative freedom. Rawls prefers to speak of specific basic liberties rather than of liberty in general: freedom of thought, liberty of conscience, the freedoms guaranteeing the liberty and integrity of one's person, and rights and liberties covered by the rule of law. Rawls' first principle also contains the political liberties that are part of Berlin's concept of positive freedom: the rights *to* participate in political life, which constituted the core of the ancient Greek ideal of freedom. In Rawls' liberal view, however, these rights do not have the overriding and obligatory character they used to have in the small city-states of antiquity. In modern times they are even attributed less intrinsic value than are the negative liberties: they are the necessary means for the preservation of equal negative liberties. Furthermore, they supply the citizens with equal opportunities to influence collective decisions that affect their well-being.

> If the state is to exercise a final and coercive authority over a certain territory, and if it is in this way to affect permanently men's prospects in life, then the constitutional process should preserve the equal representation of the original position to the degree that is feasible (ToJ, p. 222).

A constitutional regime is therefore needed with a representative legislative body, based on elections in which all citizens have a right to vote. Freedom of speech and assembly, and the liberty to form political associations must moreover be protected in the constitution. Contrary to the comprehensive ideal of the positive 'freedom of the ancients', Rawls' liberal principle of political participation only applies to institutions. 'It does not define an ideal of citizenship; nor does it lay down a duty requiring all to take active part in political affairs' (ToJ, p. 227). Rawls also emphasizes the instrumental character of political rights when he discusses how internal conflicts between different liberties are to be solved. A scheme should be provided for all the essential freedoms and rights in which they should be placed in order of importance. Their position will depend on their value in aiding individuals in determining their own concept of the good life and their sense of justice.

The second principle guarantees all citizens the material, social and economic means for deploying their freedom as equally as possible. One could view the *absence* of the means for deploying one's freedom – due to poverty or ignorance, for instance – as forming constraints as part of the definition of the concept of freedom. This would be a parallel to the standard definition of negative freedom as freedom from constraints in the form of the *presence* of external obstacles, in particular freedom from interference by others. Rawls however prefers to define the absence of such means as being extrinsic to the concept of liberty, because they merely affect the *worth* or value of liberty. Thus, in Rawls' theory, liberty is guaranteed by the first principle of justice, the worth of liberty by the second principle. If there is scarcity in the social-economic domain that is covered by the second principle, different individuals will enjoy an unequal worth of the equal freedoms of principle 1: the rich and powerful are in a better position to achieve their ends. In order to guarantee equality here, the state must play a compensatory role as indicated in the second principle. 'Taking the two principles together, the basic structure is to be arranged to maximize the worth to the least advantaged of the complete scheme of equal liberties shared by all. This defines the end of social justice' (ToJ, p. 205).

These political principles for the public domain are autonomous, not being founded in any superior *a priori* comprehensive doctrine. Nor is it their aim to exclude specific ideals of the good, although they do effectively rule out repressive perfectionist views. But Rawls rejects perfectionist doctrines as unreasonable in the light of modern pluralism.[7] They place themselves outside the public debate, and: 'This gives us the practical task of containing them – like war and disease – so that they do not overturn political justice' (p. 64, note 19). Reasonable comprehensive views are compatible with these liberal principles of political justice, even if from very different points of view. Christians may agree because they are of the opinion that true faith is based on autonomous free will, a traditional liberal because it is a political application of his comprehensive ideal of individual autonomy, and an advocate of pluralism because political freedom is a precondition for the tolerance of a plurality of world views. At the same time, political liberalism is acceptable to the non-liberal comprehensive point of view because it restricts liberal individual rights to the public sphere. In the private domain non-liberals are still free to pursue their own ideals of life.

By restricting his theory to the domain of politics and by avoiding metaphysical controversies, Rawls can counter the communitarian objection to atomistic anthropology and to classical liberalism's metaphysics of individual autonomy. Although he speaks of 'free persons' and of 'a self that is prior to its ends', he does not mean that they are free in a metaphysical or ontological sense. Rawls agrees with the communitarians that individuals do not enter society by free choice: 'We have no prior identity before being in society: it is not as if we came from nowhere but rather find ourselves growing up in this society in this social position' (1993, p. 41). He merely argues that in a plural society persons are not identical with fixed social roles and ideals of the good life. Since they can compare different comprehensive views, they are capable of a considered revision of their conceptions of the good. *Political* liberties then should not be linked to a specific moral attitude, or to specific social roles. In public life everybody has the same rights, whatever their ideals and social position. Political liberalism however does not imply the questionable comprehensive metaphysical thesis that human beings are essentially autonomous individuals, in the domain of politics as well as elsewhere. Although basic rights have priority, political liberalism does not apply to life as a whole. In the private sphere one is free to endorse illiberal doctrines. This makes Rawls' theory compatible with doctrines that deny autonomy in the non-political domain. It only requires that individuals distinguish between the comprehensive views of their private lives, and the political ideal of tolerance that rules public life.

Rawls' theory of justice also makes allowance for communitarianism in that it assumes that citizens of a 'well-ordered society' will have a sense of solidarity. If citizens were only motivated by rational self-interest, 'free riders' would soon undermine social stability. Rawls assumes therefore that they will want to cooperate on *fair* terms. Rawls' 'difference principle', the principle of justice 2b, in particular is based on the assumption that individual citizens with superior inborn talents do not consider these as personal merits that entitle them to extra income (Rawls 1993, VII, 8). Social cooperation of different individuals with differentiated specializations is in itself more than an instrument to satisfy their individual preferences. As a 'social union of social unions' the state develops into a good in itself, comparable to the shared pleasure of members of an orchestra playing together (Rawls 1993, VIII, 6). Political liberalism also presupposes that all citizens respect one another as free and equal persons. This assumption is in sharp contrast with the pre-liberal 17th century, the age of the wars of religion, when different beliefs were not tolerated. Historically speaking the politics of tolerance started as a mere *modus vivendi* in order to bring these devastating wars to an end. It was no more than an instrument to further the various private ends of all parties, a 'private society'. Based on a contingent balance of power, it is hardly a guarantee of social stability. But the liberal framework of political rights is now generally considered as a good in itself, constituting the conditions of fair cooperation and mutual respect. Most citizens of modern western states share the common political aim of furthering a just society, however divergent their overall religious and moral opinions may be (Rawls 1993, V,7; VIII, 3). Political liberalism is even affirmed by the principle of tolerance implicit in their differing reasonable and comprehensive doctrines. In other words, it has acquired a solid basis in Western political traditions.

5. Two Syntheses, Equally Reasonable?

With Taylor's politics of recognition and Rawls' political liberalism, communitarianism and liberalism have come close to each other. Both agree that fundamental negative liberties have an overriding status, and that these necessitate solidarity with a particular historical community. But their old antagonism has not dissolved completely. The main remaining difference is that Taylor's patriotic 'civic humanism' involves a comprehensive theory of the good in keeping with Berlin's concept of collective positive freedom: human beings find their essential identity when they actively participate in public life, and the state should encourage them to do so. Rawls' 'patriotism of the right' merely requires an acceptance of the liberal scheme of just cooperation in the public sphere. In "Cross-purposes: the liberal-communitarian debate" (1989) Taylor has measured himself directly against modern forms of non-atomistic, 'holistic' liberalism. He suggests that Rawls' liberal theory of the good provides too scanty a basis for social stability. Rawls answers that Taylor's patriotism makes the same error as every comprehensive doctrine that wants to monopolize state support: it is unreasonable.

This raises the question: which of the two is the more reasonable synthesis? Since Taylor and Rawls both suppose that their political ideals must have firm roots in the existing traditions of a society, I shall evaluate their doctrines in relation to three types of society that are characterized by different traditions. Firstly, the history of a community may in fact coincide with the evolution of the traditions of political liberalism. Taylor quotes the example of the history of the United States. Secondly, a traditional identity may have a non-liberal character, without however fundamentally conflicting with liberal principles of equality and freedom, as for instance the identification with French culture that occurs in Quebec. Thirdly, cultural identity may be straightforwardly illiberal. Taylor refers to Muslim fundamentalists who want to kill Rushdie (as encouraged by the present regime in Iran).

Liberal Patriotism

According to Taylor the United States 'is peculiarly fortunate in that, from its origins, patriotism combined a sense of nationality with a liberal representative regime' (1989, p. 280, note 21). When it comes down to detail, however, America's liberal traditions are open to a variety of interpretations. Rawls relates them solely and simply to his ideal of political liberalism. Taylor opposes this approach, referring to Sandel's view that the ideal of patriotic participation has traditionally played an important role too.[8] Taylor suggests that purely liberal traditions would not be substantial enough to be a proper basis for solidarity. He argues that the United States in fact probably owes its actual effectiveness as a socio-political system to a more comprehensive patriotic identification.

In an implied criticism of Rawls, Taylor invokes his 'republican thesis': he maintains that the egalitarian 'difference principle' of the liberal theory of justice requires more solidarity than Rawls can account for, because it represents 'an agreement to regard the distribution of natural talents as a common asset' (Rawls 1971, p.101) and not as personal desert.[9] The sacrifices that the difference principle demands of talented individuals, as well as the self-discipline called for by Rawls' principle of equal liberties, require a patriotism that

> is somewhere between friendship, or family feeling on one side, and altruistic dedication on the other. (...) Functioning republics are like families in this crucial respect that part of what binds people together is their common history. (p. 166)

Such patriotic republics are 'animated by a sense of a shared immediate common good' (p.169): a non-instrumental public good that is valued because of its common functioning and implications.

Taylor warns that in general Rawls' thin 'patriotism of the right' would in practice even undermine social cohesion. The common good of 'holistic' liberalism is limited to the liberal tradition of the rule of law as elaborated in Rawls' first principle of equal liberties, and to the fair distribution of opportunities and income as stated in his second principle. According to Taylor, this furthers an instrumental perspective on state institutions:

> Citizen capacity consists mainly in the power to retrieve these rights and ensure equal treatment, as well as to influence the effective decision makers. (...) That means that no value is put on participation on rule for its own sake. (p. 178-9)

This brings Taylor to his decisive question: 'can our patriotism survive the marginalization of participatory self-rule?' (p. 178). He suggests that it cannot. 'Holistic' liberalism accommodates citizens who do not participate at all in the public debate, and become 'part of an alien political universe, which one can perhaps manipulate but never identify with' (p. 179). And: 'If I win my way by manipulating the common institutions, how can I see them as reflecting a purpose common to me and those who participate in these institutions?' (p. 179). Although his theory of the liberal good is somewhat inadequately argued it can be made to tally with the central good of his civic humanism: the ideal of participatory self-rule – Berlin's collective positive freedom – given the 'republican' condition that the patriotic traditions also involve individual negative freedom. A republican-patriotic society should 'share and endorse at least this proposition about the good life' (p. 178). The public indignation during the Watergate affair indicates that the United States do in fact have such a patriotic tradition. Taylor however also recognizes that Rawls could be right in defining the American tradition exclusively in terms of non-participatory procedural liberalism, which would prove that such a tradition is actually viable.

In his turn, in "Political Liberalism" (V, 7), Rawls discusses Taylor's civic humanism. He deals implicitly with Taylor's indirect justification of patriotism as a necessary condition for an effective liberal constitution. Rawls readily agrees that political participation is one good among others that should be encouraged *as far as* it is necessary for mutual cooperation in a democratic society. Political liberalism is compatible with a non-comprehensive form of republicanism that wants the state to encourage political virtues, because democratic liberties cannot be protected 'without a widespread participation in democratic politics by a vigorous and well-informed citizen body, and certainly with a general retreat into private life' (p. 205). But civic humanism entails the more far-reaching and comprehensive Aristotelian doctrine that man is essentially a political animal, and that democratic participation is the central human good. Like all comprehensive views this overall patriotism cannot count on a reasonable consensus, so that it is unreasonable to enforce it as an overriding ideal of the good life. Of course, this leaves every individual citizen full freedom to devote himself completely to political life as a comprehensive ideal. The division of labour even requires that some citizens concentrate on politics. But others are just as likely to have other ideals of the good life.

Typical of this dispute of Taylor and Rawls is their views on education. Rawls would have the state encourage political virtues that sustain the non-instrumental liberal 'patriotism of right' by way of education (V, 6). Children should know their constitutional and civic rights.

> Moreover, their education should also prepare them to be fully cooperating members of society (...); it should also encourage the political virtues so that they want to honor the fair terms of social cooperation in their relations with the rest of society' (p. 199)

But the state may only prescribe education in the virtues of *political* liberalism. It should remain neutral as to comprehensive ideals of the good life, including the ideal of traditional 'metaphysical' liberalism. By contrast, Taylor's state would make education in a comprehensive patriotism obligatory. For example, Taylor rejects as profoundly un-American any appeal to liberal neutrality that objects to the 'pious tone with which American history and its major figures are presented to the young' (1989, p. 176). A court that upholds such protests 'would be undermining the very regime it was established to interpret' (p. 177).

Weighing up the pros and cons, I regard Rawls as having achieved a more reasonable synthesis. He is right in stressing that Taylor's essentialism requires proving. In his critique of Rawls' liberalism Taylor does not offer independent proof. He does not back up his notion of civic humanism with direct arguments; all he offers is the implicit criticism that Rawls' theory of justice requires patriotism. This 'republican thesis' is rendered vulnerable by reason of its all-or-nothing character. Taylor supposes wrongly that when patriotic participation is not the overriding human motive, an instrumental calculating attitude will take over and completely undermine political and social life. He equates social and cultural life too much with political life, which makes him think that social solidarity is impossible without political participation and an intensive state involvement.

Rawls' assumption that political solidarity can flourish without participation in public affairs being obligatory seems more realistic. Other factors can also foster solidarity. Like Taylor, Rawls stresses the resulting 'immediate common good' in his notion of fair cooperation of people with complementary skills; he even compares it with the shared joy of a musical ensemble. Moreover, the liberal constitutional regime is considered as a non-instrumental political good from the perspective of the different reasonable and comprehensive doctrines of the citizens (see also section 4).

As for political involvement, Taylor also exaggerates the dichotomy between full civic participation and asocial instrumentalism. There are many different degrees of political activity that are compatible with a non-instrumental attitude to politics. I may define the democratic constitution as being the product of organized distrust. In that case I would rather passively follow the subculture of political meetings from a critical distance, happy that the politicians leave me in peace while the political scheme of fair cooperation offers me the opportunity to devote my time to the things that I value more – for instance, playing in an orchestra. This does not mean that I lapse into mere instrumental calculation. I accept the political arrangements as good, as long as the politicians represent me reasonably fairly and continue to respect liberal rights. If they don't, I shall participate in general elections to correct them.

Moreover, Taylor's patriotism may even turn against itself, producing a breakdown in the consensus that undermines the very social cooperation it aims to ensure. If the state imposes a comprehensive ideal of civic humanism that is not voluntarily accepted, it will alienate its citizens instead of uniting them. The point of patriotic education for instance is to internalize a pious attitude to national symbols and heroes. As Taylor admits, however, national symbolism often rests on questionable historical fictions (1992/3, p. 14-5). As symbols they are open to a variety of interpretations, so that they can easily provoke bitter controversies between different national factions. William of Orange, the Dutch 'Father of the Fatherland' who led the liberation of the Netherlands from Spanish domination in the late 16th century, can be viewed as a forefather of liberal ideological tolerance. But Roman Catholic Dutchmen used to be taught that he persecuted the Catholics, who were excluded from public positions until the nineteenth century. Leaders who have gone down in history as liberals in their own countries have often acted as ruthless colonialists; the descendants of former slaves will view them as symbols of evil.

It is also incompatible with Taylor's ideal of democratic participation to instil in children a respectful attitude towards mythical national symbols. Since democracy requires that its members be capable of critical dialogue, democratic education should not be based on myths but on a spirit of open and critical inquiry. With regard to constitutional history, it should suffice to point out the reasonable character and practical benefits of a liberal regime. Taylor's advocacy of an education in patriotism is more suited to pre-modern authoritarian societies. Plato's myth of the creation of golden, silver and iron people is its model,[10] and its basis is a mistrust of the capacity of the citizens to engage in genuine debate; there is no suggestion here that they can act as democratic participants in a liberal society.[11]

Non-liberal Patriotism

Taylor also discusses a second kind of society, characterized by partly non-liberal traditions,

> where the fusion between patriotism and the free institutions is not so total as in the United States (...) modern democratic societies where patriotism centers on a national culture, which in many cases has come (sometimes late and painfully) to incorporate free institutions, but which is also defined in terms of some language or history. (1989, p. 181)

For example, the kernel of Quebec's patriotic tradition is a flourishing French culture. According to Taylor, the neutrality of political liberalism would not work here, because it would 'either not be responding to majority will, or would reflect a society so deeply demoralized as to be close to dissolution as a viable pole of patriotic allegiance' (p. 182). In an non-liberal culture like this, the homogenizing liberal 'politics of equal rights' is much less appropriate than is Taylor's romantic 'politics of difference', even though the latter entails a sacrifice of minor rights and of the equal distribution of socio-economic goods in favour of the collective right of cultural integrity.

Here again, Taylor overstates his patriotism by presenting it in an all-or-nothing way. If the majority in Quebec really identifies so strongly with French culture, why should one need any state interference other than what is necessary to guarantee equal opportunities for French-speaking citizens? Gallic culture would appear to have little vitality if it could only survive by forbidding French-speaking parents to send their children to English-language schools. Would it really demoralize the majority if the state also guaranteed the same freedoms and anti-discrimination provisions to other, non-French, citizens? Again, the reason for Taylor's overstatement is that he wrongly identifies social and cultural life with political life. Empirically speaking, however, it is implausible to argue that national cultures could not survive without

78

state encouragement and enforcement.

It could be argued, on the other hand, that a minority culture like that of Quebec is endangered by the superior economic power of the surrounding majority culture. Adequate command of English may be necessary if one is to survive in the world of Canadian business. French-speaking parents may reluctantly decide to send their children to English schools for this reason. Compulsory attendance at French schools may help to ensure the preservation of the French-Canadian language: if this obligation is applied to all French-speaking citizens, it guarantees that nobody is economically discriminated against, at least on the grounds of their language. In this way the provincial government may prevent economic factors from dominating in other areas, such as culture and education: at least *within* the French-speaking community economic competition will not be a pretext for abandoning French culture. French education however may disadavantage the Québecois people in comparison with English-speaking Canadians. To make French education obligatory would therefore imply the enforcement of a perfectionistic preference for one aspect of life (language) over another (economic development). This choice should be left to the individual citizen.

Taylor also has an unrealistic non-dynamic and atomistic view of cultural identity. Cultures consist of vital traditions that because they are in constant change cannot be protected by laws that keep them 'frozen' for future generations. Cultural change may also involve a merging or interchange with surrounding cultures. It is therefore a mistake to strive for cultural purity, as was attempted in a recent legal proposal in metropolitan France that would outlaw the public and private use of 'franglais', barbaric English words like *ok, walkman, weekend or drugstore*. (Meanwhile on the ground of liberty of expression the French *Conseil Constitutionnel* has declared that the *loi Toubon* is not applicable in the private sphere – although advertisements must still have a 'francophone character.') This is *a fortiori* the case in a multicultural community like Canada. Multicultural interaction does not necessarily lead to a homogeneous culture without any character; it is just as likely to generate a new cultural diversity as has happened in Latin America.

Furthermore, even though Taylor seems to prefer cultural differences, his stress on the power of the state to impose change suggests that his civic humanism is a far more homogenizing force than he would allow political liberalism to have. Since Taylor's 'politics of difference' has an exclusively collective character, it offers less room for individual differences, and thus it diminishes internal cultural dynamics and variety. If applied to a specific territory such as Quebec, it would also homogenize local diversity in another way in that it would protect a Canadian cultural minority by discriminating against another cultural minority: the local non-francophone citizens.

This is not the case with political liberalism. Unlike comprehensive liberalism, it does not propagate the ideal of individual autonomy in the non-public domain, which would indeed be destructive of non-liberal cultural traditions. It explicitly safeguards the cultural freedom of individuals and social groups in the private domain. If voluntary social organizations do not supply the necessary resources, the state may even create 'a just basic structure within which permissible forms of life have a fair opportunity to maintain themselves and to gain adherents over generations' (Rawls 1993, p. 198). Unlike the case with Taylor's patriotism, however, the state should not protect or encourage a comprehensive view or culture that is incapable of surviving even when protected by this 'positive discrimination'. Rawls discusses the objection that political liberalism in the public domain may unintentionally have the homogenizing effect of leading the citizens to embrace full liberalism (V, 6). His conclusion is that there are great differences between the two, although this might sometimes be the result. One might also ask why a culture deserves protection if it is incapable of surviving, not simply under conditions of equal freedom, but even when the state takes additional measures to guarantee it equal opportunities.[12]

But if a liberal state really wants to be neutral, should it not adopt a purely neutral language, say Esperanto? For instance, does the use of Dutch as the official language of the Netherlands not mean that immigrants from foreign linguistic communities (now around 5% of the population) are discrimated against in terms of equal opportunities? I think not. The introduction of Esperanto would conflict with the assumption that political liberalism must have its roots in a historical tradition. It would be like instituting freedom in a state of nature, with no more justification than the rational social contract of classical liberalism. Furthermore, the immigrants have chosen to come to this country. Therefore, a liberal state with foreign minorities has the right to preserve its traditional language, provided this does not aim to give preferential treatment to its indigenous citizens, but only treats its language as a common medium of communication to ensure mutual cooperation.[13] Another situation occurs when the state is a union of several large indigenous communities with different linguistic traditions. If they share the same territory, the best solution might be to be multilingual; if they inhabit different areas, linguistic federalism (Belgium, Switzerland) would seem to be the answer. In the case of Quebec both solutions are possible.[14] Much more complicated is the case of a minority of an indigenous people. Often they have lost the sovereignty of their land involuntarily and unjustly. This gives them at least the right to private ownership of a territory of their own that is not publicly accessible. They may also have some form of autonomous administration within the dominant liberal constitution provided this does not violate the basic liberal rights of others.[15]

Illiberal Patriotism

Only with regard to nations or cultural minorities with *illiberal* traditions are Taylor and Rawls almost fully in agreement. According to Taylor national identity may not violate *fundamental* individual rights such as Rushdie's right to life and freedom of speech. The common communitarian element in their syntheses also implies a common problem with their theory. Since both Taylor and Rawls suppose that their political ideals are rooted in the traditions of a particular community, their views would not be very convincing for representatives of other traditions.

Taylor explicitly recognizes the epistemological cultural relativism of his liberal-civic patriotism. This does not mean however that he concurs with the normative relativism of the "Statement on human rights" (see section 2). Instead, he declares that 'Liberalism is also a fighting creed', that 'has to draw the line' (1992, p. 62). He recognizes that the statement 'This is how we do things here' is not satisfactory to citizens who belong to cultural minorities with illiberal traditions. They can only experience it as a power play. Taylor presents no argument here; all he offers is a psychological strategy: 'The challenge is to deal with their sense of marginalization without compromising our basic political principles' (p. 63).[16]

Rawls too rejects normative relativism: non-reasonable comprehensive doctrines that aim to monopolize the state institutions must be 'contained'. But he is more ambiguous than Taylor with regard to the epistemological status of his political liberalism. On the one hand, he recognizes its epistemological relativity:

> (...) justification is addressed to others who disagree with us, and therefore it must always proceed from some consensus, that is, from premises we and others publicly recognize as true; or better, publicly recognize as acceptable to us for the purpose of a working agreement on the fundamental questions of political justice. (Rawls 1985, p. 229)

Rawls' justification is based on the democratic tradition of modern Western liberal culture; with this as his point of departure, he develops a complex 'deep structure' that would allow for an overlapping consensus within that culture. This means that from the very start he leaves other cultural ideals out of the discussion – for instance the notion of a hierarchical society that claims to be a reflection of a higher religious or rational order. On the other hand, he argues that his theory of justice is the most *reasonable* political doctrine in a plural society, even though it makes no attempt to prove that it is metaphysically *true*. According to Rawls, the notion of truth belongs to the realm of comprehensive metaphysical doctrines about which there can be no reasonable consensus. Rawls' political structuralism therefore neither affirms nor denies any metaphysical claims to moral truth. But this does not mean that it is arbitrary: 'Reasonableness is its standard of correctness, and given its political aims, it need not go beyond that' (1993, p. 127). For:

> Once we accept the fact that reasonable pluralism is a permanent condition of public culture under free conditions, the idea of the reasonable is more suitable as part of the basis of public justification for a constitutional regime than the idea of moral truth. (p. 129)

I prefer Taylor's straightforward epistemological relativism here. One can only condemn other cultures as being unreasonable from the point of view of one's own standards of reasonableness. This implies that the validity of Rawls' political liberalism ends where the overlapping consensus ceases to exist. In the normative field, political liberalism can only solve conflicts between incompatible ideals of the good life, for instance between Christian and Muslim ideals, in so far as their adherents share an ideal of political tolerance. But Rawls has nothing to offer to people who are not willing to differentiate between the moral and the political, because these people believe that their own moral ideals have priority over the liberal principle of tolerance. While Rawls rejects such doctrines as unreasonable, in the epistemological field his insistence on a reasonable burden of proof[17] will not be sufficient to persuade adherents of illiberal traditions who do not recognize rational consensus as their criterion of truth. If I belonged to an elitist perfectionist tradition of the Platonic kind, I would not be impressed by Rawls' argument that 'reasonable pluralism' is the normal result of the workings of a free democratic society. I would answer that this absence of moral truth is precisely what makes a free democracy bad. In short, in appealing to the traditions of his own political culture Rawls abandons any notion of debating these matters with other cultures which do not share his democratic ideals – these cultures of course form the majority of the world's population.[18]

On the other hand, I am not convinced by their arguments either. So, if illiberal perfectionists show the same fighting spirit as Taylor, I have no choice but to defend my freedom.

6. A Single Concept of Liberty

I would like to end where I started – with the conceptual question of liberty that I discussed in section 1. Berlin's conclusion was that the two traditional concepts of liberty, negative and positive freedom, should be divorced. He suggested that only the former had a right to keep the family name. Once their true character as different and potentially conflicting values was revealed, they could be reunited in a compromise. The syntheses of Taylor and Rawls offer such compromises, the former stressing positive freedom, the other negative freedom. These different compromises also lead to different notions of liberty. Which of the two is the more attractive?

Rawls devotes § 32 of "A theory of justice" to the conceptual question. He does not participate in the debate about the definition of freedom between the proponents of positive and negative liberty, because the controversy he is involved in is one of substance, not of definitions. Following MacCallum's comment on Berlin, Rawls maintains that the theme of liberty can be summed up under three headings: the agents who are free, the restrictions which they are free *from*, and what they are free *to* do.

> The general description of liberty, then, has the following form: this or that person (or persons) is free (or not free) from this or that constraint (or set of constraints) to do (or not to do) so and so. (p. 202)

The agents may be persons, associations or states.[19] The constraints may be legal duties and prohibitions as well as social sanctions. Rawls does not pay much attention to the freedom *to* do so and so, not going beyond referring to specific traditional negative liberties. The purpose of freedom of conscience for instance is to enable people to pursue their moral, philosophical or religious ideals. Rawls agrees with Berlin that positive and negative freedom refer to two different fundamental but conflicting human aspirations: the aspiration to choose one's own way of life, and the aspiration to political participation in the life of the community. To solve this conflict, a theory of justice could provide them with a scale of relative values. Rawls' theory of justice aims to do just this, in order to create a coherent whole out of the different liberties, thus resolving any conflicts implicit in them. The basic liberties of principle 1 have precedence: liberties may only be restricted on the grounds of other liberties, not for socio-economic reasons. Rawls views the latter as means to obtain an equal *worth* of the liberties, to be regulated in the subordinate principle 2. In the conflict between positive and negative liberties Rawls sympathizes more with the latter, although he does make some allowance for positive freedom. He includes part of the classical concept of positive freedom in his first principle of justice – the positive freedom to participate in democratic political life. He sees these political rights however as instrumental to the negative liberties.[20] They do not imply the ideal of citizenship and the duty of active political participation that the ancients and Taylor attach to them. Regarding other forms of positive freedom that a perfectionist government may try to enforce, such as the rationalist ones mentioned in note 3, Rawls argues that one should not tolerate intolerant individuals or groups who violate the constitutional liberties.

Taylor is of a different opinion. He not only brings liberty and solidarity together in a synthesis; he also combines them in a single concept of freedom. According to Taylor, a meaningful definition of freedom must include patriotic participatory self-rule as a central element (1989, p. 178). In "What's wrong with negative liberty" (1990, pp. 211-229) he argues against Berlin, stating that negative freedom, defined by Hobbes as the absence of external obstacles, cannot be treated as a separate concept from positive freedom. Taylor maintains first of all that the obstacles to one's freedom can also be *internal*. Hobbes' view that one is free if one can do what one wants, without others interfering, is oversimplistic in terms of moral psychology. Human beings also have secondary desires, or meta-desires concerning the hierarchy of their primary desires and purposes. This implies that a strong desire of a 'lower rank' may act as an internal obstacle to the fulfilment of higher desires. Secondly, internal obstacles can arise that the subject is unaware of. An individual can give a mistaken priority to his desires because he miscalculates his situation, for instance under the influence of irrational fears or unconscious resentment. Taylor also mentions factors like false consciousness and inner repression. Some people, like Charles Manson or Andreas Baader, even have a completely distorted sense of their fundamental goals. This second point suggests that the individual subject cannot be the final judge of whether his desires are authentic or not. Contrary then to Hobbes' definition of negative freedom, one can do what one wants and yet be unfree. The result is that the pure concept of negative freedom breaks down. Freedom also presupposes something *positive*: that one has an adequate awareness of one's fundamental purposes, which requires that one develops 'a certain condition of self-understanding (...) in order to be truly or fully free' (p. 229). Taylor concludes:

> The first step from the Hobbesian definition to a positive notion, to a view of freedom as the ability to fulfil my purposes, and as being greater the more significant the purposes, is one we cannot help taking. Whether we must also realize the second step, to a view of freedom wich sees it as realizable only within a certain form of community; (...) these are questions which must now be addressed. (p. 229)

As we have seen elsewhere, Taylor also takes the second step to full collective positive freedom as Berlin defines it. He argues that the development of individual identity depends on communal traditions, and that self-understanding requires continuous participation in the public debate that takes place in a democratic republic. Taylor's fusion of the two concepts of negative and positive freedom is replicated in his definition of liberalism: the happy marriage of the two freedoms in his civic humanism could as well be called 'liberalism' (Taylor 1989, p. 182); it is moreover a 'positive' liberalism, richer than Rawls' rather thin version.

What are we to make of this controversy of concepts? Following the analysis of Joel Feinberg, I would plead for a single concept of freedom that is broader than Berlin's definition of negative freedom as well as Rawls' combination of negative liberties and limited instrumental positive political liberties in his first principle of justice on the one hand, but that is more negative than the positive freedom of Berlin and Taylor on the other. Feinberg wants to replace Berlin's 'two concepts' analysis by a 'single concept analysis' that contains the most important insights of both negative and positive freedom in an economic frame of reference.

Feinberg extends Rawls' formula of freedom in proposing a concept of freedom in the form of a formula: *A is free from B to do (or omit, or be, or have) C.* In order to make statements about freedom understandable, Feinberg says that one has to state whose freedom is at stake, what he is free from, and what the object of this freedom is. The term A can refer to an individual or a group. The central term *free* is defined as the absence of constraints on actual and possible desires. Feinberg is basically concerned with the meaning of 'freedom' in political philosophy: 'political freedom' or 'liberty' is 'the absence of that one special kind of constraint called coercion, which is the deliberate forceful interference in the affairs of human beings by other human beings' (p. 7).

In the term 'free *from* B', the term B refers to compulsions or constraints (things that prevent one from doing something). Not all situations where one is unable to do something imply a lack of freedom. Political philosophy only takes into account situations that are directly or indirectly brought about through the coercion by others. Like Taylor, Feinberg maintains that constraints need not be external, nor 'positive'. Illness or ignorance are *internal* constraints that can be 'the indirect results of deliberately imposed and modifiable social arrangements' (p. 9). Moreover, ignorance is a *negative* constraint: one is unfree because the required knowledge is *lacking.* 'There is no doubt that some constraints are negative – lack of money, strength, skill, or knowledge can quite effectively prevent a person from doing, or having, or being something he might want' (p. 12). Poverty is an external negative constraint (the absence of money restricts one's freedom); a prison is an external positive constraint (one is unfree because of the presence of something external); headaches, obsessive thoughts and compulsive desires are internal positive restraints. The classical freedoms (Rawls' first principle of justice) guarantee freedom from positive external constraints, in particular from direct interference by others or the state. The social rights (Rawls' second principle) guarantee freedom from negative external and internal constraints, such as lack of sufficient income, shelter, health and education.

What one regards as a constraint is determined by what one strives for. This is expressed in the term 'free *to* C'. C represents the actual or hypothetical desires of A. Feinberg sees the values that are symbolized by C as external supplements to the concept of freedom as such, that are 'determined by some independent standard' (p. 19).

> Since "maximal freedom" (having as much freedom on balance as possible) is a notion that makes sense only through the application of external standards for determining the relative worth or importance of different sorts of interests and areas of activity, it is by itself a merely formal ideal that cannot stand on its own feet without the help of other values. (p. 19)

Feinberg's formula offers an important extension of, and improvement on, the negative concept of freedom that survived Berlin's analysis. I agree with Feinberg's introduction of 'negative constraints' in the term 'free from B'. It is not absurd to say that one's desires (C) can also be constrained by other *inner* inclinations or desires such as 'neurotic inhibitions, drug addiction, or subliminal needs that are not necessarily caused by direct or indirect external coercion by others. This presupposes that the desires expressed by C have to do with a concept of the person that is inherently disharmonious: the human subject has different conflicting desires that need to be ordered coherently. This is a widely accepted view that should be taken into account in any concept of liberty. According to my own *Critical Schizoism*, the human personality is split up in a number of opposite but interacting personalities – actor and spectator, for instance.[21] Freudian anthropology also implies a mildly split personality consisting of the instinctive Id, the prudent Ego and the critical Superego. The Dr Jekyll in me has to control the hidden Mr Hyde, who breaks free when I am off my guard. Feinberg rightly remarks that if the personality actually disintegrates, that is, if one ceases to have any hierarchical structure of wants, aims and ideals, any talk about freedom stops making sense. The same applies when one's system of sub-personalities collapses in cases of multiple personality disorder, or when Mr Hyde takes over, or schizoism lapses into full-blown schizofrenia.

Feinberg's single concept of freedom is also an improvement on that of Rawls who sees freedom as synonymous exclusively with the classical negative liberties and the instrumental political positive liberties of his first principle of justice. Rawls describes his second principle as external (though related) to these liberties: it aims to provide all citizens with the socio-economic means that will ensure them as equal an opportunity as possible to deploy their freedom. Feinberg on the other hand writes Rawls' second principle into his concept of freedom by which 'positive freedom' is a safeguard against 'negative constraints'.

The sub-concept of 'positive freedom' however that Feinberg adds to Berlin's negative freedom is no more than a shadow of the concept of 'positive freedom' that Berlin describes (and rejects), and which Feinberg describes (and accepts). Feinberg claims that his introduction of 'negative constraints' accommodates Berlin's two concepts in one single concept of freedom: 'negative freedom' in the sense of the absence of positive constraints, and 'positive freedom' in the sense of the absence of negative constraints. In fact, however, Feinberg's positive freedom is merely an extension of the concept of *negative* freedom: one should be free *from* negative constraints such as a lack of income, food, shelter, health or knowledge. It accommodates Rawls' second principle of justice, but fails to do so with the concept of positive freedom held by Berlin and Taylor. Feinberg's version of positive freedom, in other words, is more relevant to the debate between libertarian and egalitarian liberals than it is to the liberal-communitarian or the liberal-perfectionist debates.

Central to Berlin's concept of positive freedom is his inclusion in his definition of a notion of a positive essential human identity that one is free *to* strive towards. Taylor defines this identity as patriotic participation. In Feinberg's construct however this element appears in the phrase, 'to C'. This means that Feinberg's concept of 'positive freedom' does not include any essential human identity. Firstly, the values represented by C derive from independent standards, and are not included in Feinberg's concept of freedom. Secondly, C does not necessarily denote an essential identity. It is a blank term that refers to all actual and hypothetical desires that human beings may have. Feinberg's positive freedom therefore represents a substantial diminution of the concepts of positive freedom of Berlin and Taylor.

The term 'to C' in Feinberg's formula offers a perfect tool for exposing the nature of the controversy around the notion of negative freedom in Rawls' political liberalism on the one hand and the positive freedom of Taylor's moderate patriotic perfectionism on the other. As Feinberg indicates, 'C' is open to a whole range of interpretations, depending on one's outlook:

> One person's freedom can conflict with another's, freedom in one dimension can contrast with freedom in another, and the conflicting dimensions cannot meaningfully be combined in one scale. These conflicts and recalcitrances require that we put types of subjects, possible desires, and areas of activity into some order of importance; this in turn requires supplementing the political ideal of freedom with moral standards of other kinds. (p. 19)

According to Rawls, moral standards are based on comprehensive metaphysical views about which no reasonable consensus is possible. The state therefore should remain neutral with regard to C, leaving its citizens free to define it for themselves. Taylor objects that this is too negative, since it leaves C empty. If C does not continue to be reinterpreted in an ongoing public debate in which the whole people is involved, they will be unable to develop their identity and to fulfil themselves as human beings. Taylor therefore argues that C should be interpreted in a patriotic sense. According to his ideal of positive freedom citizens are not truly free if they are unwilling to participate in the process of democracy. Therefore the state may infringe in certain minor ways on their negative liberties in order to force them to be really free in the positive patriotic sense.

With regard to state interference in the name of freedom I again agree with Feinberg who defines *political* freedom as the absence of direct or indirect coercion by others. This implies the liberal conclusion that the state may act against constraints that are the result of such coercion. These include internal and negative constraints such as poverty, illness and ignorance that 'are the indirect result of deliberately imposed and modifiable social arrangements' (p. 9). The internal constraint of 'false consciousness' that Taylor refers to is thus a legitimate concern for the state, while attempts to counteract other inner mental restrictions such as inhibitions and irrational fears are not. The furthering of self-understanding is also not the task of the state, certainly in the patriotic sense. A paternalistic exception might be made in the case of completely perverted or addicted persons with whom it makes no sense to speak of freedom, even if they do no harm to others.

In the field of meta-ethics, Taylor's concept of positive freedom and positive liberalism should be rejected in favour of Feinberg's 'single concept'. In the ethical field Taylor's synthesis of individualism and collectivism is less reasonable than that of Rawls. Unfortunately, however, political liberalism remains a reasonable philosophy only for people who are reasonable and tolerant already.

Notes

1. I am grateful to H.J.R. Kaptein and F.C.L.M. Jacobs for their comments on an earlier draft.
2. It does not however concern the form of government. Many liberals link negative liberty with democracy, while they are both the result of the ideal of autonomous self-determination in respectively the private and the public sphere. Berlin argues that these concepts are not logically connected, because a degree of individual freedom is compatible with enlightened despotism, while an elected majority government in a democracy might leave one no personal freedom at all.
3. In the rationalist version human identity consists of a supposedly rational, 'higher' self, which is the true goal of man (Plato, Kant). If one is the slave of one's passions, one is lacking in any form of self-rule. Freedom therefore means being governed by reason, rather than by the 'lower', irrational parts of one's personality. It is freedom to do something worthwhile, to lead a good life, 'not freedom to do what is irrational, or stupid, or wrong' (p. 148). This means that paternalist advocates of the ideal of positive freedom such as Plato may propagate violations of negative freedom. If an individual is unfree as a consequence of inner mental obstacles, outward powers like the state may come to his aid and force him to be 'really' free. This coercion is viewed as fostering self-rule, because it furthers one's self-realization. Positive freedom therefore is compatible with an illiberal, perfectionist state.

   Berlin argues that there must be something wrong with the premises of positive freedom if it leads to despotism. Advocates of this variant of positive freedom wrongly suppose the existence of a harmonious rational world in which all men have only one aim, that of rational self-mastery and where they are guided by a wise elite of rulers. Since this assumption is metaphysical and therefore not demonstrable, Berlin goes on to argue that freedom in fact is not identical with rational knowledge and virtue (p. 154). This implies that negative freedom is the only acceptable concept of liberty. The nationalist version of positive freedom is similar to this despotic perfectionism in that it leads to similar illiberal conclusions. Berlin however considers it an atypical form of positive liberty because it confuses freedom with solidarity, using the misleading term, 'social freedom'. Whereas the aim of positive freedom is to keep something at bay – not outer forces as is the case with the nationalist notion of freedom, but inner irrational forces – the nationalist 'search for status' is based on a desire for recognition as a member of a worthwhile group. Nevertheless, one could still include nationalism within the concept of positive freedom when it is linked with the communitarian idea that an individual derives his true identity from his social group. Nationalism is usually the result of the suppression of a group. In the communitarian view such suppression implies that foreign powers prevent one from realizing one's true collective self. Positive freedom then in the nationalist and communitarian sense means that one is free to realize one's true self in an independent group identity, holding off foreign influences.

4. Nevertheless, in a pluralistic world view negative liberty is entitled to a special status. The freedom to have certain aspirations, while not claiming eternal validity for them, implies that there are many human goals and that these are not necessarily commensurable. 'Pluralism, with the measure of 'negative' liberty that it entails, seems to me a truer and more humane ideal than the goals of those who seek in the great, disciplined, authoritarian structures the ideal of 'positive' self-mastery by classes, or peoples, or the whole of mankind.' (p. 171)

5. Also, in contradiction with its epistemological cultural relativism, the normative relativism of the Statement itself implies a universal norm that is not shared by all cultures: the norm that the rights of other cultures must be respected.

6. Rawls in fact denies that this is his intention (Rawls 1993, p. xvii, note 6). His concern with the conditions for the stability of a liberal social order can however be read as an answer to Taylor's criticism that liberalism cannot work outside of a patriotic context.

7. Rawls opposes plain pluralism to 'reasonable pluralism' (1993, II, 3). The latter means that even after a reasonable discussion conflicting world views and ideals may still be defended, on the grounds that there is a disagreement about the validity of the arguments, because the concepts in question are inadequately defined, etc. Therefore, reasonable people – who do not appeal to their own personal interest – recognize that it is impossible to justify the truth of their view to others. The only means of achieving ideological unity is oppressive state power. It is however incompatible with public reason for a part of the citizens to possess the monopoly of state power. The state should therefore be neutral towards concepts of the moral good and it should guarantee the classical freedoms. Doctrines that do not recognize these burdens of proof are considered unreasonable.

8. Taylor 1989, p. 281, note 26. And then of course there is also the illiberal patriotic national tradition of the Moral Majority, Oliver North and Joe McCarthy.

9. In accordance with Sandel's "Liberalism and the Limits of Justice". In "A Theory of Justice", Rawls has even declared that the difference principle 'transforms the aims of the basic structure of society so that the total

scheme of institutions no longer emphasizes social efficiency and technocratic values' (p. 101), but 'provides an interpretation of the principle of fraternity' (p. 105). Fraternity, the Cinderella of the three principles of the French Revolution, is usually interpreted as an attitude of mind that involves civic friendship and social solidarity. In this sense Rawls views it as too vague to serve as a political concept since it does not express a definite requirement. Moreover, fraternity is often associated with sentiments of friendship and family ties, which it is unrealistic to expect between citizens. Fraternity can nevertheless take its place in the liberal theory of justice if it is interpreted in terms of the difference principle, as the idea that citizens only want greater advantages if it benefits others who are less well off.

10. *The State*, 414b

11. What should one think of national memorial days and public statues of national heroes? Although such symbols might conflict with liberal neutrality, they are more acceptable than patriotic education. No one is forced to show respect for these national symbols. Furthermore, the choice of symbols is open to discussion and redefinition. A statue of a colonial warlord can be replaced by one of a poet who wrote: 'Too many slaves I deducted from my income tax'. The National Monument in the Dam square in Amsterdam that commemorates the liberation of Holland in 1945 was the subject of heated controversy in the sixties when hippies used its steps as a meeting place. Conservative nationalists were shocked, but more progressive citizens argued that the architect had intended his monument of liberation to be a place of free expression.

12. Speaking personally as a Dutch national I only feel affinity with a specific part of Dutch culture. I sympathize with the Erasmian strand of Dutch culture, not with its Calvinistic element. I do not especially like the language, and have never felt homesick when abroad. I regard piety towards national symbols such as the flag or the queen as utterly ridiculous. Broadly speaking, however, I accept the obligations imposed on me by the liberal Dutch constitution, even if this means that I have to pay 60 % taxes on the highest part of my income. If I were brave enough, I would take part in the resistance against a hypothetical foreign illiberal occupation (in an underground, though I might refuse to fight in an official army). My motive is that the Dutch government functions in a fashion that is on the whole reasonable, leaving me sufficient freedom and opportunities for self-realization. If the European Community was capable of coming up with a similar model, I would not worry particularly about the preservation of Dutch culture, although it would have my sympathy if it succeeded in surviving. I would be just as happy to have the chance

to try another orchestra with a new repertoire.

As to the tension between national and international solidarity – should one make sacrifices and for instance contribute additional aid in situations such as that of to Ruanda? I would argue that the only viable arguments for reducing foreign aid are economic ones. Taylor on the other hand would probably put national interests first on the ground that only citizens of a patriotic nation experience the required sense of a common identity. I would prefer to apply Rawls' difference principle here, that only makes a concession to its egalitarian goals on the economic ground that financial inequalities stimulate the national production in favour of all citizens. Likewise, at the moment productive and fair cooperation requires socio-economic organisation in separate states.

13. While the state should remain neutral, of course private indigenous people have every right to be proud of their language and national culture. Recently in Holland many people have argued that it should be made obligatory for immigrants to learn Dutch. This is not a matter of pure enforcement, but a precondition if they are to qualify for social security. Since social security is intended as a compensation for being unemployed, it is only reasonable to expect claimants to do what they can to find work, and a command of Dutch language is a basic requirement for most jobs.

14. Inherent in the notion of linguistic federalism is that French is the official language in Quebec, while in the rest of Canada it is English. Contrary to Taylor, I would reject the making of French obligatory in the non-public domain.

15. In 1966 the United Nations issued the "International convenant of civil and political rights" that regulates the position of minorities in art. 27: 'In those States in which ethnic, religious or linguistic minorities exist, persons belonging to such minorities shall not be denied the right, in community with other members of their group, to enjoy their own culture, to profess and practice their own religion, or to use their own language'. Art. 5 confines this right to collective positive freedom within the bounds of the fundamental liberal rights that form the basis of the Convenant. In 1989 the ILO has issued an incomplete 'Indigenous and Tribal Peoples Convention'. The United Nations are working on an 'Universal Declaration of Rights of Indigenous People'.

16. Although Taylor admits that liberalism relativizes cultural values, he does not think that all cultures are equal. His argument is that all lasting cultures have something valuable to offer (1992, 66). In "Sources of the Self" (part I) he goes as far as to state that there is such a thing as an objective value.

17. See note 7.

18. Rawls' point of departure would not appeal to a Hobbesian egoist or for that matter to an adherent of Nietzsche's views. Nietzsche stated that after the 'death of God' nothing remains but an indifferent nature, where only the 'will to power' prevails. Nietzsche rejected the principle of equality because it is a levelling principle that serves to bind and inhibit anyone who exceeds the norm in genius or energy. He sees it as originating in the resentment that the petty majority feel for the strong. His aristocratic ideal of *jenseits von Gut und Böse* implies living as a heroic individual, if necessary at the expense of others.
19. Thus allowing for the concept of 'social liberty' that Berlin rejected. See note 3.
20. This means that Rawls traces a closer connection between negative freedom and democracy than Berlin did. See note 2.
21. Maris 1990 and 1993. The rationalist version of Berlin's positive freedom is a metaphysical elaboration of such views.

Literature

ANDERSON, B., *Imagined Communities; Reflections on the Origin and Spread of Nationalism*, London: Verso, 1983

BARNETT, H.G., *On Science and Human Rights*, in: *American Anthropologist*, n.s., 50, 1948, pp. 352-5

BENNETT, J.W., *Science and Human Rights: Reason and Action*, in: *American Anthropologist*, n.s., 51, 1949, pp. 329-336

BERLIN, I., *Four essays on liberty*, Oxford: Oxford University Press, 1982

BERLIN, I., *Nationalism*, in: *Against the current*, New York: Viking Press, 1980, pp.333-335

FEINBERG, J., *The concept of freedom*, in: *Social philosophy*, ENGLEWOOD CLIFFS N.J., Prentice-Hall, 1973, pp. 4-19

GELLNER, E., *Nations and nationalism*, Oxford: Blackwell, 1983

HOBSBAWN, E.J., *Nations and nationalism since 1780*, Cambridge, 1990

MACCALLUM, G.C., *Negative and Positive Freedom*, in: *Philosophical Review*, vol. 76, 1967

MARIS, C.W., *Horror vacui*, Amsterdam: 1001, 1990

MARIS, C.W., *Horror vacui and the problems of modern legal philosophy*, in: ALEXY, R. and R. DREIER (eds.), *Rechtssystem und praktische Vernunft*, Stuttgart: Franz Steiner, 1993, pp. 174-184

RAWLS, J., *Justice as fairness: political not metaphysical*, in: *Philosophy and Public Affairs* 14, Summer, 1985, pp. 223-251

RAWLS, J., *Political liberalism*, New York: Columbia, 1993

RAWLS, J., *A theory of justice*, Oxford: Belknap Press of Harvard Univ. Press, 1971

SANDEL, M.J., *Liberalism and the limits of justice*, Cambridge: Cambridge University Press, 1985

SMITH, A.D., *National identity*, London: Penguin, 1991

Statement on Human Rights of the American Anthropological Association, in: *American Anthropologist*, n.s., 49, 1947, pp. 539-543

STEWARD, J.H., *Comments on the Statement on Human Rights*, in: *American Anthropologist*, n.s., 50, 1948, pp. 351/2

TAYLOR, C., *The politics of recognition*, in: GUTMAN, A. (ed.), *Multiculturalism and "the politics of recognition"*, Princeton: Princeton University Press, 1992

TAYLOR, C., *Cross-purposes: the liberal-communitarian debate*, in: ROSENBLUM, N.L. (ed.), *Liberalism and the moral life*, Cambridge: Cambridge University Press, 1989

TAYLOR, C., *Human Agency and Language; Philosophical Papers 1*, Cambridge: Cambridge University Press, 1985

TAYLOR, C., *Philosophy and the Human Sciences; Philosophical Papers 2*, Cambridge: Cambridge University Press, 1990

TAYLOR, C., *Sources of the self: The making of modern identity*, Cambridge: Cambridge University Press, 1992

TAYLOR, C., *Wieviel Gemeinschaft braucht die Demokratie?*, in: *Transit*, Heft 5, 1992/93, pp. 5-20

Identity and Membership From a Liberal Point of View
Some Remarks on the Position of Will Kymlicka

Walter Lesch

The term 'liberalism' is rather ambiguous in modern everyday language. One may just think of so called liberal parties in Austria or Russia which do not at all have a liberal programme. On the contrary. There have always been clear differences between economic and political liberalism. European readers should further know that American liberals are not to be mixed up with 'liberals' from German speaking countries. American liberals use to be closer to European social democrats than to the representatives of economic liberalism. Such preliminary and contextual remarks may be useful before discussing some aspects of the liberal-communitarian-debate that has become prominent in the development of social philosophy of the last few years (cf. Forst 1994). My contribution in this volume refers to the work of the Canadian philosopher Will Kymlicka who tries to reflect upon the philosophical and political dimensions of community and culture from a liberal point of view. He pretends to solve the problems evoked by communitarianism with the help of the theoretical tools provided by the work of John Rawls (Kymlicka 1991).

1. Political Liberalism

The central reference of American (and European) debate is still Rawls' monumental *A Theory of Justice* (1971) which is recognized as an international modern classic of political philosophy. Rawls has meanwhile developed and modified his position in several articles without responding explicitly to his communitarian critics (Rawls 1988).

The theory of communicative action and the discourse ethics proposed by Jürgen Habermas could be regarded as a European equivalent of the theory of justice. Questions of justice are prior to particular visions of the good. When there is no longer *one* religion, *one* conception of the morally good, consensus can only be reached by rational and peaceful procedures within the framework of a democratic constitutional state limiting political concerns to a minimum of tasks, and leaving the answers to existential and practical questions to a maximum of private freedom in individual and community life (Habermas 1992).

2. The Postulate of Neutrality

Kymlicka strictly argues against the extreme version of a liberal point of view that could be presented as an objective *view from nowhere*: always neutral, just and colour-blind. In such a neutral position all kinds of affirmative action would be forbidden. A liberal state does not encourage or exclude any life-style. Only a neutral state can guarantee a pluralism of free initiatives. According to Rawls, however, the respect of civil rights automatically has non-neutral consequences. Only under conditions of individual freedom there is "a cultural market-place" on which people can present the advantages of their personal life-styles and give reasonable arguments for the superiority of their cultural offers and convictions (Kymlicka 1992: 166). Kymlicka's concept of culture is based on the economic model of competition. Fair competition is possible without any sanctions and encourages moral behaviour and social responsibility. The idea of a neutral state helps to avoid the dangerous identification of politics and culture. Cultural resources are certainly needed for the construction of personal and collective identities; but administration and economy ought to function as independent sub-systems, compatible with a multitude of ways of life.

3. An Incorrigible Individualism?

Liberalism must face the standard objections according to which individualism is a sort of egocentrism leading to social disintegration

100

and to a loss of public spirit. Kymlicka carefully discusses the dead ends of a much too simple opposition of liberals and communitarians and tries to reject three critical arguments.

First objection: Political liberalism presupposes a "possessive individualist theory of human motivation" (Kymlicka 1989: 886; this passage is not found in the shortened version of 1992). Obviously there are post-material values which cannot be reduced to the model of the *homo oeconomicus*. On the other hand material securities are an important foundation, even for idealistic projects. Those who choose non-materialistic life-styles must have a special interest in the primary goods postulated by Rawls because they could never survive without them.

Second objection: "Liberal neutrality is incapable of guaranteeing the existence of a pluralistic culture which provides people with the range of options necessary for meaningful individual choice" (Kymlicka 1992: 170). Once again Kymlicka refers to his idea of the cultural market-place as the best place where the desired plurality of goods can be produced, presented and exchanged.

Third objection: "The liberal preference for the cultural market-place over the state as an appropriate arena for evaluating different life-styles stems from an individualistic belief that judgements about the good should be made by isolated individuals, whose autonomy is ensured by protecting them from social pressures. Liberals think that autonomy is promoted when judgements about the good are taken out of the political realm. But in reality individual judgements require the sharing of experiences and the give and take of collective deliberations" (Kymlicka 1992: 173). This third argument is the most complicated one because it deals with the interdependence of individual choice and the traditions of a collective culture. It would indeed be the weakest point of liberal individualism if the glorification of freedom and independence really resulted in an absurd atomism. So Kymlicka concedes that the critics of liberalism are right in stressing the undeniable communitarian resources of deliberative democracy and the "shared social requirements of individual autonomy" (Kymlicka 1992: 177).

4. The Interaction of 'Liberalism 1' and 'Liberalism 2'

Kymlicka wisely rejects the false opposition between personal freedom and community and suggests differentiations *within* liberalism. "Despite centuries of liberal insistence on the importance of the distinction between society and state, communitarians still seem to assume that whatever is properly social must become the province of the political. (...) liberals still tend to take the existence of a tolerant and diverse culture for granted, as something which naturally arises and sustains itself (...). A culture of freedom requires a mix of both exposure and connection to existing practices, and also distance and dissent from them. Liberal neutrality may provide that mix, but that is not obviously true, and it may be true only in some times and places." (Kymlicka 1992: 178).

The same argument is used by Charles Taylor and Michael Walzer (Taylor 1992; Walzer 1990) when they differentiate between 'liberalism 1' (the state is strictly neutral) and 'liberalism 2' (the state takes measures in order to protect the continued existence of a particular culture, e.g. French language in Quebec). Classical liberals tend to prefer 'liberalism 1' because of its optimistic anthropology whereas communitarians emphasizing the importance of shared interpretations (which may be at risk) favour the sanctions and control systems of 'liberalism 2'. The second version of liberalism does of course not imply that individuals are to be enclosed in a sacrosanct cultural structure; individuals should have the opportunity to make use of an exit option, which is a necessary condition of cultural and political change. From a liberal point of view the cultural background generates possibilities of freedom, not duties.

5. Towards a Culture of Freedom: Liberalism in Multicultural Societies

The philosophical position of Will Kymlicka is an intelligent plea for

102

a political liberalism capable of incorporating often neglected cultural factors and capable of answering communitarian objections to neutrality. The mediation passes by the thick description of the individual whose integrity implies the active protection of rich cultural traditions. Nevertheless Kymlicka's new version of liberal political theory fails to be convincing in the case of cultural conflicts in immigration societies, because Kymlicka is primarily interested in the cultures of populations already living on a territory (Indians and Inuit in Canada, cf. Danley 1991). But what are the criteria for the integration of foreigners who come from completely different cultures and claim – as a matter of justice – to preserve a maximum of their traditions? What are the just conditions for their membership in the new political and cultural community? Would formal citizenship be a sufficient regulation of their status? Neither liberals nor communitarians have so far satisfied the needs of contemporary political and philosophical reflection on these challenges.

Instead of endless debates over the status of the individual we could better intensify investigations into the complex relationship of economy, state and culture (cf. Kymlicka 1992: 185). The controversy between liberals and communitarians has underlined the important question whether some aspects of cultural life belong to the domain of political regulation, while others may be subject to the Laws of the free market. Unfortunately the fiction of the homogeneous nation-state in most regions of the world still conceals the complexity of multiethnic and multicultural societies (Gutmann 1993; Habermas 1992: 632-660; Lesch 1993). The heritage of political liberalism has to be conceived as the difficult "art of separation" (Walzer) of different spheres of justice without forgetting the logic of moral learning and cultural socialisation which has little to do with the myth of the "unencumbered self", but very much with "the most pressing questions of justice and injustice in the modern world" (Kymlicka 1991: 258).

Bibliography

AVINERI, S. and A. DE-SHALIT (eds.), *Communitarianism and liberalism*, Oxford: Oxford University Press, 1992

DANLEY, J. R., *Liberalism, Aboriginal Rights, and Cultural Minorities*, in: *Philosophy & Public Affairs* 20:2, 1991, p. 168-185

FORST, R., *Kontexte der Gerechtigkeit. Politische Philosophie jenseits von Liberalismus und Kommunitarismus*, Frankfurt am Main: Suhrkamp, 1994

GUTMANN, A., *The Challenge of Multiculturalism in Political Ethics*, in: *Philosophy & Public Affairs* 22:3, 1993, p. 171-206

HABERMAS, J., *Faktizität und Geltung. Beiträge zur Diskurstheorie des Rechts und des demokratischen Rechtsstaats*, Frankfurt am Main: Suhrkamp, 1992

KYMLICKA, W., *Liberalism, Community and Culture*, Oxford: Clarendon Press, 1991 (first published in 1989)

KYMLICKA, W., *Liberal Individualism and Liberal Neutrality*, in: AVINERI/DE-SHALIT, 1992, p. 165-185 (shortened version of a text first published in: Ethics 99:4 [1989], p. 883-905)

LESCH, W., *Nationalism and the Oppression of Minorities. Is There a Right to Ethnic Identity?*, in: *Concilium. International Review of Theology* 29:4, 1993, p. 110-120

RAWLS, J., *The Priority of Right and Ideas of the Good*, in: *Philosophy & Public Affairs* 17:3, 1988, p. 251-276

TAYLOR, C., *Multiculturalism and "The Politics of Recognition"*, Princeton: Princeton University Press, 1992

WALZER, M., *The Communitarian Critique of Liberalism*, in: *Political Theory* 18:1, 1990, p. 6-23

Minority Cultures and the Cosmopolitan Alternative

Jeremy Waldron*

If it were appropriate to make dedications, this Article would be for Salman Rushdie, who a few months ago celebrated his one-thousandth day in hiding in Britain under police protection from the sentence of death passed upon him in Tehran in 1988. I want to begin with an extended quotation from an essay entitled *In Good Faith*, which Rushdie wrote in 1990 in defense of his execrated book *The Satanic Verses*:

> "If *The Satanic Verses* is anything, it is a migrant's-eye view of the world. It is written from the very experience of uprooting, disjuncture and metamorphosis (slow or rapid, painful or pleasurable) that is the migrant condition, and from which, I believe, can be derived a metaphor for all humanity.
> Standing at the centre of the novel is a group of characters most of whom are British Muslims, or not particularly religious persons of Muslim background, struggling with just the sort of great problems that have arisen to surround the book, problems of hybridization and ghettoization, of reconciling the old and the new. Those who oppose the novel most vociferously today are of the opinion that intermingling with a different culture will inevitably weaken and ruin their own. I am of the opposite opinion. The *Satanic Verses* celebrates hybridity, impurity, intermingling, the transformation that comes of new and unexpected combinations of human beings, cultures, ideas, politics, movies, songs. It rejoices in mongrelization and fears the absolutism of the Pure. *Mélange*, hotchpotch, a bit of this and a bit of that is *how newness enters the world*. It is the great possibility that mass migration gives the world, and I have tried to embrace it. *The Satanic Verses* is for change-by-fusion, change-by-conjoining.

105

It is a love-song to our mongrel selves.

(...) I was born an Indian, and not only an Indian, but a Bombayite – Bombay, most cosmopolitan, most hybrid, most hotchpotch of Indian cities. My writing and thought have therefore been as deeply influenced by Hindu myths and attitudes as Muslim ones (...) Nor is the West absent from Bombay. I was already a mongrel self, history's bastard, before London aggravated the condition."[1]

It is not my intention here to contribute further to the discussion of *The Satanic Verses* or of the price its author has paid for its publication.[2] Instead, I want to take the comments that I have just quoted as a point of departure to explore the vision of life, agency, and responsibility that is implicit in this affirmation of cosmopolitanism. I want to explore the tension between that vision and the more familiar views with which we are concerned in this symposium – views that locate the coherence and meaning of human life in each person's immersion in the culture and ethnicity of a particular community.

1. Communitarianism

What follows is in part a contribution to the debate between liberals and communitarians, though those labels are becoming rather tattered in the modern discussion.[3] Although there is a rough correlation between the liberty claimed by Rushdie and the ideal of liberal freedom, the life sketched out by Rushdie really does not answer to the more earnest or highminded characterizations of the liberal individual in modern political philosophy. Modern liberal theorists place great stress on the importance of an autonomous individual leading his life according to a chosen plan; his autonomy is evinced in the formulation and execution of a lifeplan and the adoption of ground-projects, and his rights are the liberties and protections that he needs in order to do this.[4] Liberals stress the importance of each individual's adoption of a particular conception of the good, a view about what makes life worth living, and again a person's rights are the protections he needs in order to be able to choose and follow such values on equal terms with others who are engaged in a similar enterprise.[5] The approach to life sketched out by Rushdie has little in common with this, apart from the elements of freedom and decision. It has none of the ethical unity that the autonomous Kantian individual is supposed to confer on life[6]; it is a life of kaleidoscopic tension and variety. It is not the pursuit of a chosen conception of goodness along lines indicated by Ronald Dworkin;[7] nor does its individuality consist in Rawls's words, in "a human life lived according to a plan."[8] Instead, it rightly challenges the rather compulsive rigidity of the traditional liberal picture.[9] If there is liberal autonomy in Rushdie's vision it is choice running rampant, and pluralism internalized from the relations *between* individuals to the chaotic coexistence of projects, pursuits, ideas images and snatches of culture *within* an individual.[10]

If I knew what the term meant I would say it was a "postmodern" vision of the self. But as I do not let me just call it "cosmopolitan", although this term is not supposed to indicate that the practitioner of the ethos in question is necessarily a migrant (like Rushdie), a perpetual refugee (like, for example Jean-Jacques Rousseau), or a frequent flyer (like myself). The cosmopolitan may live all his life in one city and maintain the same citizenship throughout. But he refuses to think of himself as *defined* by his location or his ancestry or his citizenship or his language. Though he may live in San Francisco and be of Irish ancestry he does not take his identity to be compromised when he learns Spanish, eats Chinese, wears clothes made in Korea, listens to arias by Verdi sung by a Maori princess on Japanese equipment, follows Ukrainian politics and practices Buddhist meditation techniques. He is a creature of modernity, conscious of living in a mixed-up world and having a mixed-up self.

I want to use the opportunity provided by Rushdie's sketch - of such a life to challenge the claims that are made by modern communitarians about the need people have for involvement in the substantive life of a particular community as a source of meaning, integrity, and character.[11] One of the things that we are going to find, as we proceed with this exploration, is the importance of pressing the communitarian on the meaning of the term "community". Many of us have been puzzled and frustrated by the absence of a clear understanding of this concept in some of the assertions made by communitarians like Alasdair Macintyre, Michael Sandel, Charles Taylor, and Michael Walzer.[12] I do not mean the absence of a precise definition. I mean the absence of any settled sense about the *scope* and *scale* of the social entity that they have in mind.

When they say that the modern individual is a creation of community[13], or that each of us owes her identity to the community in which she is brought up,[14] or that our choices necessarily are framed in the context of a community,[15] or that we must not think of ourselves as holding rights against the community,[16] or that communities must have boundaries,[17] or that justice is fidelity to shared understandings within a community,[18] what *scale* of entity are we talking about? Is "community" supposed to denote things as small as villages and neighborhoods, social relations that can sustain *gemeinschaft*-type solidarity and face-to-face friendships? What is the relation between the community and the political system? Is "community" supposed to do work comparable to "civil society," picking out the social infrastructure of whatever state or political entity we are talking about? If, as John Dunn recently has argued,[19] the concept of *the state* no longer picks out a natural kind, denoting as it does political entities as small as Fiji and as large as the United States, as tight as Singapore and as loose as the Commonwealth of Independent States (C.I.S.), is there any sense in supposing that for every state there is just one community or society to which individuals owe their being and allegiance?

Should we even suppose that communities are no bigger than states? If each of us is a product of a community, is that heritage limited to national boundaries, or is it as wide (as *world*wide) as the language, literature, and civilization that sustain us? Are we talking about particular communities, at the level of self contained ethnic groups, or are we talking about the common culture and civilization that makes it possible for a New Zealander trained at Oxford to write for a symposium in the *University of Michigan Journal of Law Reform*?[20]

108

I suspect that the popularity of modern communitarianism has depended on *not* giving unequivocal answers to these questions. I suspect that it depends on using premises that evoke community on one scale (usually large) to support conclusions requiring allegiance to community on quite a different scale (usually small).

For the purposes of this Article, I want to single out one meaning of the term as worthy of special attention. It is "community" in the sense of *ethnic* community: a particular people sharing a heritage of custom, ritual, and way of life that is in some real or imagined[21] sense immemorial, being referred back to a shared history and shared provenance or homeland. This is the sense of "community" implicated in nineteenth- and twentieth-century nationalism. I shall use community in this sense as a sort of counterpoint to my exploration of Rushdie's cosmopolitan ideal. I want to pin down the communitarian critique of the cosmopolitan style of life to something like the claim, made by the German historian Johann Gottfried Von Herder, that (in Isaiah Berlin's paraphrase) "among elementary human needs – as basic as those for food, shelter, security, procreation, communication – is the need to belong to a particular group, united by some common links – especially language, collective memories, continuous life upon the same soil", and perhaps "race, blood, religion, a sense of common mission, and the like."[22]

Some will protest that it is unfair to pin matters down in this way. Michael Sandel, they will say, is not Johann Gottfried Von Herder. But the aim is not to underestimate the subtlety of any particular philosopher's position. From time to time, it is important for us not only to read the ordinary ambiguous literature of communitarianism, but also to see how much substance there would be if various *determinate* communitarian claims were taken one by one, and their proponents were forced to abandon any reliance on vagueness and equivocation. In the end, that is the best way to evaluate the array of different meanings that are evoked in this literature. This Article is certainly not a complete execution of that task, but it is intended as a substantial beginning.

2. Minority Culture as a Human Right

There is an additional reason for being interested in social entities on this scale. In modern discussions of human rights, we are presented with the claim that particular cultures, communities, and ethnic traditions have a right to exist and a right to be protected from decay, assimilation, and desuetude. The claim is presented, in a rather modest form, in Article 27 of the International Covenant on Civil and Political Rights:

> In those States in which ethnic, religious or linguistic minorities exist, persons belonging to such minorities shall not be denied the right, in community with the other members of their group, to enjoy their own culture, to profess and practise their own religion, or to use their own language.[23]

Now, as it stands, this provision leaves quite unclear what is to count as the enjoyment of one's culture, the profession of one's religion, and the use of one's language. Are these goods secured when a dwindling band of demoralized individuals continues, against all odds, to meet occasionally to wear their national costume, recall snatches of their common history, practice their religious and ethnic rituals and speak what they can remember of what was once a flourishing tongue? Is that the *enjoyment* of their culture? Or does enjoyment require more along the lines of the active flourishing of the culture on its own terms, in something approximating the conditions under which it originally developed?

Many have thought that respect for minority cultures does require more. A recent United Nations report rejected the view that Article 27 is nothing but a nondiscrimination provision: it insisted that special measures for minority cultures (such as some form of affirmative action) are required and that such measures are as important as nondiscrimination in defending fundamental human rights in this area.[24] Such affirmative measures may include subsidies from the wider society.[25] But they also may involve the recognition that minority

110

cultures are entitled to protect themselves by placing limits on the incursion of outsiders and limits on their own members' choices about career, family, lifestyle, loyalty, and exit – limits that might be unpalatable in the wider liberal context.[26]

It is not my intention to get involved in a detailed debate about the interpretation of Article 27. Instead, I want to examine the implicit claim about human life that lies behind provisions like this. For, once again, we are dealing with the Herderian claim[27] that there is a human yearning or need to *belong*, a need that is in danger of being miserably frustrated - for example in the case of North American aboriginal groups. This is the need that scholars appeal to when they criticize or defend various interpretations of the right of cultural preservation.

3. A Thin Theory of the Good

So there are two visions to be considered – the cosmopolitan vision intimated by Salman Rushdie and the vision of belonging and immersion in the life and culture of a particular community espoused by the proponents of Article 27.

It is important to see that these are not merely different lifestyles of the sort that old-fashioned liberalism could comfortably accommodate in a pluralistic world – some like campfire, some like opera, some are Catholics, some are Methodists – that sort of thing. Instead, we are talking, as I indicated earlier, about the background view of life, agency, and responsibility that is presupposed already by any account of what it is for lifestyles to be diverse or for diversity to be tolerated.

This contrast between lifestyle and background assumptions is worth explaining a little further. Any political theory, *including* a theory of toleration or liberal neutrality, must be predicated on some view of what human life is like. This is true even if it is only what philosophers call a "thin" theory[28] – that is, a theory giving us the bare framework for conceptualizing choice and agency but leaving the specific content of choices to be filled in by individuals. We need a thin theory to tell us what goods should be at stake in a theory of justice, what liberties and rights are going to be called for, and, more broadly, what the skeletal outlines of human lives can be expected to be so that we can have some sense of how everything will fit together. For example, a liberal theory of rights needs to be able to say that religious choices and matters of conscience are very important to people (and so worthy of special protection) without begging any questions about what the content of those choices should be. A thin theory is also necessary in order to work out a subject-matter for a theory of justice: What is a just distribution ultimately a distribution *of?* Should we be interested in the just distribution of happiness, the just distribution of material resources, or the just distribution of human abilities and capacities?[29] Each society must share some consensus at this level, no matter what plurality it envisages on some other level.

Above all, we need a thin theory of choice, agency, and responsibility so that we can say something about the shape of individual lives in relation to matters like society, community, politics, and justice. We need to have some skeletal sense of how things are to fit together. Are we envisaging a society of *individuals* in some strong sense, or a community of persons bound together in some organic common life? Are we envisaging a society of equals, so that each person's claims against others are to be matched by others' reciprocal claims against him? Or are we envisaging a hierarchy, oriented functionally towards some nonegalitarian end?

We cannot make any progress at all in political philosophy unless we tie ourselves down to some extent here; certainly a liberal theory of neutrality that purports to be neutral about *everything* in this area quickly falls apart into fatuous incoherence. Critics of liberalism are fond of uncovering the assumptions made at this level, as if that were a way of discrediting the neutrality of the liberal ideal.[30] But every political theory must take some stand on what authentic human agency is like and how that relates to the fact of our location in society. The tensions that I intend to explore - between the cosmopolitan and communitarian account of human life and activities - are not merely disagreements at the level of comfortably competing lifestyles. They are not to be thought of as liberal bedfellows who have already settled the basic terms and conceptions of their association. They are tensions at a deep philosophical level.

4. Opposition and Authenticity

But are the two visions of human life that we are discussing really antagonists? It may seem odd to oppose them this starkly. Salman Rushdie is not noted as an opponent of aboriginal rights, nor are the Native American tribes particularly interested in *The Satanic Verses*. The defenders of Article 27 may frown on cultural impurity, but they are not proposing exactly to limit the freedom of those who, like Rushdie, choose to entangle their roots with foreign grafts. Not *exactly*; but the fact that one of the charges for which Rushdie was sentenced to death was apostasy is a sobering reminder of what it really may mean to insist that people must keep faith with their roots.[31]

Nor are the citizens of the world, the modernist dreamers of cosmopolis, proposing exactly to destroy minority cultures. Their apartments are quite likely to be decorated with Inuit artifacts or Maori carvings. Still, we know that a world in which deracinated cosmopolitanism flourishes is not a safe place for minority communities. Our experience has been that they wither and die in the harsh glare of modern life, and that the custodians of these dying traditions live out their lives in misery and demoralization.

We are dealing, in other words, with conceptions of man and society which, if not actually inconsistent, certainly are opposed in some important sense. Each envisions an environment in which the other is, to a certain extent, in danger.

It is also true that, although these two conceptions are not formally inconsistent, still the best case that can be made in favor of each of them tends to cast doubt upon the best case that can be made for the other.

Suppose first, that a freewheeling cosmopolitan life, lived in a kaleidoscope of cultures, is both possible and fulfilling. Suppose such a life turns out to be rich and creative, and with no more unhappiness than one expects to find anywhere in human existence. Immediately, one argument for the protection of minority cultures is undercut. It can no longer be so that all people *need* their rootedness in the particular culture in which they and their ancestors were reared in the way that they need food, clothing, and shelter.[32] People used to think they *needed* red meat in their diet. It turns out not to be true: vegetarian alternatives are available. Now some still may prefer and enjoy a carnivorous diet, but it is no longer a matter of necessity. The same – if the cosmopolitan alternative can be sustained – is true for immersion in the culture of a particular community. Such immersion may be something that particular people like and enjoy. But they no longer can claim that it is something that they need.

Of course, it does not follow from this that we are entitled to crush and destroy minority cultures. But the collapse of the Herderian argument based on distinctively human *need* seriously undercuts any claim that minority cultures might have to special support or assistance or to extraordinary provision or forbearance. At best, it leaves the right to culture roughly on the same footing as the right to religious freedom. We no longer think it true that everyone needs some religious faith or that everyone must be sustained in the faith in which he was brought up. A secular lifestyle is evidently viable, as is conversion from one church to another. Few would think it right to try to extirpate religious belief in consequence of these possibilities. But equally, few would think it right to subsidize religious sects merely in order to preserve them. If a particular church is dying out because its members are drifting away, no longer convinced by its theology or attracted by its ceremonies, that is just the way of the world. It is like the death of a fashion or a hobby, not the demise of anything that people really need.

So the sheer existence and vitality of the cosmopolitan alternative is enough to undercut an important part of the case for the preservation of minority cultures. Sometimes the cosmopolitan argument goes

114

further. The stronger claim that Salman Rushdie suggests, in the passage we began with, is that the hybrid lifestyle of the true cosmopolitan is in fact the only appropriate response to the modern world in which we live.[33] We live in a world formed by technology and trade; by economic, religious, and political imperialism and their offspring; by mass migration and the dispersion of cultural influences. In this context, to immerse oneself in the traditional practices of, say, an aboriginal culture might be a fascinating anthropological experiment, but it involves an artificial dislocation from what actually is going on in the world. That it is an artifice is evidenced by the fact that such immersion often requires special subsidization and extraordinary provision by those who live in the real world, where cultures and practices are not so sealed off from one another. The charge, in other words, is one of *inauthenticity*.

Let me state it provocatively. From a cosmopolitan point of view, immersion in the traditions of a particular community in the modern world is like living in Disneyland and thinking that one's surroundings epitomize what it is for a culture really to exist. Worse still, it is like demanding the funds to live in Disneyland and the protection of modern society for the boundaries of Disneyland, while still managing to convince oneself that what happens inside Disneyland is all there is to an adequate and fulfilling life. It is like thinking that what every person most deeply needs is for one of the Magic Kingdoms to provide a framework for her choices and her beliefs, completely neglecting the fact that the framework of Disneyland depends on commitments, structures, and infrastructures that far outstrip the character of any particular facade. It is to imagine that one could belong to Disneyland while professing complete indifference towards, or even disdain for, Los Angeles.

That is the case from one side. Suppose, on the other hand, that we accept what defenders of minority culture often say – that there *is* a universal human need for rootedness in the life of a particular community and that this communal belonging confers character and depth on our choices and our actions.[34] Then the freedom that Rushdie claims looks deviant and marginal, an odd or eccentric exercise of license rather than a consummation of human liberty. It sometimes is said that claims of freedom must be made with respect to actions that make sense and that unintelligibility rather than hostility is the first obstacle to toleration.[35] If anything like this is correct, then the more credence that we give to the communitarian thesis, the less intelligible the claim to cosmopolitan freedom becomes.

From the point of view of community, the cosmopolitan freedom that Rushdie extols – the freedom to renounce his heritage and just play with it, mixing it with imagery and movies and jokes and obscenities – is like the freedom claimed by any other oddball: the freedom to sail the Atlantic in a bathtub or the freedom to steer one's way through a bewildering series of marriages and divorces. Those who hop from one community to another, merging their roots and never settling down into any stable practices and traditions may, like the bathtub sailor or the matrimonial athlete, excite our sneaking admiration. But when things go wrong for them, our pitying response will be, "Well, what did you expect?"

A moment ago, we considered the view that immersion in the life of a minority culture is like hiding in Disneyland and that it is an inauthentic way of evading the complex actualities of the world as it is. But the charge of inauthenticity is likely to be returned with interest by the proponents of minority culture. From their point of view, it is the Rushdian life of shifting and tangled attachments that is the shallow and inauthentic way of living in the world. The cosmopolitan ideal, they will say, embodies all the worst aspects of classic liberalism - atomism, abstraction, alienation from one's roots, vacuity of commitment, indeterminacy of character, and ambivalence towards the good. The accusation is implicit in the undertones of words like "deracinated" and "alienated" or in the terminology that Rushdie turns bravely to his own purposes in the passage quoted earlier: "hybrid," "impurity," "hotchpotch," "mélange," and "mongrelization."[36] It is no accident that these terms, which so accurately describe the cosmopolitan ideal, are fraught with negative and cautionary connotations.

116

The same point can be put another way. There is a question about how seriously we should regard the threat to Rushdie's work. Certainly, the threat to his life should be taken seriously. But how seriously should we take the "chilling effect" that the threat might have on Rushdie's subsequent writing, on his publishers and booksellers, and on other authors who might be tempted into similarly "offensive" prose? To answer this question, one must make a qualitative judgment about the worth or value of the freedom that is exercised in cases like these. Not all freedoms are on a par; we need, as I said earlier[37], a theory of the good to tell us which are important and which not. As Charles Taylor puts it:

"There are discriminations to be made; some restrictions are more serious than others, some are utterly trivial. About many, there is of course controversy. But what the judgement turns on is some sense of what is significant for human life. Restricting the expression of people's religious and ethical convictions is more significant than restricting their movement around uninhabited parts of the country; and both are more significant than the trivia of traffic control."[38]

Even with regard to speech and writing, we may want to draw distinctions. The publication of a serious political or philosophical tract is one thing, the publication of cheap magazine aimed at corrupt titillation is another; a moral argument for free speech is notoriously much more difficult to make in the case of pornography than in the case of "serious" writing.[39] Rushdie's enemies claim that *The Satanic Verses* and similar writings fall into exactly the category of pornography, and they think that it is not a particularly serious matter (it may even be a good thing) if writing of this kind is chilled or deterred. This is the case that must be answered if the cosmopolitan vision is to be sustained.

5. Cosmopolitan Isolation

I want to begin the detailed discussion by exploring the communitarian view of the cosmopolitan as a lone and alienated figure. Look at Salman Rushdie himself, living the cosmopolitan experience in hiding, by himself, deliberately isolated from friends, disaffected from his wife, Marianne Wiggins, rushed from anonymous safe house to safe house in unmarked police cars, unreachable by anyone except through the most protracted arrangements. Now that perhaps is an unfair case; a self-fulfilling prophecy by the particular communitarians who proclaimed the *fatwa*. Rushdie, on all accounts, lived a rich and fulfilling life until he was threatened with execution.

Still the image lingers. Even at its best, the cosmopolitan rejection of specific community evokes a sense of isolation. Think of the opening words of the *Reveries of the Solitary Walker,* written by the deracinated Jean-Jacques Rousseau just before his death:

> "So now I am alone in the world, with no brother, neighbour or friend, nor any company left me but my own (...) So now they are strangers and foreigners to me; they no longer exist for me (...) But I, detached as I am from them and from the whole world, what am I? (...) Wrenched somehow out of the natural order, I have been plunged into an incomprehensible chaos where I can make nothing out, and the more I think about my present situation, the less I can understand what has become of me."[40]

Is this the cosmopolitan destiny?

The pathos of such a figure is heightened by reference to the traditional Aristotelean conception of man as *zoon politikon*, one whose nature is to live in a particular state.[41] Man, said Aristotle, is the least self-sufficient of the animals.[42] But the human individual is not merely an animal who happens to lack self-sufficiency; he is an animal whose essence it is to lack self sufficiency. We *need* each other, and it is Aristotle's task to make, as it were, a virtue of this necessity. The life of belonging to a *polis* is not only a grudging dependence, but a positive and essentialist embrace of interdependence.

From this perspective, there is something *monstrous* about the aloofness, the isolation, or the independence of the man without a culture:

"The man who is isolated – who is unable to share in the benefits of political association, or has no need to share because he is already self-sufficient – is no part of the polis, and must therefore be either a beast or a god (...)

(...) [H]e is like the man of whom Homer wrote in denunciation: "Clanless and lawless and heartless is he." The man who is such by nature at once plunges into a passion for war; he is in the position of a solitary advanced piece in a game of draughts."[43]

The hearthless man, Aristotle argued, can never attain true happiness or felicity (*eudaemonia*):

"Surely it is strange, too, to make the supremely happy man a solitary; for no one would choose the whole world on condition of being alone, since man is a political creature and one whose nature is to live with others."[44]

To be happy, Aristotle argued, is to revel in goodness and in the enjoyment of virtuous activity as such.[45] One cannot be sure that it is the good life *as such* that one is enjoying (as opposed to a selfish preoccupation with getting through one's own life) unless one has an opportunity to enjoy it also in the being and thus in the company of others:

"[A]s his own being is desirable for each man, so, or almost so, is that of his friend. Now his being was seen to be desirable because he perceived his own goodness, and such perception is pleasant in itself. He needs, therefore, to be conscious of the existence of his friend as well, and this will be realized in their living together and sharing in discussion and thought; for this is what living together would seem to mean in the case of man, and not, as in the case of cattle, feeding in the same place."[46]

However, being without roots in a particular community is not necessarily the same as being isolated or friendless. In order to ascertain the importance of community (as we are understanding it) for the social and political aspects of man's nature, we must look a little closer at the Aristotelean thesis of interdependence. In the following sections, I shall examine two possible interpretations of the interdependence thesis – economic and moral – and I shall ask how far the relation of one life to others, along either of these dimensions, is undermined by the cosmopolitan renunciation of allegiance to any particular culture.

It may be worth adding that I take Aristotle's thesis as a point of departure, not because he is necessarily to be regarded as a final authority on these matters, but because the Aristotelean tradition of political philosophy (including *modern* Aristoteleanism) comprises the most challenging body of thought with which to confront the assumptions of the liberal ideal. Of course, Aristotelean conceptions of friendship, community, and *polis* were formed in the context of city-states not much larger than a small American town. In what follows, therefore it often will be necessary to distinguish the *concepts* of Aristotelean friendship and interdependence from the particular *conceptions* of those concepts that were appropriate for the social context in which he lived.[47] The plausibility of communitarian critiques of modern society often rests on the claim that Aristotelean conceptions of friendship and community have no place in modern society; the critics seldom are interested in asking whether there is any distinctively modern conception answering to the concepts underlying Aristotle's particular views.

6. Interdependence

Economic Interdependence

It is true that his is not a life immersed in the intense economic activity of a particular community, working alongside and exchanging things with fellow members of his group on a face-to-face basis. He is not a member of an aboriginal hunting band or a community of Amish farmers. But those are fanciful pictures of anything other than a tiny fraction of modern economic relations. As Adam Smith noted, our interdependence far outstrips our ability to sustain face-to-face friendship:

120

"In civilized society [man] stands at all times in need of the co-operation and assistance of great multitudes, while his whole life is scarce sufficient to gain the friendship of a few persons."[48]

Given the true state of our connection with others – economic interdependence that goes far beyond the boundaries of particular communities, far indeed beyond the boundaries of particular nation-states – cosmopolitanism conveys a much more accurate sense of our involvement with others than immersion in the bucolic idyll of communalist *Gemeinschaft*.

Lest the reference to Adam Smith be thought to load the dice unduly in favor of world capitalism, the same point can be made on the basis of Karl Marx's work. The early Marx is noted for his concern that the capitalist economy was alienating man from his fellows in the conditions of production.[49] But the alienation that Marx worried about was not a sense of alienation that could be remedied by immersing people more fully in the productive life of a face-to-face community. Rather, Marx feared alienation from the entire human species. When he insisted that "productive life is species-life,"[50] he meant not merely that creative and cooperative production was essential or specific to human nature, but also that human production took place, in the modern era, on a truly species-wide scale, relating man to man, not in a particular community, but across the world. This truly global interdependence, he argued, was initially the achievement of capitalism, but it was also the indispensable condition for socialism:

"The bourgeoisie has through its exploitation of the worldmarket given a cosmopolitan character to production and consumption in every country. To the great chagrin of Reactionists, it has drawn from under the feet of industry the national ground on which it stood. All old-established national industries have been destroyed or are daily being destroyed. They are dislodged by new industries, whose introduction becomes a life-and-death question for all civilized nations, by industries that no longer work up indigenous raw material, but raw material drawn from the remotest zones; industries whose products are consumed, not only at home, but in every quarter of the globe. In place of the old wants, satisfied by the productions of the country, we find new wants, requiring for their satisfaction the products of distant lands and climes. In place of the old local and national seclusion and self-sufficiency, we have intercourse in every direction, universal inter-dependence of nations."[51]

At the beginning of his analysis, Aristotle argued that what was distinctive about the Greek *polis* was its self-sufficiency;[52] unlike the family or the village, the members of the *polis* found that they were dependent on one another but not dependent upon outsiders. It was for this reason that the *polis* was considered the appropriate location for the highest forms of human cooperation: But the arguments from Smith and Marx just cited indicate that this is no longer the case. The full extent of human interdependence is now global, not national (and certainly not civic or parochial). To insist, then, that Aristotelean interdependence for the modern world must be realized in a social entity as small as the Athenian *polis* would distort seriously the values underlying Aristotle's argument; we would be ignoring his concept of the link between human good and full interdependence in favor of a radically obsolete conception of that concept.

Moral and Political Interdependence
Our interdependence is not only economic. It is also moral and political. Here the case against cosmopolitanism is more subtle. Aristotle again:

"The reason why man is a being meant for political association, in a higher degree than bees or other gregarious animals can ever associate, is evident. Nature, according to our theory, makes nothing in vain; and man alone of the animals is furnished with the faculty of language. The mere making of sounds serves to indicate pleasure and pain, and is thus a faculty that belongs to animals in general (...) But language serves to declare what is advantageous and what is the reverse, and it therefore serves to declare what is just and what is unjust."[53]

122

We are most distinctively human, according to the Aristotelean tradition, when we talk with one another and come to share common views about the social good, about right and wrong, about justice and injustice. It is important to understand that this use of speech, for Aristotle, is not just the unanimous murmuring or chanting of accepted nostrums. It is a matter of conversation, debate in the *agora*, articulate discussion. The interdependence of humans in this context indicates the ability of a multitude to converse together and, through discussion and the concatenation of different perspectives and experiences, to arrive collectively at a better view than any individual could have attained on her own. In other words, man's nature as a *speaking being* is revealed most profoundly in Aristotle's doctrine of the collective wisdom of the multitude:

> "There is this to be said for the Many. Each of them by himself may not be of a good quality; but when they all come together it is possible that they may surpass – collectively and as a body, although not individually – the quality of the few best. Feasts to which many contribute may excel those provided at one man's expense. In the same way, when there are many [who contribute to the process of deliberation], each can bring his share of goodness and moral prudence; and when all meet together the people may thus become something in the nature of a single person, who – as he has many feet, many hands, and many senses – may also have many qualities of character and intelligence."[54]

There may be one or two people of great insight who can work out the demands of justice and morality on their own, apart from the company of discussants and critics. For most of us however, isolated thought on these matters leads nowhere. We must address them in the company of others.[55]

Does this mean that issues of justice may be addressed only in the *polis*, that is, only in the particular communities from which our protagonist has by his cosmopolitanism isolated himself?

There has been some suggestion to this effect in modern political philosophy. Michael Walzer, for example, has argued that social justice is relative to the meanings and understandings implicit in the life of each society, and he has maintained that only those who are privy to, or participate in, local understandings can grasp in each context what justice really requires. Certainly, according to Walzer, the philosopher's armchair, which might be anywhere from Oxford, to Ann Arbor, to a business–class cabin, is a hopeless vantage point. There are, he says, no a priori or universal principles: "Every substantive account of distributive justice is a local account."[56]

"There are an infinite number of possible lives, shaped by an infinite number of possible cultures, religions, political arrangements, geographical conditions, and so on. A given society is just if its substantive life is lived in a certain way – that is, in a way faithful to the shared understandings of the members."[57]

Walzer went on, notoriously, to infer that in a hierarchical society, "justice will come to the aid of inequality"[58], and to insist that it would be nothing short of tyrannical to oppose local understandings of caste, gender, or differential status in the name of universal egalitarian ideals.[59]

Even John Rawls has adopted this parochial line of late. He characterizes his own enterprise as follows:

"[W]e are not trying to find a conception of justice suitable for all societies regardless of their particular social or historical circumstances (...) We look to ourselves and to our future, and reflect upon our disputes since, let's say, the Declaration of Independence. How far the conclusions we reach are of interest in a wider context is a separate question (...)

(...) What justifies a conception of justice is not its being true to an order antecedent to and given to us, but its congruence with our deeper understanding of ourselves and our aspirations, and our realization that, given our history and the traditions embedded in our

124

public life, it is the most reasonable doctrine for us."[60]

Now to strike for a moment a personal note, these are disturbing thoughts for one who first read *A Theory of Justice* on the other side of the world, who studied and taught it in New Zealand and Britain for fifteen years before coming to the particular society cozily connoted by Rawls's use of the first "We look to ourselves (...) and reflect upon our disputes since, let's say, the Declaration of Independence." Until I read that particular passage, it never occurred to me that Rawls's theory was supposed to be confined to understandings and ideas embedded locally in the United States of America. I never doubted that Rawls intended to address problems about freedom and equality *everywhere* in the modern world, not just in the particular society from which he was writing.

Of course that *is* the life of the book, whatever its author says. There are reasons why Rawls's work was and is studied in New Zealand and in Britain as well as in Cambridge, Massachusetts, why it has been translated into French and Italian, why it is discussed in Athens and Delhi, Warsaw and Singapore. It is not that these societies are particularly interested in the dilemmas of *American* community. It is rather that all advanced societies share certain general problems about property, freedom, welfare, and equality, and they are *aware* of sharing these problems. The problems may differ somewhat in shape and detail from society to society and different societies do have different histories of dealing with them and somewhat different (though overlapping) resources in their respective political cultures. But, in every society, there is also a consciousness that these problems or similar problems occur elsewhere, that they are common difficulties, and that any attempt to solve them necessarily must have an eye to what has been tried with success or failure in other societies. The Americans and the Australian look at what the Swedes are doing. The lessons of what we used to call the Soviet Union are taken to be lessons for us all. The British read Milton Friedman from Chicago, who read F.A. Hayek from Austria, who reads Adam Smith from Scotland. Any characterization by Rawls or Walzer which failed to take this international character of the modern debate about justice into account would be plainly inadequate – inadequate even as an account of local meanings and local understandings.

In each of these societies, the debate about justice plainly depends upon comparisons with other systems and thus on the abstractions and extrapolations that make comparisons possible.[61] There is certainly no reason to suppose that the cosmopolitan personality is in any worse position to participate in such debates than her more grounded and parochial opponent. On the contrary, she may have the advantage of actually being acquainted firsthand with the workings of more than one social system and thus be in a better position to contribute to a debate in which comparisons are of the essence.

All this is to say nothing of the fact that these days, the questions themselves are as much international as national in character. One difficulty with Michael Walzer's insistence that "[t]he theory of justice is (...) sensitive to boundaries"[62] is that *issues* of justice are typically *not* so sensitive. For many of the global issues that we face, such as redistribution, pollution, and resource depletion, the localism of Walzer's approach would be catastrophic. Even particular social problems spill over from society to society in the form of war, refugees, and mass migration. These are not things that can be resolved by the nostalgia of *Gemeinschaft* or at a New England town meeting. Certainly what is needed is some form of community; but it is community on a global scale, a bringing together of a diversity of perspectives and ideas in the formation of common solutions to common problems. I suspect that those who are currently contributing most to the solution of these problems are, in many cases, people whose primary allegiance is to some international agency – who are genuinely and effectively citizens of the world – rather than those who pride themselves on their local acculturation and on the narrow parochialism of their understandings.

Once again, I must caution against a superficial deployment of the Aristotelean tradition. Aristotle argued that we should attempt to reach

126

a common view about justice with those for whom issues of justice are pressing.[63] For him, these were our fellow citizens in the polis. But for us, conscious as we are that the great issues of justice transcend communal boundaries, the Aristotelean concept of justice requires the repudiation of narrow parochialism in favor of a genuine attempt to work out what we owe one another on a global scale. A confined sensitivity to strictly local understandings, along the lines suggested by Walzer, may be attractive for other reasons (mainly literary and anthropological); but it is a travesty of the Aristotelean view of what the virtue of justice requires in the circumstances of the real world.

7. Our Debt to Global Community

One advantage of our focus on the cosmopolitan vision is that it forces us to think a little more grandly about the scale on which community and friendship are available for the constitution of the individual and the sustenance of friendship and interdependence. Talk of community in the nostalgic first-person plural of belonging, is, as I have said, apt to evoke images of small-scale community, neighborhood, or intimacy – the aboriginal hunting band, the Athenian city-state, or the misty dawn in a Germanic village.

Think honestly, however, of the real communities to which many of us owe our allegiance and in which we pursue our values and live large parts of our lives: the international community of scholars (defined in terms of some shared specialization), the scientific community, the human rights community, the artistic community, the feminist movement, what's left of international socialism, and so on. These structures of action and interaction, dependence and interdependence, effortlessly transcend national and ethnic boundaries and allow men and women the opportunity to pursue common and important projects under conditions of goodwill, cooperation, and exchange throughout the world. Of course, one should not paint too rosy a picture of this interaction. Such groupings exhibit rivalry, suspicion, and divisive controversy as well; but no more than any common enterprise and certainly no more than the gossip or backbiting one finds in smaller, more localized entities. It is community on this global scale which is the modern realization of Aristotelean friendship: equals who are good at orienting themselves in common to the pursuit of virtue. This form of community is quite missed by those who lament the loss of true friendship in modern life.[65]

Once we recognize this, the simple Herderian picture of the constitution of an individual through his belonging to a homogenous group begins to fall apart. Think how much we owe in history and heritage – in the culture, or the cultures that have formed us – to the international communities that have existed among merchants, clerics, lawyers, agitators, scholars, scientists, writers, and diplomats. We are not the self-made atoms of liberal fantasy, certainly, but neither are we exclusively products or artifacts of single national or ethnic communities. We are made by our languages, our literature, our cultures, our science, our religions, our civilization – and these are human entities that go far beyond national boundaries and exist, if they exist anywhere, simply *in the world*. If, as the communitarians insist, we owe a debt of provenance to the social structures that have formed us, then we owe a debt to the world and to the global community and civilization, as well as whatever we owe to any particular region, country, nation, or tribe.

The argument that we must not think of our individuality as self-made, but that we must own up to the role that society has played in the constitution of our selves and cultivate a sense of allegiance and obligation that is appropriate to that social provenance has been a staple of modern communitarian thought. It finds its most eloquent recent expression in a paper by Charles Taylor, entitled *Atomism*,[66] though I fear that in that article Taylor is guilty of exactly the equivocation I mentioned earlier: tracing our debt to society, in the sense of a whole civilization, and inferring an obligation to society, in the sense of a particular nation-state.[67]

Be that as it may, Taylor's argument is one that can be turned as easily against the partisans of small-scale community as against the advocates

128

of atomistic individualism. For just as the allegedly self made individual needs to be brought to a proper awareness of her dependence on social, communal, and cultural structures, so too in the modern world particular cultures and national communities have an obligation to recognize their dependence on the wider social, political, international, and civilizational structures that sustain *them*.

This is obvious in the case of indigenous communities in countries like the United States, Canada, Australia, and New Zealand. Indigenous communities make their claims for special provision and for the autonomous direction of their own affairs in the context of the wider political life of the countries where they are situated, and by the logic of Taylor's argument they must accept some responsibility to participate in and sustain this wider life. They are not entitled to accept the benefits of its protection and subsidization and at the same time disparage and neglect the structures, institutions, and activities that make it possible for indigenous communities to secure the aid, toleration, and forbearance of the large numbers of other citizens and other small communities by which they are surrounded.

Indigenous communities of course will lament that they are thus at the mercy of larger polities and that they have to make a case for the existence of their culture to fellow citizens who do not necessarily share their ethnic allegiance. They may yearn for the days of their own self-sufficiency, the days when the question of sharing their lands with anyone else simply did not arise.[68] They have that in common, I think, with Nozickian individualists who yearn for the days when the individual person was not so much at the mercy of the community and did not owe so much to the state, and who resent the processes that have brought them to this point.[69] Yet here we all are. Our lives or practices, whether individual or communal, are in fact no longer self-sufficient. We may pretend to be self-sufficient atoms, and behave as we are supposed to behave in the fantasies of individualistic economics; but the pretense easily is exposed by the reality of our communal life. And similarly – though we may drape ourselves in the distinctive costumes of our ethnic heritage and immure ourselves in an environment designed to minimize our sense of relation to the outside world – no honest account of our being will be complete without an account of our dependence on larger social and political structures that goes far beyond the particular community with which we pretend to identify ourselves.

If this is true of the relation of indigenous minorities to the larger state, it applies also to the relation of particular cultures and nations to the world order as a whole. The point is evident enough from the ironies of Article 27 of the International Covenant on Civil and Political Rights, quoted earlier, which claims the integrity of indigenous cultures as a matter of human rights.[70] One hardly can maintain that immersion in a particular community is all that people need in the way of connection with others when the very form in which that claim is couched – the twenty-seventh article of one of a succession of human rights charters administered and scrutinized by international agencies from Ottawa to Geneva – indicates an organized social context that already takes us far beyond a specific nation, community, or ethnicity. The point is not that we should all therefore abandon our tribal allegiances and realign ourselves under the flag of the United Nations. The theoretical point is simply that it ill behooves the partisans of a particular community to sneer at and to disparage those whose cosmopolitan commitments make possible the lives that they are seeking to lead. The activity of these international organizations does not happen by magic; it presupposes large numbers of men and women who are prepared to devote themselves to issues of human and communal values in general and who are prepared to pursue that commitment in abstraction from the details of their own particular heritage.

So far I have developed the *instrumental* side of Taylor's argument: just as individuals need communal structures in order to develop and exercise the capacities that their rights protect, so minority communities need larger political and international structures to protect and to sustain the cultural goods that they pursue. But Taylor's critique of individualist atomism also goes deeper than this. The very idea of individuality and autonomy, he argues, is a social artifact, a way of thinking about and managing the self that is sustained in a particular social and historical context.[71] I am sure that he is right about that. But we must not assume, simply because individuality is an artifact, that the social structures that are said to produce it are necessarily natural. Certainly there is nothing natural about communitarian, ethnic, or nationalist ideas. The idea of a small-scale national community is as much a product (and indeed a quite recent product) of civilization, growing and flourishing as the convergence of a number of disparate currents under particular conditions in a particular era, as is the idea of the autonomous individual.[72] Certainly, ethnic nationality is an idea which postulates or dreams its own naturalness, its own antiquity, its immemorial cultivation of a certain patch of soil. Each national community, in Benedict Anderson's phrase, *imagines* itself as something that can be traced to the misty dawn of time.[73] But so did *individuals* dream themselves, as the natural units of mankind, in the heyday of atomistic philosophy.[74] The claim that we always have belonged to specific, defined, and culturally homogenous peoples – the staple claim of modern nationalism – needs to be treated with the same caution as individualist fantasies about the state of nature: useful, perhaps, as a hypothesis for some theoretical purpose, but entirely misleading for others.

8. Kymlicka's View of the Social World

The Importance of Cultural Membership
In all of this, the cosmopolitan strategy is not to deny the role of culture in the constitution of human life, but to question, first, the assumption that the social world divides up neatly into particular distinct cultures, one to every community, and secondly, the assumption that what everyone needs is just *one* of these entities – a single, coherent culture – to give shape and meaning to his life.

That assumption, I am afraid, pervades Will Kymlicka's recent book on community and culture,[75] and it is to his argument that I now want to turn. Kymlicka's aim is to show that liberal theorists, such as John

Rawls and Ronald Dworkin, have underestimated radically the importance of culture as a primary good for the self-constitution of individual
lives.[76] He wants to fill that gap and to enlist liberal theories in the
cause of the preservation of minority cultures.[77]

Thus, Kymlicka's starting point is not so much the Herderian urge to
belong, but a Rawlsian conviction about the importance to people of
the freedom to form reform and revise their individual beliefs about
what makes life worth living.[78] To sustain that freedom one needs a
certain amount of self-respect, and one needs the familiar protections,
guarantees, opportunities, and access to the means of life – all the
things that figure already on Rawls's list of the primary goods to be
governed by a theory of justice.[79] In order to make the case that culture
is also one of these primary goods, Kymlicka argues that people cannot
choose a conception of the good for themselves in isolation, but that
they need a clear sense of an established range of options to choose
from.

> "In deciding how to lead our lives, we do not start *de novo*, but
> rather we examine "definite ideals and forms of life that have been
> developed and tested by innumerable individuals, sometimes for
> generations". The decision about how to lead our lives must ultima-
> tely be ours alone, but this decision is always a matter of selecting
> what we believe to be most valuable from the various options availa-
> ble, selecting from a context of choice which provides us with
> different ways of life."[80]

Kymlicka elaborates the point by insisting that what we choose among
are not ways of life understood simply as different physical patterns of
behavior.

> "The physical movements only have meaning to us because they are
> identified as having significance by our culture, because they fit into
> some pattern of activities which is culturally recognized as a way of
> leading one's life. We learn about these patterns of activity through
> their presence in stories we've heard about the lives, real or

imaginary, of others (...) We decide how to lead our lives by situating ourselves in these cultural narratives, by adopting roles that have struck us as worthwhile ones, as ones worth living (which may, of course, include the roles we were brought up to occupy)."[81]

"What follows from this?" Kymlicka asks.

"Liberals should be concerned with the fate of cultural structures, not because they have some moral status of their own, but because it's only through having a rich and secure cultural structure that people can become aware, in a vivid way, of the options available to them, and intelligently examine their value."[82]

On the face of it, the argument is a convincing one. Of course, choice takes place in a cultural context, among options that have culturally defined meanings. But in developing his case, Kymlicka is guilty of something like the fallacy of composition. From the fact that each option must have a cultural meaning, it does not follow that there must be one cultural framework in which each available option is assigned a meaning. Meaningful options may come to us as items or fragments from a variety of cultural sources. Kymlicka is moving too quickly when he says that each item is given its significance by some entity called "our culture", and he is not entitled to infer from that that there are things called "cultural structures" whose integrity must be guaranteed in order for people to have meaningful choices. His argument shows that people need cultural materials; it does not show that what people need is "a rich and secure cultural structure." It shows the importance of access to a variety of stories and roles; but it does not, as he claims, show the importance of something called *membership* in a culture.

Kymlicka's claim about the difference between physically and culturally defined options was an echo of an argument made earlier by Alasdair Macintyre, and it may reinforce my point to discuss that argument as well. According to Macintyre:

"We enter human society (...) with one or more imputed characters – roles into which we have been drafted – and we have to learn what they are in order to be able to understand how others respond to us and how our responses to them are apt to be construed. It is through hearing stories about wicked stepmothers, lost children, good but misguided kings, wolves that suckle twin boys, youngest sons who receive no inheritance but must make their own way in the world and eldest sons who waste their inheritance on riotous living and go into exile to live with the swine, that children learn or mislearn both what a child and what a parent is, what the cast of characters may be in the drama into which they have been born and what the ways of the world are. Deprive children of stories and you leave them unscripted, anxious stutterers in their actions as in their words."[83]

Again, it is important to see that these are heterogenous characters drawn from a variety of disparate cultural sources: from first-century Palestine, from the heritage of Germanic folklore, and from the mythology of the Roman Republic. They do not come from some *thing* called "the structure of our culture." They are familiar to us because of the immense variety of cultural materials, various in their provenance as well as their character, that are in fact available to us. But neither their familiarity nor their availability constitute them as part of a single cultural matrix. Indeed, if we were to insist that they are all part of the same matrix because they are all available to us, we would trivialize the individuation of cultures beyond any sociological interest. Any array of materials would count as part of a single culture whenever they were familiar to one and the same person. It would then be *logically* impossible for an individual to have access to more than one cultural framework.

Someone may object to the picture of cultural heterogeneity I am painting: "Doesn't each item take its full character from the integrity of the surrounding cultural context, so that it is a distortion to isolate it from that context and juxtapose it with disparate materials?" Maybe that is true, for certain purposes. If we were making an anthropological study of each item, we *would* want to explore the detail of its context

134

and provenance; we would look at the tale of the prodigal son in the context of Aramaic storytelling, and we would confine the children lost in the wood to the Germanic villages from which the Grimm brothers drew their collection of folklore. But that is absurd as an account of how cultural materials enter into the lives and choices of ordinary people. For that purpose, the materials are simply *available*, from all corners of the world, as more or less meaningful fragments, images, and snatches of stories. Their significance for each person consists in large part in the countless occasions on which they have been (from the anthropological purist's point of view) misread and misinterpreted, wrenched from a wider context and juxtaposed to other fragments with which they may have very little in common. Since this in fact is the way in which cultural meanings enter people's lives, Salman Rushdie's description of a life lived in the shadow of Hindu gods, Muslim film stars, Kipling, Christ, Nabokov, and the *Mabharata*[84] is at least as authentic as Kymlicka's insistence on the purity of a particular cultural heritage.[85]

If all this is correct, then membership in a particular community, defined by its identification with a single cultural frame or matrix, has none of the importance that Kymlicka claims it does. We need cultural meanings, but we do not need homogenous cultural frameworks. We need to understand our choices in the contexts in which they make sense, but we do not need any single context to structure all our choices: To put it crudely, we need culture, but we do not need cultural integrity. Since none of us needs a homogenous cultural framework or the integrity of a particular set of meanings, none of us needs to be immersed in one of the small-scale communities which, according to Kymlicka and others, are alone capable of securing this integrity and homogeneity. Some, of course, still may prefer such immersion, and welcome the social subsidization of their preference. But it is not, as Kymlicka maintained, a necessary presupposition of rational and meaningful choice.

Evaluation and Cultural Security
In addition to the claim (which I have just criticized) that each person needs to be a member of a particular cultural community, Kymlicka

also argues that each person needs some assurance of the *security* of the cultural framework or frameworks from which she makes her choices.[86] This seems to me a self-defeating claim.

Kymlicka's liberal individual is supposed to be making not just a choice, but an evaluation: "Which of the roles presented to me by the cultural materials at hand is a good role or an attractive one (for me)?" Now evaluation is a practical and, in part, a comparative matter. I choose role A because it seems a better way of living and relating to others than role B. It is difficult to see how one can make these comparisons without the ability to take a role, defined by a given culture, and compare it with what one might term loosely other ways of doing roughly the same sort of thing. For example, a traditional culture may define the role of *male elder*, a patriarchal position of tribal power, as a source of authority and the embodiment of tradition. Is this something for a young man to aspire to? One thing he may want to know is that the politics of patriarchal authority have, in almost all other social contexts, come under fierce challenge, and that people have developed other means of authoritative governance that do not embody male power and fatherhood in the same way. But to the extent that our young man can know this, he is not choosing from a cultural framework which is secure, in Kymlicka's sense. He only can make his choice a genuine *evaluation* to the extent that the culture he is scrutinizing is vulnerable to challenge and comparison from the outside. Unless the culture is vulnerable to his evaluation (and other evaluations like it), his evaluation will have no practical effect; and unless it has been vulnerable in this way in the past, he will have no basis for an informed and sensible choice.

To preserve a culture – to insist that it must be *secure,* come what may – is to insulate it from the very forces and tendencies that allow it to operate in a context of genuine choice. How does one tell, for example, whether the gender roles defined in a given culture structure have value? One way is to see whether the culture erodes and collapses as a way of life in a world once different ways of doing things are perceived. The possibility of the erosion of allegiance, or of the need

136

to compromise a culture beyond all recognition in order to retain allegiance and prevent mass exodus, is the key to cultural evaluation. It is what cultures do, under pressure, as contexts of genuine choice. But if that is so, we cannot *guarantee* at the same time the integrity of a given community and say that its culture (or the fate of its culture) can *tell* people about the value and viability of this particular way of life. Either people learn about value from the dynamics of their culture and its interactions with others or their culture can operate for them at most as a museum display on which they can pride themselves. There is, I suppose, nothing wrong with such fierce nostalgic pride, but it certainly should not be confused with genuine choice and evaluation. To confer meaning on one's life is to take risks with one's culture, and these are risks that dismay those whose interest is the preservation of some sort of cultural purity.[87]

In general, there is something artificial about a commitment to *preserve* minority cultures. Cultures live and grow, change and sometimes wither away; they amalgamate with other cultures, or they adapt themselves to geographical or demographic necessity. To *preserve* a culture is often to take a favored "snapshot" version of it, and insist that this version must persist at all costs, in its defined purity, irrespective of the surrounding social, economic, and political circumstances. But the *stasis* envisaged by such preservation is seldom itself a feature of the society in question, or if it is, it is itself a circumstantial feature. A society may have remained static for centuries precisely because it did not come into contact with the influences from which now people are proposing to protect it. If stasis is not an inherent feature, it may be important to consider, as part of *that very culture*, the ability it has to adapt to changes in circumstances. To preserve or protect it or some favored version of it, artificially, in the face of that change, is precisely to cripple the mechanisms of adaptation and compromise (from warfare to commerce to amalgamation) with which all societies confront the outside world. It is to preserve part of the culture, but not what many would regard as its most fascinating feature: its ability to generate *a history*.

10. The Cosmopolitan Self

I have argued that the "mongrelization" of identity that Salman Rushdie celebrated in the passage with which we began has none of the inauthenticity that the communitarian critique tends to suggest. I think it may well be a richer, more honest, and more authentic response to the world in which we live than a retreat into the confined sphere of a particular community.

But what becomes of *the self* in the cosmopolitan picture? This is the final question that I want to consider. If we live the cosmopolitan life, we draw our allegiances from here, there, and everywhere. Bits of cultures come into our lives from different sources, and there is no guarantee that they will all fit together. At least if a person draws his identity, as Kymlicka suggests, from a single culture, he will obtain for himself a certain degree of coherence or integrity. The coherence which makes his particular community a single cultural entity will confer a corresponding degree of integrity on the individual self that is constituted under its auspices.[88] By contrast, the self constituted under the auspices of a multiplicity of cultures might strike us as chaotic, confused, even schizophrenic.

The point is an important one. The cosmopolitan, as we have seen, is not in the business of disputing that people are formed by attachments and involvements, by culture and community. She acknowledges it, but acknowledges it – as it were – *too much* for the communitarian's comfort. For she shows how each person has or can have a variety, a multiplicity of different and perhaps disparate communal allegiances. Such integrity as the cosmopolitan individual has therefore requires *management*. Cultural structures cannot provide that management for her because too many of them are implicated in her identity, and they are too differently shaped.

The trouble is, if we talk too much about management, we fall into the trap of postulating the existence of a managerial entity, an agent existing in distinction from each of the disparate elements that together constitute the person in question. We have to postulate the "I", the true self who contrives somehow to keep the whole house in order. But who or what is this entity? How does it make its decisions? How does it know what sort of order to maintain?

One dominant theme in recent communitarian writing has been a critique of this picture of the independent self – the cosmopolitan manager, standing back a little from each of the items on the smorgasbord of its personality. In order to manage the disparate commitments, to see that they fit with one another, and to evaluate each item and compare it with others on the cultural menu, the self would have to be an ethereal sort of entity, without any content or commitments of its own. Michael Sandel quite properly has raised the question whether this is really the way that we want to view our personality and our character:

> "[W]e cannot regard ourselves as independent in this way without great cost to those loyalties and convictions whose moral force consists partly in the fact that living by them is inseparable from understanding ourselves as the particular persons we are – as members of this family or community or nation or people, as bearers of this history, as sons and daughters of that revolution, as citizens of this republic. Allegiances such as these are more than values I happen to have or aims I 'espouse at any given time' (...) To imagine a person incapable of constitutive attachments such as these is not to conceive an ideally free and rational agent, but to imagine a person wholly without character, without moral depth. For to have character is to know that I move in a history I neither summon nor command, which carries consequences none the less for my choices and conduct."[89]

Sandel's critique seems to present the defender of cosmopolitanism with an unhappy dilemma. Either he must embrace the ethereal self of liberal deontology – the self that chooses but is not identified with any of its choices; or he must admit that the self can have a substantial character of its own, a character essential to its identity. If he chooses the former, he gives a wholly unrealistic account of choice; for on what basis can this ghost choose if it has no values, commitments, or projects of its own? If, on the other hand, he opts for the picture of a self with a substantial essence in order to avoid the imputed shallowness of the former conception, then cosmopolitanism begins to look unsatisfactory. For now the self must have not just cultural characteristics in all their plurality and variety, but a *distinct character*, and it has not been proven that the cosmopolitan mode of engaging with the world can provide that.[90]

To avoid the dilemma, we should go back and question the image of *management* and the assumptions about *identity* that are presupposed in this critique. So long as we think that the management of the self is like the personal governance of a community or a corporation, we will be driven to ask embarrassing questions about the specific character of the "I" in its capacity as manager. But suppose we think instead about a personal identity, not in terms of hierarchical management, but in terms of the democratic self-government of a pluralistic population. Maybe the person is nothing but a set of commitments and involvements, and maybe the governance of the self is just the more or less comfortable (or at times more or less chaotic) coexistence of these elements. The threat, of course, is what we vulgarly call schizophrenia; but that may be better understood as radical conflict or dissonance rather than mere unregulated plurality. An image that may help to dispel this threat is that of the self-governance of a group of friends living and working together. Each friend has a character of her own and strengths and weaknesses of her own; they are quite different, but their variety and their frictions may be the key to their association and to their ability to undertake different projects and enterprises. No one, I hope, thinks that a friendship can be sustained only if one or the other friend is recognized as being *in charge* or only to the extent that all parties are agreed on some specific common purpose or charter. Friendship does not work like that, nor I think do the internal politics of the self. There may be, on occasions, antagonisms within the self (as indeed there are among friends); all of us, even, the most culturally and psychologically secure, have the experience of inner conflict. But far from detracting from the self's integrity, the possibility of such conflict, and the variety

140

and open texture of character that make it possible, seem indispensable to a healthy personality. It may be this limitless diversity of character – Rushdie's *melange* or hotchpotch – that makes it possible for each of us to respond to a multifaceted world in new and creative ways.

These are mere speculations, and they need to be matched more closely to the empirical psychology of personality. However, I hope that they indicate how misleading it may be to indict a picture of human life or action, such as the cosmopolitan vision that I have outlined, on the basis of simplistic and rigid assumptions about what the self *must* be like. Human identity is not a simple thing. The openness and diversity of the cosmopolitan way of life may well hold more of a key to understanding the role of character and creativity in a changing world than the assumption of Sandel's critique that character is to be identified compulsively with a single pre-established cultural role.

Conclusion

At the beginning of this paper, I set out a quotation from Salman Rushdie's defense of *The Satanic Verses* in his collection *Imaginary Homelands*.[91] Let me conclude with another passage from *In Good Faith*, the essay in which Rushdie reflects on the politics of his own cultural roots:

"To be an Indian of my generation was also to be convinced of the vital importance of Jawaharlal Nehru's vision of a secular India. Secularism, for India, is not simply a point of view; it is a question of survival. If what Indians call "communalism", sectarian religious politics, were to be allowed to take control of the polity, the results would be too horrifying to imagine. Many Indians fear that that moment may now be very near. I have fought against communal politics all my adult life. The Labour Party in Britain would do well to look at the consequences of Indian politicians' willingness to play the communalist card, and consider whether some Labour politicians' apparent willingness to do the same in Britain, for the same reason (votes), is entirely wise."[92]

I have chosen not to talk in this Article about the warning that Rushdie is sounding here, but to discuss more affirmatively the image of the modern self that he conveys. Still, I hope that we do not lose sight of the warning. The communitarianism that can sound cozy and attractive in a book by Robert Bellah or Michael Sandel can be blinding, dangerous, and disruptive in the real world, where communities do not come ready-packaged and where communal allegiances are as much ancient hatreds of one's neighbors as immemorial traditions of culture.

Rushdie wrote his piece originally for an English newspaper (hence his reference to the Labour Party). He said in effect that the British people, in the tensions of their new pluralism, had a right to expect something more from politicians, particularly on the Left, than a return to ethnic sectarianism. Something similar, I think, is true of legal and political philosophy. It is no secret that the old individualist paradigms are in crisis and that something must be done to repair or replace the tattered remnants of liberalism. But as shells rain down on Sarajevo[93], as Georgia announces that it will withhold citizenship rights from inhabitants who cannot prove that their ancestors were Georgian speakers and lived in the territory before 1801[94], as the long lines of refugees, in consequence, begin their fearful trudge toward the only homelands where they can expect to be welcomed or tolerated, as "community" even in North America becomes increasingly a code word for the class and ethnic exclusivity of wealthy home-owner's associations[95] – in the midst of all that, I suggest that people have a right to expect something better from their political philosophers than a turn away from the real world into the cultural exclusiveness of the identity politics of community. I hope that, at any rate, the vision of cosmopolitanism developed here can provide the basis of an alternative way of thinking – one that embraces the aspects of modernity with which we all have to live and welcomes the diversity and mixture that for most people is their destiny, whatever the communitarians say.

Notes

* This article originally appeared in the *University of Michigan Journal of Law Reform,* Vol.25: 3&4, pp. 751-793

1. RUSHDIE, SALMAN, *In Good Faith,* in: *Imaginary Homelands,* pp. 393, 394, 404 (1991)
2. See WALDRON, JEREMY, *Religion and the Imagination in a Global Community,* The Times Literary Supplement (London), Mar. 10-16, 1989, at p. 248 (discussing the Salman Rushdie affair)
3. See, e.g.,TAYLOR, CHARLES, *Cross-Purposes: The LiberalCommunitarian Debate,* in: *Liberalism and the moral life,* p. 159 (Nancy L. Rosenblum ed., 1989) (discussing both the independence and interdependence between ontological issues and advocacy issues which confuse the debate between communitarianism and liberalism in social theory).
4. E.g., RAWLS, JOHN, *A Theory of Justice,* 1971, pp. 395-439.
5. See LOMASKY, LOREN E., *Persons, Rights, and the Moral Community,* 1987, pp. 37-83
6. See id. at p. 42
7. See DWORKIN, RONALD, *A Matter of Principle,* 1985, p. 191. (referring to a theory of equality in which government is neutral as to "goodness" since each person's conception of what gives value to life differs).
8. RAWLS, supra note 4, at p. 408
9. Mackie presents a less rigid conception of a liberal life:
   "People differ radically about the kinds of life that they choose to pursue. Even this way of putting it is misleading: in general people do not and cannot make an overall choice of a total plan of life. They choose successively to pursue various activities from time to time, not once and for all." MACKIE, J.L., *Can There Be a Right-Based Moral Theory?,* in: WALDRON, JEREMY (ed.), *Theories of Right,* 1984. Raz expresses a similar idea:
   "The autonomous person is part author of his life. The image this metaphor is meant to conjure up is not that of the regimented, compulsive person who decides when young what life to have and spends the rest of it living it out according to plan (...) [Autonomy] does not require an attempt to impose any special unity on one's life. The autonomous life may consist of diverse and heterogeneous pursuits. And a person who frequently changes his tastes can be as autonomous as one who never shakes off his adolescent preferences."
   RAZ, JOSEPH, *The Morality of Freedom,* 1986, pp. 370-71. There is a strong temptation in traditional liberalism to take the form of an Aristotele-

143

an theory of ethical well-being and convert it to the purposes of liberalism. Instead of a single conception of the good life, authoritatively enunciated by Aristotle in *Nicomachean Ethics* p. 283 (bk. X, ch. 7) (David Ross trans., 1954), there are many such conceptions, and each person should be free to choose one. With Raz and Mackie, I think that the freedom of the modern self is less constrained than that: it is the freedom to make a variety of choices, not the freedom to choose just one out of a number of ethical conceptions.

10. Nietzsche too embraces this pluralistic view:

    "But for the enrichment of knowledge it may be of more value not to reduce oneself to uniformity in this way, but to listen instead to the gentle voice of each of life's different situations; these will suggest the attitude of mind appropriate to them. Through thus ceasing to treat oneself as a *single* rigid and unchanging individuum one takes an intelligent interest in the life and being of many others."

    NIETZSCHE, FRIEDRICH, *Human, All too Human: A Book for Free Spirits*, p. 196 (R.J. Hollingdale trans., 1986)

11. The communitarian works I have in mind include, most prominently, MACINTYRE, ALISDAIR, *After Virtue: A Study in Moral Theory*, 1984, 2d ed.; SANDEL, MICHAEL J., *Liberalism and the Limits of Justice*, 1982; TAYLOR, CHARLES, *Atomism*, in 2 Philosophical Papers: *Philosophy and the Human Sciences* 1985, 187 and WALZER, MICHAEL, *Spheres of Justice*, 1983; see also the extracts collected in: SANDEL, MICHAEL J. (ed.), *Liberalism and its Critics*, 1984.

12. See supra note 11

13. MARX, KARL, *Grundrisse*, in: MCLELLAN, DAVID (ed.), *Selected Writings*, 1977

14. SANDEL, supra note 11, at pp. 179-80

15. KYMLICKA, WILL, *Liberalism, Community and Culture*, 1989, p. 165

16. TAYLOR, supra note 11, at p. 198

17. POST, ROBERT C., The Social Foundations of Defamation Law, 1986, 74 CAL.L.REV., pp. 691 and 736

18. WALZER, supra note 11, at p. 313

19. DUNN, JOHN, *Interpreting Political Responsibility*, 1990, p.124

20. WALDRON, JEREMY, *Particular Values and Critical Morality*, 1989, 77 CAL.L.REV. pp. 561, 582; see also IGNATIEFF, MICHAEL, *The Needs of Strangers*, 1985, pp. 139-40. ("Our political images of civic belonging remain haunted by the classical polis, by Athens, Rome and Florence. Is there a language of belonging adequate to Los Angeles?").

21. For "imagined", see the excellent discussion in ANDERSON, BENEDICT, *Imagined Communities: Reflections on the Origin and Spread of*

Nationalism, 1983, pp. 15-16. Anderson stresses, quite rightly, that "imagined" does not imply "fabricated" Id. at 15.

22. BERLIN, ISAIAH, *Benjamin Disraeli, Karl Marx and the Search for Identity*, in: HARDY, HENRY (ed.), *Against the Current*, 1980, pp. 252 and 257

23. International Covenant on Civil and Political Rights, adopted Dec. 19, 1966, art. 27, 999 U.N.T.S. 172, 179

24. CAPOTORTI, FRANCESCO, *Study on the Rights of Persons Belonging to Ethnic, Religious and Linguistic Minorities*, pp. 40-41 and 98-99, U.N. Doc. E/CN.4/Sub. 2/384/Rev. 1, 1979

25. Id. at pp. 98-99

26. For example, Canadian legislation places restrictions on the ability of non-Indians to reside on or use Indian lands:

"[A] deed, lease, contract, instrument, document or agreement of any kind, whether written or oral, by which a band or a member of a band purports to permit a person other than a member of that band to occupy or use a reserve or to reside or otherwise exercise any rights on a reserve is void." Indian Act, R.S.C., ch. 1-5, § 28(1), 1985 (Can.). Some aboriginal leaders in Canada have proposed a variety of changes in local electoral requirements to assure recognition of the political rights of aboriginal peoples, regardless of the ethnic composition of the majority in a given region. See ASCH, MICHAEL, *Home and Native Land: Aboriginal Rights and the Canadian Constitution*, 1984, pp. 102-04; see also KYMLICKA, supra note 15, at pp. 148-49. Proposed changes include the imposition of residency requirements of between three and ten years before newcomers can vote for or hold public office in aboriginal communities. ASCH, supra at p. 103. In both the United States and Canada, participants in mixed marriages may suffer certain disabilities even when they reside on reservations or in aboriginal territories. For a general discussion, see KYMLICKA, supra note 15, pp. 148-49. The United States Supreme Court has recognized the jurisdiction of tribal authorities over Native American children born off the reservation in a case where a Native American mother had purposely given birth off the reservation in order to be able to relinquish her children to non-Native American adoptive parents. See *Mississippi Band of Choctaw Indians v. Holyfield*, 490 U.S. 30, 1989, pp. 51-53. This is about as far as the claims have gone in the context of aboriginal cultural rights in the United States. But of course it would be irresponsible to advance general theses about minority cultures without also recognizing their tendency to shade into nationalist claims for regional autonomy and self-determination, claims that throw boundaries and general political stability seriously into question. See infra text accompanying note 92.

27. See supra note 22 and accompanying text

28. For a general discussion of a "thin theory" of human good, see RAWLS, supra note 4, at p. 396

29. See id. at pp. 90-95 (discussing "primary goods"); see also DWORKIN, RONALD, *What Is Equality?* (pts. 1 & 2) 10 PHIL. & PUB. AFF. 186, 283, 1981 (discussing "equality of welfare" and "equality of resources"); SEN, AMARTYA, *Equality of What?*, in: MCMURRIN, STERLING M., *Liberty, Equality, and Law*, 1987, p. 137

30. Thomas Nagel, for example, says the following about Rawls's construction:

"The model contains a strong individualistic bias, which is further strengthened by the motivational assumptions of mutual disinterest and absence of envy. These assumptions have the effect of discounting the claims of conceptions of the good that depend heavily on the relation between one's own position and that of others (...) The original position seems to presuppose not just a neutral theory of the good, but a liberal, individualistic conception according to which the best that can be wished for someone is the unimpeded pursuit of his own path, provided it does not interfere with the rights of others."

NAGEL, THOMAS, *Rawls on Justice*, in: DANIELS, NORMAN (ed.), *Reading Rawls: Critical Studies on Rawls' A Theory of Justice 1*, 1975, pp. 9-10. Nagel is right that Rawls makes these assumptions. They constitute his thin theory of human choice and agency. They *are* controversial; but the existence of that controversy no more undermines the claim to liberal neutrality than the existence of a controversy about what counts as a hostile act undermines a claim to neutrality in international law. See WALDRON, JEREMY, *Legislation and Moral Neutrality*, in: GOODIN, ROBERT E. & ANDREW REEVE (eds.), *Liberal Neutrality 61*, 1989, pp. 78-81

31. RUSHDIE, supra note 1, at p. 405 ("I do not accept the charge of apostasy, because I have never in my adult life affirmed any belief; and what one has not affirmed one cannot be said to have apostasized [sic] from.").

32. Cf. supra note 22 and accompanying text

33. See supra note 1 and accompanying text

34. See supra notes 11, 22 and accompanying text

35. For example, Benn and Weinstein argue that "it is apposite to discuss" whether an action is free

"only if [the end it pursues] is a possible object of reasonable choice; cutting off one's ears is not the sort of thing anyone, in a standard range of conditions, would reasonably do, i.e. "no one in his senses would think

146

of doing such a thing (even though some people have, in fact, done it). It is not a question of logical absurdity; rather, to see the point of saying that one is (or is not) free to do X, we must be able to see that there might be some point in doing it
BENN, S.I. and W.L. WEINSTEIN, *Being Free to Act, and Being a Free Man*, 80 *Mind*, 1971, pp. 194, 195

36. See supra text accompanying note 1
37. See supra notes 28-30 and accompanying text
38. TAYLOR, CHARLES, *What's Wrong with Negative Liberty*, in: RYAN, ALAN (ed.), *The Idea of Freedom: Essays in Honour of Isaiah Berlin*, 1979, pp. 175, 182-83
39. For a discussion, see WILLIAM, BERNARD (ed.), *Obscenity and Film Censorship: An Abridgement of the Williams Report*, 1981, pp. 54-57.
40. ROUSSEAU, JEAN-JACQUES, *Reveries of the Solitary Walker*, 1783, p. 27 (Peter France trans., 1979). But it is worth noting that Rousseau, like Rushdie, thought of himself as an outcast rather than a misanthrope: "The most sociable and loving of men has with one accord been cast out by all the rest. With all the ingenuity of hate they have sought out the cruellest torture for my sensitive soul, and have violently broken all the threads that bound me to them." Id.
41. ARISTOTLE, *The Politics*, p. 5 (bk.I, ch.2) (Ernest Barker trans., 1979) ("[T]he polis belongs to the class of things that exist by nature, and that man is by nature an animal intended to live in a polis.").
42. Id. at pp. 5-6 ("[M]an is a being meant for political association, in a higher degree than bees or other gregarious animals (...) Not being self-sufficient when they are isolated, all individuals are so many parts all equally depending on the whole (...)").
43. Id. at p. 6, 5
44. ARISTOTLE, supra note 9, at p. 238 (bk. IX, ch. 9)
45. Id. at p. 263 (bk. X, ch. 6)
46. Id. at p. 241 (bk. IX. ch. 9)
47. For this distinction between concept and conception, see DWORKIN, RONALD, *Taking Rights Seriously*, 1978, pp. 134-36. Thus, for example, we may want to distinguish the concept of "cruel and unusual punishment" from the Founders' particular conception of that concept.
48. SMITH, ADAM, *The Wealth of Nations*, 1776, p.18. (Edwin Cannan (ed.), 1976).
49. See MARX, KARL, *Economic and Philosophical Manuscripts*, in: *Selected Writings*, supra note 13, at p. 83 ("An immediate consequence of man's alienation from the product of his work (...) is the alienation of man from man.")

50. Id. at 82

51. MARX, KARL & FRIEDRICH ENGELS, *The Communist Manifesto*, in: *Selected Writings,* supra note 13, at p. 224. This passage is of course part of the more general celebration of the dissolution of traditional ways of life. *The Communist Manifesto* is in many ways a manifesto of modernism:

"All fixed, fast-frozen relations, with their train of ancient and venerable prejudices and opinions, are swept away, all new-formed ones become antiquated before they can ossify. All that is solid melts into air, all that is holy is profaned, and man is at last compelled to face with sober senses, his real conditions of life, and his relations with his kind."

Id. Anyone who thinks that Marx is lamenting or condemning this state of affairs is, of course, confusing him with the "Reactionary Socialist" he excoriates later in the *Manifesto*, ignoring his insistence on the progressive role of the bourgeoisie, and ignoring also the connection between this global interdependence and the economic and philosophic basis of his own political claims about communist internationalism. See also BERMAN, MARSHALL, *All that is Solid Melts into Air: The Experience of Modernity*, 1982, pp. 19-21, for this cosmopolitan view of Marx.

52. ARISTOTLE, supra note 41, at p. 4 (bk I, ch. 2) ("When we come to the final and perfect association, formed from a number of villages, we have already reached the polis – an association which may be said to have reached the height of full self-sufficiency (...)").

53. Id. at pp. 5-6 (bk I, ch.2)

54. Id. at p. 123 (bk. III, ch. 11) (translator's alteration)

55. As John Stuart Mill wrote:

"Truth, in the great practical concerns of life, is so much a question of the reconciling and combining of opposites that very few have minds sufficiently capacious and impartial to make the adjustment with an approach to correctness, and it has to be made by the rough process of a struggle between combatants fighting under hostile banners."

MILL, JOHN STUART, *On Liberty*, 1859, p. 58 (Currin V. Shields (ed.), 1956)

56. WALZER, supra note 11, at p. 314

57. Id. at p. 313

58. Id.

59. Id. at pp. 313-14

60. RAWLS, JOHN, *Kantian Constructivism in Moral Theory,* 77 *J. Phil.,* 1980, pp. 516, 618-19

61. Cf. ARISTOTLE, supra note 41, at p. 39 (bk. II, ch. 1) ("We must begin by investigating ideal forms of government other than our own; and we

must investigate not only forms which are actually practised by states that are accounted to be well governed, but also forms of a different order which have been designed by theorists and are held in good repute.")

62. WALZER, supra note 11, at p. 315

63. ARISTOTLE, supra note 9, at p. 106-09 (bk. V, ch. 1)

64. Id. at p. 196 (bk. VIII, ch. 3)

65. Cf. BELLAH, ROBERT N., et al., *Habits of the Heart,* 1985, pp. 115-16 ("The conception of friendship put forward by Aristotle (...) had three essential components. Friends must enjoy one another's company, they must be useful to one another, and they must share a common commitment to the good.")

66. TAYLOR, supra note 11

67. Id. at 197-98 ("[P]roof that [our distinctively human] capacities can only develop in society (...) is a proof that we ought to belong to or sustain society (...)")

68. For the dangers of taking this yearning as a basis for rectificatory justice, see WALDRON, JEREMY, *Superseding Historic Injustice*, 103 *Ethics*, 1992, p. 103; see also WALDRON, JEREMY, *Historic Injustice: Its Remembrance and Supersession*, in: ODDIE, GRAHAM & ROY W. PERRETT (eds.), *Justice, Ethics and New Zealand Society*, 1992, p. 139

69. See generally NOZICK, ROBERT, *Anarchy, State, and Utopia*, 1974

70. See supra note 23 and accompanying text

71. See TAYLOR, CHARLES, *Sources of the Self*, 1989. Taylor has traced the provenance of these individualist ways of thinking in this massive and important book.

72. See ANDERSON, supra note 21, at pp. 50-65, 80-103 (describing the role of imperialist administration in creating not only national entities but also national consciousness in what used to be imperial colonies).

73. See id. at pp. 129-40

74. Cf. LOCKE, JOHN, *Two Treatises of Government,* 3d ed. 1698, p. 269 (Peter Laslett (ed.),student ed. 1988) ("To understand Political Power right, and derive it from its Original, we must consider what State all Men are naturally in, and that is, a *State of perfect Freedom* to order their Actions, and dispose of their Possessions, and Persons as they think fit, within the bounds of the Law of Nature, without asking leave, or depending upon the Will of any other Man.")

75. KYMLICKA, supra note 15

76. Id. at pp. 162-66

77. Id.

78. See RAWLS, supra note 4, at pp. 407-24; see also RAWLS, JOHN, *Reply to Alexander and Musgrave*, 88 *Q.J. Econ.,* 1974, pp. 639, 641 ("[F]ree

persons conceive of themselves as beings who can revise and alter their final ends and who give first priority to preserving their liberty in these matters.")

79. RAWLS, supra note 4, at pp 90-95
80. KYMLICKA, supra note 15, at p. 164 (quoting RAWLS, supra note 4, at pp. 563-64) (citation omitted).
81. Id. at p. 165
82. Id.
83. MACINTYRE, supra note 11, at p. 216; but cf. OKIN, SUSAN M., *Humanist Liberalism*, in: ROSENBLUM, NANCY L. (ed.), *Liberalism and the Moral Life*, 1989, pp. 39, 48 ("Macintyre gives, with no apparent consciousness of its sexism, a list of the characters 'we' need as the models around which to shape our lives as narratives. The only female characters in the list are a wicked stepmother and a suckling wolf.")
84. See RUSHDIE, supra note 1, at p. 404
85. But cf. POST, supra note 17, at p. 736 ("A community without boundaries is without shape or identity (...)").
86. KYMLICKA, supra note 15, at p. 169
87. I think what this shows, by the way, is that Kymlicka's strategy (arguing from liberal premises) is simply a dangerous one for the proponents of cultural preservation to adopt. The liberal conception of autonomous choice evokes a spirit of discernment, restlessness, and comparison. It is, I think, simply antithetical to the idea that certain structures of community are to be *preserved* in their integral character. As long as cultures depend for their existence on people's allegiance and support, their use as frameworks of choice for individual lives is always liable to cut across the interest we have in preserving them.
88. But this can be exaggerated. However we define and individuate cultures, can we simply assume that each culture is coherent in this sense? Aren't some cultures, even some traditional ones, riven by contradictions? And isn't the artifice of "preservation" likely to heighten any contradictions that exist as well as to introduce new ones? Moreover, are we really in a position to assume that coherence means the same in the context of a social entity, like a cultural framework, and an individual entity, like a person constituting a life? I leave these challenging questions for another occasion, noting only that they seldom are addressed by those who insist on the communitarian provenance of the self.
89. SANDEL, supra note 11, at p. 179; see also TAYLOR, CHARLES, *Hegel and Modern Society*, 1979, p. 157 ("The self which has arrived at freedom by setting aside all external obstacles and impingements is characterless, and hence without defined purpose, however much this is hidden by such

150

seemingly positive terms as 'rationality' or 'creativity'.")

90. Macintyre makes a similar suggestion:

"[W]e all approach our own circumstances as bearers of a particular social identity. I am someone's son or daughter, someone else's cousin or uncle; I am a citizen of this or that city, a member of this or that guild or profession; I belong to this clan, that tribe, this nation. Hence what is good for me has to be the good for one who inhabits these roles. As such, I inherit from the past of my family, my city, my tribe, my nation, a variety of debts, inheritances, rightful expectations and obligations. These constitute the given of my life, my moral starting point. This is in part what gives my life its own moral particularity.

This thought is likely to appear alien (...) from the standpoint of modern individualism. From the standpoint of individualism I am what I myself choose to be. I can always, if I wish to, put in question what are taken to be the merely contingent social features of my existence."

MACINTYRE, supra note 11, at p. 220

91. See supra note 1 and accompanying text

92. Id. at p. 404

93. See *Serbs Step Up Fighting for Piece of Bosnia Capital*, N.Y. Times, Apr. 23. 1992, at A10

94. See HOBSBAWM, ERIC, *Grand Illusions: The Perils of the New Nationalism*, in: 253 *Nation*, pp. 537, 555 (Nov. 4, 1991)

95. See DAVIES, MIKE, *City of Quartz: Excavating the Future in Los Angeles*, 1990, pp. 153-56

Political Principles of Respect for Both the Individual and the Group Identities

Hans Joachim Türk

1. Two Forms of Respect for the Individual: an Individualistic one and a Group Orientated One

1.1 The topic I have been given contains a contrast and on closer inspection a real contradiction. According to the tradition of the European Enlightenment, the philosophy of human rights, the political liberalism and the constitutional state to which we are accustomed, the connection between respect for the individual and respect for the identity of a certain cultural or ethnical group appears to be a contradiction in terms. Within this tradition of thought respect for the individual includes an universalistic ethics of equal treatment of each person. At present Charles Taylor and his commentators such as Amy Gutmann and Michael Walzer describe this problem.[1] Within the discours about recognition of others a policy of universalism has arisen. Accordingly dignity is something which all citizens are entitled to and which aims towards assimilation and adjustment of rights and duties. Therefore a division of society into first and second class citizens should be avoided at all costs. Michael Walzer calls this kind of recognition *liberalism 1* and concludes from the recognition of equal rights that the Government is not allowed to aim at certain cultural or religious projects or collective goals which exceed the personal freedom, welfare and security of citizens. The commitment to such aims can be called (in agreement with Taylor) *procedural*, whereas the policy which pursues a certain idea or essence of a morally good life should be termed *substantial*. According to American liberalism only a procedural society deserves to be called *liberal*. By the way the U.S.A. sees itself, by philosophers such as Ronald Dworkin, John Rawls, Jürgen Habermas and many supporters of a multicultural society and of the dual nationality this kind of liberalism is represented. In this sense only the individual as an autonomous being creates the state and other communities, but together with other individuals. All forms of communities including the state and the Government are created by contracts, not by nature or by authorities. It is not a patriotism of birth or nationality which counts, but the patriotism to one's constitution ("Verfassungspatriotismus"). This is founded more in a rational way than in an emotional one and figures as an antidote against nationalism and chauvinism.

After the fall of Soviet communism in the East, liberalism and the doctrine of individual human rights as well as the democratic state founded by contract and consent seemed to be victorious. This was said to be the end of history by Francis Fukuyama, because enemies no longer exist. A new world order appears to emerge. Nevertheless everywhere in the world regional, national, ethnic and religious movements or even revolts can to be seen which nobody ever believed to be possible now or in the future. Besides all the problems of liberal and individualistic society, formerly hidden, now came up, as the supposed rival of Western civilization disappeared.

The sociologist Friedrich Tenbruck already diagnosed the problem in 1989: "Der vermeintlich vorgezeichnete Weg zur allgemeinen Menschheitskultur wurde fraglich, als sich die nationalen Besonderheiten verstärkten. Erst recht zerrann die erhoffte Einigkeit in Werten und Idealen vor dem organisierten sozialen Dissens der Interessen und im verstärkten Kampf der Ideologien und Weltanschauungen. Im Gegenteil zeigte sich, daß die Reste gemeinsamer Überzeugungen und Überlieferungen durch rationale Reflexion, historische Relativierung und naturalistische Erklärung aufgelöst wurden."[2] One has the impression that all tendencies towards unity of man are confined to the surface of telecommunication and the behavior of consumers of Coke and Big Macs and of tourists all over the world. On the other hand the Western society falls apart into pieces, i.e. into different groups of diverse lifestyles, moral standards and ideologies. We pass through a process of a society in which the range of culture and morals disintegrates into pieces. The benefit of individual liberty no doubt leads to deliverance from the compulsion of nature and the restraint of society, but can result in the destruction of both. In this sense the German political scientist Ludger Kühnhardt says: "Nicht länger gilt unangefochten als gewiß, ob der universale Anspruch der Menschenrechtsidee einem kulturellen Relativismus und Pluralismus standhält, ob die engen Begegnungen unterschiedlicher Weltkulturen einen moralischen Dialog noch möglich sein lassen."[3] His American colleague Samuel Huntington agrees with him and goes beyond Kühnhardt's statement in his wellknown article in "Foreign Affairs" in 1993 predicting a clash of different civilizations in the future. Instead of a universal and unified world culture, there will be various forms of civilization, namely the Western, the Islamic, the Confucian, the Hindu, the Japanese, the Latin-American and the Slavic-Orthodox. Leaving out the worldwide telecommunication and the superficial common way of acting, there won't be a universal civilization in the near future. At best we can expect a co-existence of the above-mentioned diverse civilizations.

Because the political development and the course of things don't confirm the assumptions of individualistic liberalism and its anthropology and man doesn't like to live in an atomized and lonely mass (like in a big Hotel), the liberal conception of the individual and of the relationship between him and the community has to be modified. The German writer and poet Hans Magnus Enzensberger remarks in his new essay "Aussichten auf den Bürgerkrieg": "Spezifisch für den Westen ist jedoch die Rhetorik des Universalismus. Die Postulate, die damit aufgestellt worden sind, sollen ausnahmslos und ohne Unterschied für alle gelten. Der Universalismus kennt keine Differenz von Nähe und Ferne; er ist unbedingt und abstrakt. Die Idee der Menschenrechte erlegt jedermann eine Verpflichtung auf, die prinzipiell grenzenlos ist. Darin zeigt sich ihr theologischer Kern, der alle Säkularisierungen überstanden hat. Jeder soll für alle verantwortlich sein. In diesem Verlangen ist die Pflicht enthalten, Gott ähnlich zu werden; denn es setzt Allgegenwart, ja Allmacht voraus. Da aber alle unsere Handlungsmöglichkeiten endlich sind, öffnet sich die Schere zwischen Anspruch und Wirklichkeit immer weiter. Bald ist die Grenze zur objektiven Heuchelei überschritten; dann erweist sich der Universalismus als moralische Falle."[4] Similarly the Oxford philosopher

Leszek Kolakowski stated at the philosophy congress in Berlin, 1993, that Western liberalism rather than communism has destroyed the basis of our social life.

1.2 Against these universalized and at the same time individualized constructions in a contemporary debate (not only in America but also in Europe) some arguments are advanced particularly by the so-called "communitarianism". The supporters of communitarianism, sociologists, political scientists and philosophers, should not be identified with the political right wing, as is sometimes done. They belong to a different political school. Moreover not all of them are absolutely opposed to liberalism, some rather want to correct it. On the one hand, the communitarians criticize the trends towards individualism and hedonism in American society, which destroy the very foundations of common values and common sense. They take the Greek *polis* as an example of living together and continue the ethics of Aristotle, who founded morals in real communities and not in abstract ideas. On the other hand, the revival of particular values such as nation, native country, region, dialects and traditional customs everywhere, above all in the former communist countries, forms the basis of the philosophy of communitarianism. The nation and other social fabrics create intermediary communities between the individual and the state: All these communities and social groups, the minorities too, are worthy of respect. Therefore the political correctness of speaking has gained acceptance from the opinion leaders in the field of politics and universities. Another motive for communitarian thinking is that one can find the breakdown of the multicultural living together in many different places and countries. Multiculturalism seems to be possible between highly motivated individuals of the cultivated class or at certain places of work. Otherwise it is restricted to the areas of tourism and the catering trade. Now it is obvious that for instance the U.S.A. is not a melting pot but a fractioned society, divided into ethnic, religious and social groups. As far as Germany is concerned, recently the sociologist Gerhard Schulze noted in his research[5] that German society is split in five environments or *milieus*, which differ from each other so much that they find it extremely difficult to communicate.

The axiom of communitarianism means that the identity of an individual neither comes from himself as an autonomous human being nor from his affiliation to mankind in the abstract but from his belonging to a certain group or community. Therefore this community which shapes the identity of an individual deserves respect too. The question is now how to combine the indispensable essentials of liberalism and the principle of communitarianism. In reference to this, Taylor proposes some plausible thoughts as a kind of synthesis of both liberalism and communitarianism, which Walzer calls *liberalism 2*. According to Taylor, the policy of universal dignity of man aims at something universal, equal to all individuals. In contrast to that, the policy of difference, in spite of its universalist basis, recognition of everyone's equal dignity, means something else: " (...) with the politics of difference, what we are asked to recognize is the unique identity of this individual or group, their distinctness from everyone else. The idea is that it is precisely this distinctness that has been ignored, glossed over, assimilated to a dominant majority identity. And this assimilation is the cardinal sin against the ideal of authenticity."[6] In this way the universal recognition of every individual changes into the recognition of difference! "Or, put otherwise, we give due acknowledgment only to what is universally present – everyone has an identity – through recognizing what is peculiar to each: The universal demand powers an acknowledgment of specificity."[7] Rüdiger Bubner names such groups (as e.g. nations) *partikularisierte Allgemeinheiten*. Not only personal characteristics but also the affiliation to certain social, ethnic, religious groups rank among those differences. Identity is based on the universal and equal dignity of everyone as well as on the acknowledgment and recognition of the groups the individuals belong to. Both claim respect; in addition moral respect implies also political entitlements and duties.

2. Documents of International Law

2.1 The idea of human rights has developed in a strange way from the French Revolution and from the "Declaration des Droits de l'Homme et du Citoyen". At the beginning individual freedom and equal rights constituted the basis for all the political goals of the revolution.

Because equality before the law had not yet been achieved, equality rather than liberty was becoming the focus of attention. Equality became even an end in itself. Liberty played a minor role, unlike the U.S.A. In this country equality of all citizens (with the exception of slaves) was a matter of fact and therefore the prerequisite for the "Bill of Rights" of Virginia in 1776, which declares the right to liberty, property, happiness and security. Here the roots of the abovementioned *liberalism 1* can be found, and not in France. These ideas of liberty are reflected in the United Nations Charter on 26.6.1945 (art. 1,3), in the Human Rights Conventions and Covenants of the UN on 10.12.1948 and on 19.12.1966, and also in the documents of the Conference on Security and Cooperation in Europe (the Final Act of 1.8.1975 and the following meetings in Madrid 1983, in Vienna 1986, in Copenhagen 1990), and also in the Convention of the Council of Europe on 4.11.1950 and so on. Many of them became national or international law by ratification proceedings. Meanwhile the international community has come to believe that severe violations of human rights give the UN cause for intervening, despite the right of self-determination of the nations concerned. The analysis of these documents shows that the approach is a historic and classic one: Only the respect for the individual and for his entitlements is protected. These basic human rights entitle and protect everyone against interference from governments or from other persons. According to current political theories only in some cases the individual hands over certain rights to the government, namely by social contract. The frequently quoted ban on discrimination against race, religion, nation and gender relates only to individuals who belong to such a group, but never relates to the group itself. The guarantee and protection apply to the individual person.

2.2 On the other hand, the right of self-determination of nations and peoples is recognized by many covenants, treaties and conventions. Apart from the special situation of decolonization (Banjul Charter on 27.6.1982, art. 20), only those nations that are established states are officially recognized subjects of self-determination. This results in the inviolability of their territorial sovereignty and in the commitment to non-aggression (UN Charter, art. 2,4 and 7). Comments on minorities, ethnic and religious groups can be found in the CSCE documents (Final Act of Helsinki VII, Copenhagen Conference IV). However this only means that members of these groups should not be discriminated and that these members are entitled to maintain their individual rights: The signatory states have to take note of the "ethnic, cultural, religious, linguistic identity" (Copenhagen, no. 35). It's not possible to justify aggression against the sovereignty of these states and their territory, not even in the interest of minority rights (no. 37). No secession of a minority which wants to decide its own affairs is provided for in national or in international law; such action is regarded as high treason till today. Respect of minorities is restricted to legal protection of individuals belonging to minorities, this because of universal human rights, and not because of group affiliation. The second part of our subject ("respect for group identities") cannot be found in binding statements of international law. Groups are only considered to be constitutional states or voluntary unions of individuals according to civil law. The relations between the individuals, groups and the states, particularly the legal status of minority groups which don't belong to the majority nation, are legally and politically unsettled. Collective rights are missing. Unlike the traditional theories of contract the documents of international law even fall back to a mere individualism, since they take the existing states for granted and acknowledge only the human rights of individuals.

3. The Ethical Foundation and the Political Implementation of the Respect for Group Identity

3.1 We don't have to talk about the individual human rights based on a universal perspective (even though the grounds for it vary); but the question is how to combine the equal treatment of every single citizen with the right of having a certain group identity; the "droit à la différence" of a "communauté" (as the saying goes in French) within an existing state that contains a particular minority in addition to the majority nation. Three social levels have to be taken in account which form the identity of a person: the immediate vicinity and the milieu in which one grows up, the freely chosen associations or communities and the political community, that can be a state which comprises a variety of nationalities like the U.S.A. or a pure nation state or a state made up of majority nation and one or more ethnic minorities.

The notion of *nation* is very unclear, also in foreign languages. A generally accepted definition doesn't exist. But at the moment two esssentials of nation are becoming more and more common among political scientists: Firstly a historic and cultural continuity (which is not necessarily an ethnic one) the individual takes part in; secondly a deliberate assent to a certain form of community, which can be politically very different (it must not be identical to the state this "nation", i.e. ethnic group, belongs to). In this sense Ernest Renan defined nation in a famous speech at the Sorbonne (Paris, 11.3.1882) as follows: "le consentement, le désir clairement exprimé de continuer la vie commune".[8] Nation is something more than citizenship, more than "Verfassungspatriotismus" as defined by the German intellectuals Dolf Sternberger and Jürgen Habermas, less than a mythical patriotism identifying state, culture, language and race, a fact that particularly in Germany and in the Slavic nations has led to the nation state as the unique form of state and finally to imperialistic nationalism. Nation in the said sense participates in the above mentioned three social levels and is somewhere between the state and the immediate environment of the individual. It's very similar to the Greek *polis*. The ethical relevance of nation is based on the so-called *ethos*, which means that the way of ethical thinking, the moral attitudes and the norms emerge from the social environment and the *community* and even the "nation" that the individual grows up in.[9] Nation contributes a lot to the moral identity, which nevertheless leaves open the possibility of correction and further development by rationally improved ethics.

In order to avoid misunderstanding, it can't be emphasized enough that the time and the justification of the sovereign nation state are past for three reasons: There are supranational structures because of economic, technical and communicative requirements, also because of subsidiary communities and social subsystems below the level of the state, finally there is on this level itself the coexistence of minorities, possibly

160

together with a majority nationality.

Some political problems develop from the ethical foundation of group identity: Is a government authorized to give preferential treatment to the majority nation, which fears for its own identity, e.g., because of imminent immigration and foreign infiltration? To what extent does a cultural or ethnic minority (i.e. a certain "nationality") have to align itself with the majority ("acculturation")? What cultural and political self-determination should be granted to the minorities? Should a minority or ethnic group be supported, in the face of the risk of loosing its identity? Under which circumstances has a minority the right to gain freedom from the oppressing majority and its state (which to this day has been a matter of fact and power only)? What about multiculturalism within a state? Maybe all these questions can be summarized as follows: Is a certain group entitled to ostracize another group, either majority or minority, from its area of life, in order to maintain or even to save its own identity?

3.2 Provided that we don't lapse back into the idea of nation state or even into a new kind of nationalism (which makes the nation state an absolute one), we'll plead in accordance with Taylor for a policy of recognition and of difference. A policy of equal human rights is not sufficient. Nationalism is not a counterargument against the ethical implications of nation. Nation shares the ambivalence with other social structures such as sports clubs, areas of towns, blocks and neighbouring villages etc. Violence is not a specific characteristic of national consciousness but an anthropological constant factor which can be combined with different social phenomena. This has been recently described by the German writer Hans Magnus Enzensberger in reference to the nationalist acts of violence in the Balkans and elsewhere.[10] On this theme Shlomo Avineri said: "Der Nationalismus ist eine Kreatur mit Januskopf: Einerseits hat er ein großes emanzipatorisches Potential, andererseits trägt er Gefahren in sich. Es ist Selbstbestimmung, wenn man in einem selbsterrichteten Gemeinwesen lebt, mit seiner eigenen Geschichte, Sprache, Kultur, manchmal auch Religion in Einklang steht – und wenn man sich über die Möglichkeiten freut, diese Traditionen an seine Nachkommen weiterzugeben. Soweit damit die Bereitschaft verbunden ist, ähnliche Gefühle anderer zu respektieren, ist das die harmonische Version Manzinis. Aber Nationalismus kann auch fremdenfeindlich, intolerant, aggressiv, hegemonial, autoritär sein, wenn die Bereitschaft fehlt, dem anderen das zuzugestehen, was man für sich selbst fordert: Das ist die Version Treitschkes. Die große Gefahr dabei ist, daß man von der fremdenfeindlichen Version des Nationalismus so schockiert und erschüttert ist, daß man sein emanzipatorisches Potential übersieht – und dadurch kann man viele Menschen in die aggressive Richtung des Nationalismus drängen, weil man ihnen seine harmonische Seite vorenthält."[11] The statement Avineri makes about nationalism applies to all groups, minorities as well as majorities. Once again: It would be fatal to consider the universalistic and equal respect for every individual and the recognition of group identities and particularities as an alternative. We must not choose between universal and particular values. We have to hold to them both. And this is not only a question of political opportunity, but also of ethics, which consists of universalized norms as well as of particular values and habits. Without the former, morals would end in relativism and scepticism, no matter how the fundamental values (e.g. the dignity of man, human rights, the "golden rule") are to be founded – at least one of the diverse theories of foundation must be true. The latter morals are based on the above particular *ethos* which belongs to a specific group. Taylor refered to the two forms of ethics and politics: "These forms do call for the invariant defense of *certain* rights, of course. There would be no question of cultural differences determining the application of *habeas corpus*, for example. But they distinguish these fundamental rights from the broad range of immunities and presumptions of uniform treatment that have sprung up in modern cultures of judicial review. They are willing to weigh the importance of certain forms of uniform treatment against the importance of cultural survival, and opt sometimes in favor of the latter. They are thus in the end not procedural models of liberalism, but are grounded very much on judgements about what makes a good life – judgments in which the integrity of cultures has an important place."[12] Taylor goes back (similar to other communitarians like e.g.

162

Alasdair McIntyre) to Aristotle's ethics who based morals on the conditions of the good life in the *polis*. But he transfers the right of peculiarity and of its recognition also to minority groups within a community or a state, without giving the minorities the right to establish their own nation state. Once more Taylor: "(...) a society can be organized around a definition of the good life, whithout this being seen as a depreciation of those who do not personally share this definition. Where the nature of the good requires that it be sought in common, this is the reason for its being a matter of public policy. According to this conception, a liberal society singles itself out as such by the way in which it treats minorities, including those who do not share public definitions of the good; and above all by the rights it accords to all of its members."[13]

It must be added that the ethical claim to cultural, social and administrative group rights as collective ones (e.g. the usage of the native language at school and on trial, special supports etc.) has to be legally founded by national and by international law. Only by this way the ambivalence and the danger of nationalism can be avoided and the respect for the individual and for the group identity has to be combined. In the past, nations had the tendency to form a nation state, but at present and in the future, governments have to strive for granting special rights to ethnic groups within their territories. In this sense the "Responsive Communitarian Platform"* wants to reconcile universal human values and rights with the particular values, norms and habits of a certain community. Therefore not only politics of abstract and universal equality, but also of difference is required.

Notes

* in: *The Responsive Community,* Vol. 2, Iss. 1, Winter 1991/92.

1. TAYLOR C., *Multiculturalism and 'The Politics of Recognition', An Essay by Charles Taylor,* with commentary by Amy Gutman, Steven C. Rockefeller, Michael Walzer and Susan Wolf, Princeton, 1992. In the German version (TAYLOR, C., *Multikulturalismus und die Politik der Anerkennung,* Frankfurt am Main, 1993) also a contribution of Jürgen Habermas.

2. TENBRUCK, F., *Die kulturellen Grundlagen der Gesellschaft. Der Fall der Moderne,* Opladen: Westdeutscher Verlag, 1990, p. 271

3. KÜHNHARDT, L., *Die Universalität der Menschenrechte,* Bonn: Olzog, 1991, p. 100

4. ENZENSBERGER, H.M., *Aussichten auf den Bürgerkrieg,* Frankfurt am Main: Suhrkamp, 1993, pp. 73-74; cf. pp. 86-91

5. SCHULZE, G., *Die Erlebnisgesellschaft. Kultursoziologie der Gegenwart,* Frankfurt am Main/New York: Campus, 1993, pp. 277-333

6. TAYLOR, C., *The Politics of Recognition,* loc. cit. p. 38

7. loc. cit. p. 39

8. RENAN, E., Qu'est-ce qu'une nation? Oeuvres Complètes I, Paris, 1947-1961, p. 904

9. cf. KLUXEN-PYTA, D., *Nation und Ethos. Die Moral des Patriotismus,* Freiburg/München, 1991, esp. pp. 120-133

10. ENZENSBERGER, H.M., loc. cit. pp. 18-28

11. AVINERI, S., *Eine neue Welt – oder die Wiederkehr der alten? Über Postkommunismus, Nationalismus und das vermeintliche 'Ende der Geschichte',* in: *Frankfurter Allgemeine Zeitung,* 2.2.1993 (No.27), p. 10

12. TAYLOR, C., loc. cit. p. 61

13. loc. cit. p. 59

Special Rights for Minorities
The Muddy Waters of Collective Rights

Marlies Galenkamp

1. Introduction

Over the last few years, we have been witnessing a growing world-wide sensitivity to the identity of minority groups. Among ethicists too, group identity has become a major issue. One may refer to Charles Taylor's *Multiculturalism and 'The Politics of Recognition'* (1992). In this book, Taylor argues that non-recognition of the identity of minority groups may inflict harm and even result in a form of oppression, imprisoning those groups in a false and distorted mode of being. Presupposing the importance of group identities, the question arises how we are to protect those identities.

The answer to this question is often sought in the attribution of special rights to minority groups. Those special rights are generally considered to be 'collective rights.' That is, these rights are ascribed to groups as such, in order to protect their group characteristics (Galenkamp 1991 and 1993a). Underlying the defense of collective rights, is a criticism of the predominantly individualistic human rights approach. This approach is viewed to be not apt to cope with problems of group discrimination. Hereby, the assumption seems to be that the attribution of special rights to some groups might help to overcome some of their problems, since it might provide a more adequate protection of their threatened, communal identity. Thus, it is small wonder that the idea of collective rights is often defended by communitarian ethicists, although not exclusively so (see e.g. Kymlicka's (1989) liberal-philosophical defense of collective rights).

In this paper, I shall raise some doubts on this assumption. I shall focus on one specific collective right: the right to preserve one's cultural identity, which receives considerable attention these days. In section 3, I shall discuss some of the problems which may arise by proclaiming such a collective right. In the next section, some of the presuppositions of this right will be critically appraised. Finally, section 5 is a re-evaluation of the individualistic human rights framework.

2. Justifying the Collective Right to Preserve One's Cultural Identity

Why should some groups have special rights? Or more specifically: why should minority groups have a right to preserve their group identity? The argumentation is mostly based on a criticism of the individualistic human rights framework. The alleged shortcomings of this framework could be summarized as follows.

Human rights are generally defined as rights which human beings have *qua* human beings, regardless their belonging to a specific, communal setting. The principles of individualism, universalism and formal equality are its basis. Main assumption of the human rights doctrine is that it is the similarity among persons – the universal core of human dignity or, in the words of Taylor (1992: p. 40) 'the universal human potential' – rather than the differences among them, that is of moral importance. According to Taylor, this potential, rather than anything a person may have made of it, ensures that each person deserves respect. The focus on the similarity among persons, however, can only be obtained through a process of abstraction and formalization. In the human rights model, the presence of groups and various group identities, such as race, ethnic origin or sex, are temporarily bracketed. Group differences are considered to be contingent rather than constitutive of the individual's identity. As Van Dyke (1974: p. 72) notes, such blindness to group differences is often accompanied by a neglect of the actual presence of different groups. An undifferentiated and homogeneous population seems to be implied.

Up until now, the individualistic, (formal) egalitarian and universalistic line of thinking has been predominant in international legal practice.

166

The postwar minority protection may illustrate this. Since World War II, public international law has been designed to integrate the minority issue in individualistic, 'non-discrimination' clauses. One may refer here to article 27 of the International Covenant on Civil and Political Rights of 1966. This article reads as follows: "In those States in which ethnic, religious or linguistic minorities exist, persons belonging to such minorities shall not be denied the right in community with the other members of their group, to enjoy their own culture, to profess and practice their own religion or to use their own language." The 'minority right' expressed here adheres to "persons belonging to minorities." Emphasis is put on the backward position of individuals belonging to minority groups rather than on the disadvantaged position of the groups as such. Current international regulations of the minority issue seem to be characterized by two propositions. The first is that an inferior position of a minority group may be redressed by pressing for equal rights for any individual member of the group. As Glazer (1978: p. 91) notes: "If Brown could not be segregated on the basis of race, neither could White, nor Wilkens, nor any black." A second assumption is that minority groups whose members enjoy individual equality of treatment, do not need additional facilities for the maintenance of their ethnic particularity as a group.

It is these two assumptions of the human rights discourse, that have been the main target of criticism by advocates of the collective right to preserve one's cultural identity. The abstract and egalitarian discourse is blamed for being inappropriate to redress the backward position of minority groups. Besides and more fundamentally, it is blamed for falling short of preserving those distinctive, specific characteristics of minority groups that are highly valued by their members. In spite of the current universal adoption of the human rights doctrine, in many parts of the world one may find a marginalization and a forced assimilation of individuals, belonging to minority groups.

Processes of marginalization illustrate that in a 'group-differentiated society' (Young 1989: p. 258), the principle of formal equality and a policy of non-discrimination do not automatically lead to substantive equality. As critics argue, when some groups are privileged and others are marginalized, a policy of formal equality (equality *de jure*) does not suffice, for it is likely to result in a practice of substantive inequality (inequality *de facto*). Adherence to the principle of formal equality serves the purposes of dominant groups in a society: it perpetuates rather than undermines oppression. (Van Dyke 1979: p. 56) One may illustrate this by referring to the current position of indigenous peoples all over the world. Indigenous peoples are less advanced and weaker than people in the dominant community. They are unable to protect and promote their own interests in open, competitive relationships with outsiders. These groups face inequalities, not as a result of their choice, but due to circumstances. Rectification may require a policy of preferential treatment of the group as a group and the provision of some additional rights to those groups. As Young (1989: p. 268) puts it: "To the degree that there are group differences that disadvantage, fairness seems to call for acknowledging rather than being blind to them. Instead of always formulating rights in universalistic terms that are blind to differences, some groups sometimes deserve special rights." Hence, one argues for *preferential* rather than *equal* treatment. Note that this argument is not inspired by the wish to give minority groups permanent advantages. Rather, it aims to restore them to a substantively equal position with those in the dominant culture.

Yet for another and more fundamental reason, human rights critics argue that the notion of equality falls short. Here, the idea of equality itself is at stake. The current processes of assimilation of individual members of indigenous peoples to a dominant society signals the disadvantages of merely thinking in formal egalitarian and universalistic phrases, such as: "if everyone is treated alike, there should be no need for specific measures to protect minority groups." According to critics, this statement misses the point, since it fails to account for precisely those differences among groups which are distinctive. In the words of Taylor (1992: p. 38), by adopting such a homogenizing framework "the distinctness is ignored, glossed over, assimilated to the dominant identity." As mentioned earlier, in the universalistic human rights model, differences between people – as of race, sex or national origin – are temporarily bracketed. Bracketing is possible, since these differences are believed to be contingent rather than constitutive of an individual's identity. This picture of contingent differences is the main target of the critics of equality. As they note, group differences, rather than being contingent, are constitutive of an individual's identity. Note the 'communitarian' outlook of the argument: the cultural identity of a community is said to be the main – or even sole – basis of the individual's identity. Because of this, bracketing differences between people would lead to uniformization and levelling, and consequently to silencing, suppression and exclusion of any distinctive characteristics. If some groups are to preserve these characteristics, they may need something more than just equality. The preservation of those distinctive characteristics arguably is the main rationale of the collective right to preserve one's cultural identity. Its distinction from the human rights framework can be summarized by the distinction Taylor (*ibid.*: p. 42) makes between "respecting the universal human potential" and "respecting actually evolved cultures." In the first case, all humans *potentially* are equally valued, in the second instance what they have *actually* made of this potential is equally valued.

The importance of the need to protect one's group identity is often illustrated by referring to the present plight of indigenous peoples. In the last few centuries, most of them, from being the original inhabitants of their land, have been reduced to fringe elements in modern societies. Though they are often victims of human rights violations, experience has shown that the special problems facing indigenous peoples cannot be adequately solved by a human rights approach alone. It is not sufficient to say that a government does not make distinctions based upon race, religion, language or ethnicity. First, such an individualistic approach can not cope with disadvantages which these groups face as a group. It is unattentive to their need for preserving their distinctive characteristics, that is, their group identity. Moreover, the individualistic rights approach itself may be argued to have changed their group identity, perhaps even destroyed it. As Donnelly (1990: p. 56) notes, it is the social homogenization of formal egalitarian measures which threaten the specific group identity of those peoples. Their specific identity is particularly vulnerable in that it may be outbid or outvoted by majority decisions, a problem that members of a majority culture do not face. Hence, the protection of indigenous peoples against assimilation can not be subsumed under the heading of discrimination alone, for the goal in the fight against discrimination is equality, whereas the goal of indigenous peoples exceeds equality: it is the preservation of their specific identity. According to advocates of collective rights, the best way to maintain this distinctiveness would be to establish a collective right for those vulnerable groups to preserve their cultural identity. Only this group approach of rights ensures an appropriate remedy for the protection of their specific identity.

These developments – marginalization and forced assimilation of individuals belonging to marginalized groups – shed light on the rationale of the collective right to preserve one's cultural identity. They also make clear that this right has a Janusface. On the one hand, the goal seems to be a situation of material equality. Due to the substantive egalitarian outlook, it expresses the need to treat individuals as equals, given their specific group-linked differences. In this respect, the provision of this collective right may be seen as a temporary measure, since it is meant to be an protective device during a transitional period, that is, until the goal of equality has been achieved. This egalitarian picture is not complete, however, for the collective right to preserve one's cultural identity goes beyond the idea of equality. In contradistinction to universalistic and egalitarian human rights – rights which are said to be "indifferent to differences" -, the collective right to preserve one's cultural identity may be reformulated as a particularistic "right to difference." It aims at the preservation and protection of the specific identity of certain groups. It may be labeled as particularistic, since this right asks to give acknowledgment and status to something that is not universally shared.

The main distinction between, as Taylor (1992: p. 38) calls it, the "human rights politics of equal dignity" and the "politics of difference" should be clear by now: "With the politics of equal dignity, what is established is meant to be universally the same, an identical basket of rights and immunities. With the politics of difference, what we are asked to recognize is the unique identity of this individual or group, their distinctness from everyone else" (*ibid.*: p. 38). A second distinction concerns the fact that the politics of difference is meant to be a permanent rather than an temporary one. Taylor (*ibid.*: p. 40) therefore concludes: "Collective rights go beyond a mere positive action. The goal of those rights is not to bring us back to an eventual difference-blind social space, but, on the contrary, to maintain and cherish distinctness, not juist now, but forever. After all, if we're concerned with identity, then what is more legitimate than one's aspiration that it never be lost?"

3. The Muddy Waters of Collective Rights

The plea for collective rights, and more specifically for a collective right to preserve one's cultural identity, has not gone uncontested. One may refer to Habermas (1993: p. 158), who recently used the expression "systemfremde kollektive Rechte." In view of the above analysis, this critical attitude is not that strange. Due to their 'communitarian' outlook, collective rights seem to be at odds with the key presuppositions of the predominant, liberal-philosophical doctrine in ethics. The waters surrounding the isle of collective rights seem to be rather muddy. In this section I shall discuss some of the problems that – seen from a liberal-philosophical perspective – may result from attributing special rights to some groups, and more specifically, by proclaiming a collective right to preserve one's cultural identity as a group. One may distinguish two kinds of criticism: pragmatic ones and arguments of principle. In the end, the arguments come down to the following trio: special rights for some groups are neither feasible, nor desirable, nor needed.

Let us begin with the first cluster of arguments, the pragmatic ones. Collective rights seem to have been introduced to solve some of the problems of an individualistic rights model. It may be doubted, however whether collective rights may rightly be seen as a solution to those problems. As critics of collective rights rightly argue, the main problem with the current human rights protection is the proper enforcement of human rights in all states of the world. In many states containing minority groups, the human rights of the members of these minority groups are often violated. This being so, it seems to be rather unlikely that states would recognize and protect special rights for some groups. We should not so much press for additional rights for some groups, but rather stick to a better enforcement of human rights for all members of minority groups.

A second pragmatic argument concerns the confusion when it comes to determining the subject of collective rights. Collective rights are rights a group has qua group. It will be obvious, however, that not any group, consisting of two or more persons, automatically is a bearer of collective rights. One could ask which groups are sufficiently qualified to get some additional rights. Which specific criteria have to be met in order to be qualified as a collective rights bearer? In the literature on collective rights to date, there is no unanimously agreed answer. One may refer to the criteria which are put forward by scholars who have written on the issue of collective rights: Kymlicka, Taylor and Donnelly. Is it the plight of aboriginal people, being disadvantaged due to the encroachment of a predominant, modern society (Kymlicka 1989: p. 187)? Is it the specific character of a community – and the wish to protect it – such as in the French-speaking community of Quebec in Canada (Taylor 1992: p. 53)? Or is it the traditional outlook of a community (Donnelly 1990: p. 52) that legitimizes the ascription of some special rights? A related issue concerns the topic as to the content of those rights. Should these groups have the right to national self-determination, or merely the right to preserve their cultural identity? Finally, there is the problem of determining the membership of minority groups, qualified as special rights-bearers. Defenders of collective rights often mistakenly assume that individuals may be neatly divided into distinct communities. What to do, however, with the second or third generation of ethnic minorities, for example within The Netherlands or Germany? Should we regard them as members of their former, 'native' community, or as citizens of the country in which they happen to live at present? As Michael Ignatieff asks in his latest book,

Blood and Belonging. Journeys into the New Nationalism (1993, p. 130): "Does the Quebecois nation comprise all those who live there or only those who were born French-speaking? (...) Is Croatia the nation of the Croatian people or of all those – they may include Serbs – who chose to make Croatia their home? Is Germany the nation of the German people, or of the Turks, Yugoslavs, Portugese, Spaniards, Romanians and Poles who have chosen Germany as their home?"

The main theme of the arguments of principle against special rights is that the ascription of special rights to some groups is at odds with non-discrimination clauses, upon which liberal-political systems are based. As Van Dyke (1974: p. 740) notes: "Potential contradictions obviously exist between the proposition that individuals are entitled to equality without distinction as to race, language or religion and the proposition that groups, identified by these characteristics may have special legal status and rights." Speaking of collective rights seems to involve a kind of *apartheid*. Individuals are no longer seen as principally equal: rather, belonging to a certain group may result in a different status for different persons.

One may distinguish four kinds of arguments of principle against the ascription of special rights, and more specifically, the ascription of the collective right to preserve one's cultural identity. The first two raise doubts on the underlying objective of this right. As we have seen, the rationale of the collective right to preserve one's cultural identity is in the preservation of the specific identity of minority groups. First, such a juridicial formalization of distinctions between groups suggests – at least implicitly – that minority groups actually have distinctive identities, which remain intact and unchanged in time. This seems to be a rather static view of cultural identity. Jeremy Waldron (1991: p. 787) denotes the wish for the preservation of one's cultural identity as an artificial one: "Cultures live and grow, change and sometimes wither away; they amalgamate with other cultures or adapt themselves to geographical or democratic necessity. (...) To preserve or protect it (a culture, MG), or some favored version of it, artificially, in the face of that change, is precisely to cripple the mechanisms of adaptation and compromise. (...) It is to preserve part of the culture, but not what many would regard as its most fascinating feature: its ability to generate a history." Another problem concerns the implicit suggestion of the collective right to preserve one's cultural identity that any actual group identity – whatever its nature – should be cherished. It is doubtful whether all actual group identities deserve a likewise romantic glorification. For what to do, for example, with a group identity based on a fascist or racist ideology? Deriving a right to preserve one's cultural identity from the actual presence of different group identities, advocates, in fact, commit the so-called 'naturalistic fallacy.' Normative evaluations are derived from factual statements. The fact that there are different group identities does not automatically imply a positive evaluation of those identities.

The two remaining criticisms of principle of the collective right to preserve one's cultural identity focus on the 'internal' and 'external' level. From the inside of minority groups, the idea of preservation of group identity may be used as a license to lock up individuals within their closed community. From the outside of the groups concerned, it may lead to a far-reaching exclusivism. Let us take these two aspects in order.

With regard to the internal level, as we have seen in section 2, the argument for a right to preserve one's cultural identity is generally based on the constitutive role of the community. Individuals are supposedly embedded within a particular tradition. This viewpoint may render the individual to a vulnerable position, however, for embeddedness may mean being struck. That is, individuals may be forced to adjust to a homogeneous community. This may lead to the repression of dissenting ways of life as well as to rigidization of traditional structures. In other words, the appeal to "a cultural identity of the group" may not do enough justice to group-internal differentiation. It may imply the consolidation of elite values at the cost of minority values within this community. As Finkielkraut (1987: p. 107) notes, the proclamation of a community's right to preserve its cultural identity easily ends up as an individual's right to be repressed by his or her culture. A group

174

approach of rights may result in a restriction of the possibility to develop oneself as an individual. The current civil war in former Yugoslavia is illustrative. People who have always defined themselves in terms of their education, profession or gender, now have been stripped of all those defining marks of identity, in order to have merely one single identity: either being a Croatian, a Serb, or a Muslim.

As to the 'external' level, the argument for a collective right to preserve one's cultural identity is predicated on the importance of group membership. Group membership is seen as constitutive for the individual's identity. No doubt, this emphasis on one's belonging to a community may dispell a sense of anomy and strengthen feelings of being at home. The emphasis on group membership is a mixed blessing, however. Thinking in terms of group membership implies that some people are members, while others are not. It may increase the solidarity within groups, but at the same time decrease the solidarity and tolerance among groups. Hence, it may lead to a disintegration of societies (Schlesinger 1992: p. 4). The threat of disintegration is even greater, since communal identities are often exclusionary itself. It should be emphasized that this exclusion is not merely accidental, but rather endemic to a group approach. At whatever level we call ourselves brothers and sisters, some are more so than others. There is no way to overcome this logic: any 'us' will imply the presence of a 'them.' Besides, a strong community seems to be best created by a hostile approach towards outsiders. What better way to create a community – a cynic might say – than to wage a holy war against others?

These mechanisms of segregation and exclusion are even more problematic because of their in-built tendency of restricting the community's scope. Communitarian values themselves are incapable of determining at which level they should operate. In the end, nationalistic splitting up *in infinitum* of heterogeneous multicultural societies and ex-communication of dissenters, may be the result of the wish for communal homogeneity. Ignatieff (1994: p. 30) describes the logic of this process quoting a fictitious Yugoslavian warlord: "If we cannot trust our neighbours, we must rid ourselves of them. If we cannot live together in a single state, we must create clean states of our own." He continues: "The logic of ethnic cleansing is not just motivated by nationalist hatred. Cleansing is the warlord's coldly rational solution to the war of all against all. Rid yourself of your neighbours, the warlord says, and you no longer have to fear them. Live among your own, and you can live in peace." Since there are no objective criteria to determine which groups are qualified for special rights and which groups are not, violence and force may become the ultimate arbiters. That is: only a group able to enforce its will in a given constellation will get its right to self-determination.

It should be clear by now that the attribution of collective rights to some minorities inevitably comes down to a nationalist 'solution' of the minority issue: the infinite division of multi-cultural societies in smaller national groups, tearing apart the structure of inter-ethnic accomodation and producing a new order of partitioned, supposedly homogeneous states. As the bloody practices of 'ethnic cleansing' in former Yugoslavia demonstrate, this 'postmodern tribalism' (Franck 1993) is no solution at all.

4. The Paradox of Difference

We can now put some question marks at one of the main assumptions of the collective rights debate itself. As we have seen, the plea for special rights for certain groups is often aimed at a more adequate pro-tection of marginalized groups. The assumption is the specific group identity of those groups might only be protected by ascribing special rights to those groups. It is doubtful, however, whether this assumption is a viable one.

As we have seen in section 2, a collective right to preserve one's cultural identity is generally proposed in response to the (formal) egalitarian and individualistic rights approach. This approach is blamed for not being able to provide material equality, and moreover, for not being able to preserve the peculiar identity of some communities. The

176

implicit proposition is that an emphasis on the abstract value of equality within the individualistic rights approach will inevitably lead to a 'whitewashing' of concrete differences and of specific identities of communities. That is, the focus on egalitarian human rights is thought to result in a policy of forced assimilation and homogenization. Accordingly, critics deduce that one should not adopt egalitarian measures, but emphasize differences by proclaiming a collective right to preserve one's cultural identity. Means and ends are thus viewed to coincide. Measures based on the value of 'equality' are said to lead to a homogenization, a levelling down of society, whereas measures based on the value of 'difference' would result in a colourful society in which differences among people are cherished. However, as we have seen in the former section, emphasizing specific differences between people is not without costs. We encounter a 'dilemma of difference', since both the neglect and the emphasis on actual differences among people have their disadvantages. Neglecting the differences between people, by focussing on the value of equality, may imply a forced assimilation and a loss of the specific, cultural identity of minority groups. However, accentuating specific group characteristics by proclaiming a collective right to preserve one's cultural identity may lead to an exaltation of communal identities, eventually imprisoning individual members within their group. When it comes to this dilemma, the main question we may ask is, in the words of Todorov (1982: p. 249), whether "we can speak of equality without hereby whitewashing all differences by presupposing one common identity."

In my view we can. In this respect we may counter the hidden assumptions of critics of the individualistic rights discourse. Firstly, the focus on 'differential' measures, for example the ascription of special rights for specific groups, may not result in a 'differential' outcome. Secondly, the adoption of '(formal) egalitarian' measures does not automatically lead to a homogenization or assimilation. I shall explain these two aspects in order.

As far as the first aspect is concerned, at face value no doubt the proclamation of the collective right to preserve one's cultural identity may enable the heterogenization of identities in society, in that it may offer specific communities an opportunity to evade forced assimilation and to choose their own group identity. At closer inspection, however, proclamation of group identities may leave individuals powerless to reject the communal identity that others – e.g. the elites of their community or outsiders – have defined for them. Hence, what at first sight may seem to be an appropriate measure for expressing one's sensitivity to various differences *among* communities, and thus for the preservation of pluralism within a society, may have dreadful side-effects. It may lead to a forceful repression of differences *within* communities and, in the end, to an ethnic homogenization of societies. What we hoped for was diversity, but what we get is homogeneity.

As regards the second aspect, the application of the abstract and egalitarian mood of thinking at first sight may lead to a neglect of differences among people. That is to say, universalistic thinking is likely to result in a homogenization of society. This is not the end of the story, however. In my view, emphasizing the abstract value of equality within the individualistic rights approach can result in a maximalization of space for differences and otherness. A multi-cultural society, based on liberal principles, does not necessarily imply a levelling of distinctive group characteristics. The explanation is to be found in the endemically abstract character of liberal values, such as 'equality.' Rather than describing an actual state of affairs, the notion of equality is a 'counterfactual' one (Foqué and 't Hart 1990: p. 139). 'Equality' of individuals is obtained by abstracting from practice. That is, equality is an artificial attribute acquired by individuals entering the public realm. This view of equality is abstract, since it assumes human beings to be temporarily separated from their contingent characteristics.

This abstraction marks an important departure from the communitarian view, on which the collective right to preserve one's cultural identity is generally based. The communitarian perspective of individuals is reflected by the well-known proverbial saying that "it is the coat which makes the gentleman." In the communitarian viewpoint, the individual's identity is said to be mainly determined by his or her membership of

178

and his or her role within a constitutive community. Liberal-philosophical discourse, on the other hand, focusses on the modern and abstract notion of the 'nude man'. It may be argued that this abstraction is its main advantage rather than – as sometimes suggested – its disadvantage. For one, only abstraction from concrete identities and differences may pave the way for all-inclusiveness and a non-discriminatory policy, not only towards fellow members of the community, but towards strangers as well. Secondly, only by focussing on the abstract value of equality can we prevent an essentialistic 'dressing up' of concrete men and women, since it is left to individuals themselves to decide what kind of persons they want to be. We may thus prevent a process of ethnic homogenization, since individuals are not locked up within their own culture. Only by focussing on the abstract value of equality can we protect cultural diversity.

Summarizing, the 'dilemma of difference' has actually turned out to be a 'paradox of difference.' In doing justice to actual differences among people, one should not focus too much on those differences, for this may have the opposite effect: homogenization rather than heterogenization of society. In the end, in order to preserve concrete differences and distinctive group characteristics, emphasis on the abstract value of equality may be more suitable. As to the collective right to preserve one's cultural identity, one may indeed speak of "equality without hereby whitewashing the differences among people." Only by presupposing abstract equality may we prevent the whitewashing of concrete differences. If we want to preserve *concrete* differences and distinctive characteristics as much as possible, we are better off sticking to the *abstract* value of equality. The abstract value of equality is not incompatible with actual pluralism; rather, they go hand in hand (Galenkamp 1993b: p. 309).

5. Human Rights Revised

This brings us to the third and last set of critical arguments against the ascription of special rights to minority groups, by claiming those rights to be redundant. There is no need for additional collective rights, since the existing individual human rights suffice. Let us assess this claim by re-evaluating the individualistic human rights framework and the related liberal-democratic approach.

In the former section, we have encountered a 'paradox of difference:' in order to preserve actual differences among people, we had better not focus too much on those actual differences. Sticking to the abstract value of equality might be better. This argument can be argued to be the core of any liberal-democratic political system. As Rockefeller (1992: p. 92) notes, the objective of liberal-democratic systems is to respect and not to repress ethnic identities. This does not imply that in those systems much explicit attention is paid to different ethnic identities. On the contrary, one may say by bearing in mind the paradox: only the focus on the abstract value of equality may do justice to actual and specific identities. That way, a multi-cultural society, rather than a nationalistic division of society, is feasible. Within multi-cultural or 'pluralistic' societies, any citizen may require to receive respect, regardless his specific background and his membership of a specific sub-community. Ignatieff (1994: p. 4) calls this pluralistic model of society a form of 'civic nationalism', in contradistinction to a society of 'ethnic nationalism.' What gives unity to a nation in the first sense, what makes it a home, is the cold contrivance of shared rights, instead of people's pre-existing ethnic characteristics. Ignatieff (ibid.: p. 4): "According to the civic nationalist creed, what holds a society together is not common roots, but law. By subscribing to a set of democratic procedures and values, individuals can reconcile their right to shape their own lives with the need to belong to a community."

In such a pluralistic, political system, then, the equal value of the different cultures is respected by pressing for equal citizenship, that is, by ascribing equal individual rights to all members of various minority groups. As Habermas (1993: p. 173) recently noted, we should recognize and respect the individual members of minority groups rather than the groups as such. Doing otherwise would come down to a conservation of cultures and a shutting up of individuals within their closed community. Ultimately, only individuals belonging to a culture

180

should decide whether their culture is worth preserving. Hence, in Habermas' view, so-called 'cultural rights', such as the right to speak one's own language and to enjoy one's own culture, should be seen as rights of individuals rather than of minority groups as such. I think we should endorse this liberal-philosophical viewpoint: the one legitimate minority protection is the protection of the individual members of minority groups.

As we have seen, the present plight of minority groups has been an important background of the collective rights debate. At present, in many political systems world-wide, members of minority groups are seriously hindered in their exercise of human rights. In view of the above, these problems are not to be addressed by attributing special rights to those groups. We better press for an unqualified ascription and guarantee of human rights for the members of those groups. Hence, in contradistinction to what is suggested by critics of individual human rights discourse, the main problem with the current minority protection is not so much that the protection of the individual human rights of the members of minority groups is insufficient for the preservation of the specific identity of those groups. The main problem is that the individual human rights of the members of those groups have not been taken seriously enough.

Let us conclude. No doubt, the recognition of separate and coherent group identities might be of primordial importance to an individual, something which has generally been overlooked in liberal-philosophical theories. But even so, it may be doubted whether this importance should be followed up by ascribing some special, collective rights to marginalized groups, for instance the collective right to preserve one's cultural identity. The recognition of the importance of cultural pluralism within a society should not incite us to a recognition of special rights for some groups. Quite on the contrary. As I have attempted to show, cultural pluralism within a society will be guaranteed best by sticking to a human rights protection for all individuals, irrespective of their specific, cultural background. One should take human rights much more seriously than has been done to date. There is no viable alternative to individual human rights. Here, I do not suggest that human rights will solve all problems of minority groups. Some of their problems – such as their marginalized status qua group – will remain. The ascription of special rights to minority groups is no solution at all to their problems, however. The ascription of special rights to minority groups is undesirable. Apart from that, it is unfeasible and superfluous. All members of minority groups – just like any individual – should have rights qua person. We should not ask for more, but we could not do with less.

Bibliography

BERTING, J. (et al.), *Human Rights in a Pluralist World. Individuals and Collectivities*, Westport/London: Meckler, 1990

DONNELLY, J., *Human Rights, Individual Rights and Collective Rights*, 1990, in: *Berting*, pp. 39-62

DYKE, V. VAN, *Human Rights and the Rights of Groups*, in: *American Journal of Political Science*, 1974/18, pp. 725-741

DYKE, V. VAN, *The Individual, the State and Ethnic Communities in Political Theory*, in: KOMMERS, D.P. and G. D. LOESCHER (eds.), *Human Rights and American Foreign Policy*, London, 1979, pp. 36-62

DYKE, V. VAN, *Human Rights, Ethnicity and Discrimination*, London: Greenwood, 1985

FINKIELKRAUT, A., *La défaite de la pensée*, Paris: Gallimard, 1987

FRANCK, T., *Postmodern Tribalism and the Right to Secession*, in: BRÖLLMANN, C., R. LEFEBER and M. ZIECK (eds.), *Peoples and Minorities in International Law*, Dordrecht/Boston/London: Martinus Nijhoff, 1993, pp. 3-28

FOQUÉ, R. and 'T HART, A.C., *Instrumentaliteit en rechtsbescherming. Grondslagen van een strafrechtelijke waardendiscussie*, Arnhem: Gouda Quint, 1990

GALENKAMP, M., *Collective Rights: Much Ado About Nothing? A Review Essay*, in: *Netherlands Quarterly of Human Rights*, 1991/9, 3, pp. 291-307

GALENKAMP, M., *Individualism Versus Collectivism. The Concept of Collective Rights (PhD. thesis)*, Rotterdam: Erasmus Universiteit, 1993

GALENKAMP, M., *Seyla Benhabib. Feitelijke inbedding en liberale distantie*, in: KLINK, B. VAN, P. VAN SETERS and W. WITTEVEEN (eds.), *Gedeelde normen. Gemeenschapsdenken en het recht*, Zwolle: W.E.J. Tjeenk Willink, 1993, pp. 297-310

GLAZER, N., *Individual Rights Against Group Rights*, in: Eugene Kamenka en Alice Erh-Soon Tay, *Human Rights*, London: Arnold, 1979, pp. 87-103

HABERMAS, J., *Anerkennungskämpfe im demokratischen Rechtsstaat*, in: Charles Taylor, *Multikulturalismus und die Politik der Anerkennung*, Frankfurt am Main, 1993, pp. 147-196

IGNATIEFF, M., *Blood and Belonging. Journeys into the New Nationalism*, London: BBC Books, 1993

KYMLICKA, W., *Liberalism, Community and Culture*, Oxford: Clarendon Press, 1989

ROCKEFELLER, S. C., *Comment*, in: Taylor, 1992, pp. 87-98

SCHLESINGER, A.M. Jr., *The Disuniting of America. Reflections on a Multicultural Society*, New York/London: Norton, 1992

TAYLOR, C., *Multiculturalism and 'The Politics of Recognition'*, Princeton: Princeton University Press, 1992

TODOROV, T., *The Conquest of America*, New York: Harper & Row, 1982

YOUNG, I.M., *Polity and Group Difference: A Critique of the Ideal of Universal Citizenship*, in: *Ethics*, 1989/99, pp. 250-274

WALDRON, J., *Minority Cultures and the Cosmopolitan Alternative*, in: *University of Michigan Journal of Law Reform*, 1991/25, 3/4, pp. 751-781 (reprinted in this volume)

WAL, G.A. VAN DER, *Collective Human Rights: A Western View*, in: BERTING, 1990, pp. 83-98

State without Nation
Reconsidering the Nation-State Concept

Thomas Fleiner

1. State and Social Contract

Poisoned Gift of "People's Sovereignty"

The legitimacy of the modern state is based upon the principle of social contract. As Prometheus, who has stolen from God the fire in order to give to individual human beings sovereignty over nature, so did Hobbes by means of the social contract theory steal from God its authority over human society and gave full and total sovereignty to the "Leviathan, State and the contracting people".[1] However, Hobbes did not define the human society, he did not determine the border lines between the communities of human society having full sovereignty. He did not decide whether the compact has been made between the "natural community" made by God in the sense of Herder[2] or whether it is a community made by the citizens of whatever territory considering themselves as equal and free in the sense of the French revolution, nor did he assume, that the contract can be made by immigrants occupying a new country and excluding the indigenous people of the new territory from the contract.

So the gift of sovereignty given to mankind has been a poisoned gift and the question is, whether we have to give back the gift and return to the authority "by the grace of God", or whether we can remove this poison by clarifying the notion of the nation, or by changing simply the concept of sovereignty or the concept of the state.

The main thesis of this paper will be, that we have no other choice but to remove the poison and to reconsider the social contract theory. As the contract is in any way a fictitious contract I propose that the contract is not made by a specific people but by "Mankind" in the sense of Althusius. Further I propose that conciliation between state and nation is only possible if we reconsider also the function and the purpose of the state and give up any kind of open or hidden totalitarian view of the state.

Nationalism: Tribalism of the Past?
First I will demonstrate, that the notion of nation as ethnic or cultural natural entity will always be contradictory and conflicting as long as it is taken as the only entity legitimatized to create a state, in other words: as it is linked to a ethno-totalitarian view of the state. Nation is a sentimental and emotional value, which realistically will never fade away. It is part of the mind and thinking of men or women. Men or women who have no nation can be compared with Chamisso's Peter Schlemihl[3], who has sold his shadow to the devil. Without nation they also would have lost their shadow.[4] As nobody can destroy his shadow, nobody can destroy the nation and national feelings of men or women. "Ich will, dass meine Seele auf Romanisch in den Himmel kommt" recently a strong advocate for the defense of the Romontsch language in Graubünden, Switzerland, exclaimed.

What we have to take care of on the other hand, is to avoid that the shadow will start to control men or women, that the shadow becomes more important than men or women themselves, that it starts to determine their behavior. Such objectives, however, can only be achieved if the concept of the nation and particularly of the state will be reconsidered.

Karl Popper may be fully right, when he accuses Nationalism as Tribalism:

> "Nationalism appeals to our tribal instincts, to passion and to prejudice, and to our nostalgic desire to be relieved from the strain of individual responsibility which it attempts to replace by a collective or group responsibility" (...) "None of the theories which maintain that a nation is united by a common origin, or a common

history, is acceptable, or applicable in practice. The principle of the national state is not only inapplicable but it has never been clearly conceived. It is a myth. It is an irrational, a romantic and Utopian dream, a dream of naturalism and of tribal collectivism."[5]

However, we have to be realistic and to accept that we have to live with this essential component of modern democracy. As long as society has been ruled by aristocracy, the common feeling of the rulers has been status and birth. Now that people are supposed to rule themselves the common feeling is language, history, religion or culture. And as the tyranny of the majority does not need any further legitimacy this authority is more totalitarian than aristocracy. So we have to face this reality in the sense of Isaiah Berlin:

"It would not be an exaggeration to say that no political movement today, at any rate outside the western world, seems likely to succeed unless it allies itself to national sentiment."[6]

2. The Conflicting Elements of the Definition of the Nation

Before the French Revolution Abbé Sieyes defined the nation as the unity of citizens living under the same laws and represented by the same parliament.[7] According to this concept the nation has a political aim, the nation is the constitution making body, the body of equal citizens and the body to legitimize state power. All residents living at that time in France were considered citizens. Sieyes wanted to free the French citizens treated unequally in different regions, social groups and geographic areas. All of them were however part of the French people. He was not concerned about Catalonians, Basques, Welsh or Corsican people.

This concept of a political nation composed of equal citizens is still valid, but it gives no answers to the crucial modern problems of the nation as a cultural and ethnic unity. We shall therefore emphasize in the following the more problematic concept of the nation as an ethnic cultural unity and we will base our analysis on a modern definition made by Otto Dann. This definition contains at least 6 fundamental conflicting elements which show, that this newly again used concept of the ethnic cultural nation as political unity, will lead us finally to endless conflicts all over the world.

"Als Nation bezeichnen wir eine Gesellschaft, die aufgrund gemeinsamer geschichtlicher Herkunft eine politische Willensgemeinschaft bildet. Eine Nation versteht sich als Solidargemeinschaft, und sie geht aus von der Rechtsgleichheit ihrer Mitglieder. Sie ist angewiesen auf einen Grundkonsens in ihrer politischen Kultur. Nationen sind stets auf ein bestimmtes Territorium orientiert, auf ihr Vaterland. Ihr wichtigstes Ziel ist die eigenverantwortliche Gestaltung ihrer Lebensverhältnisse, politische Selbstverwaltung (Souveränität) innerhalb ihres Territoriums, ein eigener Nationalstaat."[8]

History and Political Will: Contradiction No. 1:
"A nation is a society which during its common history built up a political community fermented by its political will."

This definition is rooted in the German perception of the notion of nation, however it is not clear at all, what is to be meant by *common history*. Are the Germans living in Eastern countries part of the German nation, or are they part of the nation into which they have been integrated through centuries? Is the notion of common history bound to the territory the particular society is living in, is it bound to a common language, to a common alphabet or to a common religion? If it is the territory, then the total island of southern and northern Ireland according to article 2 of the Irish constitution has created a nation. But this "nation" lacks the political will of an important part: the Unionist. Can it therefore be denied the nation status? The Jewish community is scattered all over the world. Does it still have a common history? If Jewish people have no common history, they have at least a common political will to be united as a nation. Does this make history irrelevant?

Does the community of the nation therefore primarily depend on the political will? Are the Albanians then a nation, because they have political will, common history and common language, although not a common religion? Are the Serbs a nation, and if so, what has to be done with the Serbs in Bosnia and those in Croatia?

Abchasians, Ossetians and Georgians have common history, but they seem not to have a common political will. Will they be nonetheless a nation, and if not, do they have to be separated? Tutsis and Hutus in Rwanda have a common history made by colonialism. Are they a nation or do they have to be separated? Russians and Ukrainians have common history in Ukraine. Did they build up a common nation? Scottish, Welsh and Englishmen or woman have had common history at least since several centuries. Are they one nation or three different nations? How long must common historical fate last: 50 years (Israel), 70 years (Yugoslavia) or at least 500 years (England and France)?

Some Bulgarians claim that the Macedonians of Macedonia are not an independent nation, but part of the Bulgarian Nation. Why did Bulgaria still recognize Macedonia, although the nation had a common history?

In what sense are Ecuador and Venezuela, which seceded 1830 from Colombia and Panama which seceded 1903 from Colombia, separate nations? Had they already been different nations when they seceded from each other or did they become separate nations, because they have become sovereign and independent states for almost 100 years? New Zealanders are more unanimous to be part of the English nation than some people in Northern Ireland although they are separated by thousands of miles from their mother-island. Still they are a separate and sovereign state while the Scottish, Welsh and Cornwallers are not. Why are Norwegians a separate nation which could secede from Sweden in 1905 and why has neither Greenland a right of secession from Denmark nor the Swedish minority from Finland?

White and black Americans share a common history with the Indians. Do they form a common nation, although Indians have to live in special territories and certainly lack political will to form a common nation? English Canadians and Quebequiens share a common history. They still have the will to build a state, although Quebequiens claim to be a separate nation.

If Europe will be once created as a state, will it be a state of separate nations or will it be a state of a new political nation because of the common will? Will this "European nation" make disappear the existing nations as the French, German, British or Italian Nation? Or will it be like Switzerland a nation based on the common political will of different existing cultural nations? Or will it be like Spain a new nation of Spaniards composed of nationalities (Catalonians, Basques, Gallicianes, Castillians etc.)[9], or like the Russian federation based on a multinational people, or like the British nation composed of the English, Scottish, Welsh[10] and Cornwall nation?

Equality: Contradiction No. 2:
  "A nation defines itself as a community based on solidarity, which recognizes the equality of its members."

This definition contains enormous problems. Does it require from a nation to treat all those not being part of the nation as inferior? Does it justify the discrimination of Russians in the Baltic states, does it justify the discrimination of the Serbs in Slovenia and Croatia? Does it justify the discrimination of foreigners in Western Europe?

On the other hand: does equality create a nation? Are Corsicans part of the French nation, because they are French citizens with full rights as French nationals although they would like to be treated differently as with regard to their language and culture? Are the Curds no nation, because they are Turkish citizens with full rights and equal treatment, although they would prefer to be considered as a separate nation? Are the Muslims in the Serbian and Montenegrin Sandjak a different nation although they are treated as Serbs with equal rights?

Two historically most important nations claim to be the people chosen

190

by God: the Jewish and the Japanese. While this claim is logically and structurally inherent in the concept of the Jewish state, it is much more emotional and amorphous within the Japanese tradition. Both nations live actually under secularized rules. If they would translate their national feelings into their constitution, this fundamentally would mean discrimination with regard to non-nationals. And, if we observe the struggle of both nations for secularization and equal rights to non-national citizens, we are aware of the enormous political and emotional tensions to be calmed down by the necessity to create a civil society.

The need for solidarity is often the fundamental reason to require non-nationals to assimilate with the language, culture and/or religion of the mother-nation. Assimilation requires individuals to replace part of their identity with a new identity. If such assimilation is forced with state and political power, it is inhumane and contrary to fundamental human rights. States and nations should only promote integration based on the free and personal choice of those individuals, who seek a stronger social communication of the general society.

Consensus: Contradiction No. 3:
  "A nation depends on a fundamental consensus upon its political culture."

Does this mean, that if the political consensus is lacking, the nation falls apart? Does this imply the right of secession? Can Hungarians in Romania, in Slovakia and in Ukraine and Serbia claim the right of secession, because they have no fundamental political consensus with the great bulk of the state-society they actually belong to? Does this imply the right of the Boer nation in South Africa to create a Volksstaat, because they do not have fundamental consensus with the big majority of the blacks and the whites of English origin?

Does this on the other hand give the nation the right to force assimilation in order to integrate the minorities and to get their enforced consensus or implement ethnic cleansing by expelling those who do not agree with the fundamental political culture from the territory?

The fundamental consensus means also total loyalty towards the nation. This has as consequence that most states still do not allow double citizenship. One can only be loyal to one nation, not to different nations. This concept of total loyalty divides societies in different religious, language or alphabet communities. It excludes small religious or cultural communities from the society as the Jewish community in Western countries or the Korean minority in Japan. It has been the reason of secession between India and Pakistan and is a major threat for societies in Eastern countries divided between Orthodox, Islamic and Catholic communities.

As long as state statutes on citizenship, as for instance in Germany, require from those, who apply for citizenship, to renounce their old citizenship, those laws testify of an exclusive ethnic concept of statehood and thus go hand in hand with nationalistic feelings within the country. Only if we accept, that double citizenship is possible, we accept also double loyalty and renounce the "friend-enemy" concept of the state, final bases for a peaceful international society.

Territory: Contradiction No. 4:
   "Nations are always oriented to a specific territory, their 'fatherland'."

This is the most problematic part of the definition. It somehow includes that nations have a right to a specific territory. What solutions can be found, if this right contradicts other rights? Has the "American Nation", *a nation of immigrants*, a right to a territory, while the Indians have no right? Do the Afrikaners in South Africa who historically (17th century) where the first settlers in this territory have a primary right to the territory of South Africa, or does this right belong to the blacks, because the continent of Africa belongs to the blacks, or does it belong to all people living in South Africa? Article 2 of the Irish constitution claims the territory of the entire Island as part of the state. Has the Irish or the British nation a right to this territory? Greece is fearing that by recognizing the Macedonian state, it would also recognize the right of the nation of this state to the entire Macedonian territory, which is

192

actually Greek territory, and at the same time it would indirectly renounce the right of the Greek nation, which it considers as actually Macedonian nation, to have territory and state.

What can be the good solution if territories are overlapping? Who can claim better rights to the territory of Kosovo: Albanians or Serbs? Who has a better right to Palestine, the Palestinians who claim to have been in the territory already 4000 years B.C. or the Jewish people, who settled 1000 years later?

Does the right to territory also imply that nations have the right to have two or even more states with different territories? Are Austrians a different nation from Germans because they live in different territories, or are they part of the German nation, which has the right to have two different states and territories? Some Albanians in Kosovo do not seek a unification with Albania. They rather prefer to have a separate state, a state of Kosovo. Is this right legitimate or void because Albanians already have their state?

The so-called right to territory often gives different nations overlapping rights, which reasonably cannot be questioned. It often depends on what historical period is more relevant. But just because there is no clear criterion to distribute territories among nations, the conflicts on territories are merciless, because every nation claims to have total legitimate rights to the territory. This creates Greek tragedies.

Closely linked to these arguments are also statements concerning the artificiality of states. Yugoslavia is considered to be an artificial state, because it came into being only after World War I. If such arguments are legitimate, then almost all colonial and maybe quite a few Latin-American states are artificial. Do artificial states have less recognized sovereignty than others? This means open conflict for all so-called artificial states from Switzerland to Sri-Lanka, Turkey and South Africa.

Sovereignty: Contradiction No. 5:
"Their most important aim is the possibility to decide in their own

responsibility their fate and their living conditions, their political independence (Sovereignty) within their territory."

Already the Italian Pasquale Mancini said, that a state in which different nationalities live together is not a political organization, but a monster which cannot survive.[11] According to this concept Switzerland would not exist anymore. Europe has no chance to be ever united as a federation, the United States, Canada and Australia will not survive as "melting-pots". Such an exclusive linkage between nation and state is detrimental for the survival of mankind and for the respect of fundamental human rights.

Does this concept for instance exclude non-nationals from the decision-making process? The Constitutional Court in Germany denied the Land Schleswig-Holstein the power to grant foreigners a limited right to participate in the decision-making process, because the German Fundamental Law (Constitution) requires that state-power and -authority is rooted in the German nation. If this is the case, could then the German Constitution legitimately renounce the (natural) right of the entire German people to the eastern territories?

The notion of sovereignty is full of ambiguity. Does it mean absolute sovereignty? In this case, does the nation have the natural inalienable right of self-determination? Does this include that every nation has the "pouvoir constituant" which cannot be withheld from the nation, not even by a international organization such as the European Union, as has been pointed out by the Constitutional Court of Germany in the Maastricht decision? This would have as a consequence that whatever the member states of the Union decide, they cannot abolish their constitution-making power to the European Union, they will always have a natural right to secession.

What is to be done, when this right to sovereignty is also claimed by other nations and minorities living in the same territory? Why do the Turks, the Irakiens, the Iranians and the people from Syria have the right of self-determination but not the Curds living in all those territories? Are they denied to be a "nation" because Ataturk has defined the nation as a unity of equal citizens according to the French tradition and therefore the Curds do not exit as a nation but only as individual citizens? Why does Turkey not observe the same principle when it defends the interests of Turkish minorities in Bulgaria or Cyprus?

Self-determination: Contradiction No. 6:
  "Right to own Nation-State."

Does the German people have a right to be divided in two or even three nation states: Germany, Austria (and Switzerland)? Did the people of the GDR have the right to create an own nation or was it part of the right to self-determination of the entire German nation? Does this right accordingly imply the right of the German nation to unify with Austria? Is the unification of Germany a consequence of this concept and did it justify to unify Germany without democratic referendum? Does it also imply, that no German Land may ever have the right to secession? What has to be done with Switzerland? Does this concept deny the right of Switzerland to exist, because it unifies nations belonging all except the romantsch culturally to their neighbor-states; does it deny the right of Singapore to exist as a state of several cultural nations, does it deny the right of United States to exist as a melting pot of immigrants from Europe and Africa?

In the Caucus of the Russian federation about 33 nations do exist according to this definition. Do they all have a right to a nation-state? Is this right compatible with the rights of other nations possibly also affected by a unilateral secession? Does the Curds nation have a right to create a nation-state notwithstanding that this does also affect the Turkish and all other nations of the concerned territory? Do the Tuaregs in Niger have a right to create a nation-state notwithstanding other tribes affected by the secession? How can this right include also minority rights of minority nations living within the new territory? Do the Turks living in the territory of the Curds, the Serbs living in the territory of Kosovo, the Georgians living in the territory of Abchasia on their own behalf have again a right to unilateral secession? When is this right denied? When the minority has less than a million, 100,000 or 50,000 members? When the state can survive? Liechtenstein is a small sovereign state with only 30,000 inhabitants!

3. Nation and State

With the following statements I will argue, that we can overcome the fundamental problem of nationalism only if we reconsider the totalitarian concept of the state. The state has to be limited to the political, civil society and it has to be open for all human beings part of mankind. States should never become hostages of their nations. The national community therefore has to be separated from the state. Its right to self-determination must be limited to self-determination of cultural and educational values but not of political aims.

Necessity of a New Concept of the State

Once again: the nation is the shadow of every men or woman. We cannot destroy this shadow. But the shadow should not control the societies and replace the rational *reflection and choice* of men or woman by their emotions. Thus we have to accept the reality of the nation. The only question which remains is, what we can do with the state, so long strongly connected with the nation.

The definition of the nation would not have as far reaching consequences, if it would not be in direct connection to the concept of the modern state in the sense of Max Weber, who defines it as the agency within society, which holds the monopoly of legitimate violence (Gewaltmonopol).[12] Since the development of the social contract theory the modern state has gained its full legitimacy only within the people as the party of the fundamental contract. This contract gives, according to Hobbes, all legitimacy to whatever decision the state should make. It gives the state full sovereignty and does not require any justification of its decision. Of course Hobbes has been "overruled" by Locke, who complemented the compact theory by the concept of the inalienable rights of the citizens. Those, specially Anglo-Saxon states, which followed Locke, accept the rule of law as a limit even to the sovereignty of the constitution making power (pouvoir constituant), because of the inalienable rights of the citizens. However with regard to foreign policy and also to foreigners the concept of limited sovereignty has not so much impact.

The contract theory according to Hobbes, Rousseau, Locke and many others secularized the legitimacy of the state and the state power, but it did not solve the very crucial question what people, citizens, bourgeois, residents, inhabitants have the right, the power or the "legitimacy" to legitimatize the constitution making of a new state or simply any kind of action of an existing state agency.

However this seems to be the most crucial and unsolved problem of this century and, I fear, specially also of the next century. If in the sense of Max Weber the state is the only agency which can use power and violence in order to enforce its rules, then the question, who can make a state, is becoming fundamental.

If for instance every nation has the right to make a state, it can also use, without being obliged to justify its decisions, all its force and power to implement its interest with regard to other nations and other citizens. This right cannot be questioned, it needs no justification. The power is sovereign and therefore absolute.

If a private person kills somebody, it is murder, if the soldier kills, it is military necessity and therefore allowed, if the executioner hangs the condemned he fulfills a justified state judgment. So if the nation has as part of its *natural* right to self-determination the right to be a state, it can require all sorts of actions of its citizens or civil servants, and all those actions need not to be justified.

Thus the link of an ambiguous definition of the nation with a totalitarian concept of the state is detrimental for the survival of mankind. It justifies the war of nations against all nations and gives the most powerful nation the right to dominate the others. The prohibition of aggression according to the Charter of United Nations becomes meaningless, because the ambiguous notion of nation gives every nation a fair possibility to accuse the other nation as aggressor. What in the Middle Ages was necessary to limit the autarchy of individuals will be necessary today with regard to the nations.

However the above already explained statements of the contradictory elements of the notion of the nation have shown very clearly that it will not be possible to solve the problem by clear nation concepts. Those concepts will always remain ambiguous, they will always contain confronting elements and nations will always be overlapping and infringing on minority nations.

Thus one can overcome the possible conflicts of the future only if one does focus on the concept of the state and the concept of self-determination.

The Concept of Limited State Sovereignty

As long as the state is based on the concept of absolute sovereignty one cannot solve the problem of conflicting nation and state interests. Besides the concept of absolute sovereignty of the state does not fit any more to the modern interdependently globalized world community. This is an obvious statement made by many scholars. However, there is until now no clear alternative to the concept of sovereignty. So as everybody questions the concept, almost everybody establishes his ideas on constitution making, international law, justification of state power, distinction between international, supranational and state organization finally on the concept of absolute sovereignty.

The concept of absolute sovereignty is based on the social contract principle. This principle has been developed by theories based on the presumption, that people can only live together and survive, when they have concluded a contract to convey to the state the power to regulate order and to protect them. This isolation of a state has become the crucial problem, because the interdependence of the world community has become so intense, that no state can as isolated state anymore protect

198

its nationals. Further we have to be aware, that the anarchy and the chaos of London in the 1640ies, which instructed Hobbes to develop his social contract theory, may have been similar to the anarchy we are actually going through on the global level. Although I do not share Hobbes' one-dimensional view of the egoistic men, I would sustain, that nations and their states behave totally irresponsible and unrealistic, if they are not controlled by a larger body, the international law.

Thus we have to enlarge the fiction, not to a real or fictitious borderline, but to mankind. Environment and actual conflicts are such that we have to base our theory on a fictitious social contract of mankind. Mankind is not a political entity, although it is about to develop a certain kind of common interest, namely to survive.

This does not mean, that we have to come to the idea of the world state, but it is the necessary fiction, which limits the power of single states. Mankind is divided into different states, the major agencies to act on behalf of the common interest of mankind and of its inhabitants. The states are having a specific mandate in order to develop welfare and happiness of all human beings living within their territory. This mandate is limited. It cannot arbitrarily discriminate foreign citizens or non-nationals, all belonging to the human race of mankind. It can of course pursue the public interest of all people living in this territory. It cannot pursue any objectives which could be detrimental for the survival of mankind and/or of future generations.

Of course states can divide the mandate and give part of it to local municipalities, to federal subjects and even to international organizations. The "mandate concept" is an open concept, because it does not give absolute authority but only limited authority to the agencies. As states have a mandate from mankind, they must treat all human beings primarily equal. Equal treatment means of course that for instance taxpayers may be treated differently with regard to foreigners traveling within the country. Refugees and asylum seekers must be given shelter if their live is in danger. Because the interest of mankind is in the interest of every state. States are not limited to pursue interests of their own people but also interests of mankind.

The limited mandate given to the states means also that states have an international responsibility to require of states which do heavily violate fundamental human rights, to observe their obligations. This is not a general justification of violence and war against mandate-breakers. Such justification would finally exclude the most powerful states from any control and it would give them the possibility to abuse the power of "Leviathan" for their own strategies. But the violation of a mandate by a state creates an obligation of all other states to find common grounds by negotiations for correcting the state responsible for violating the mandate.

This means with regard to nations controlling their state power, that they have no right to exclude principally non-nationals from citizenship, from participating in the decision-making process. Non-nationals are part of general mankind, they are human beings to be treated equally. The state composed by the great bulk of the society of nationals has no specific mandate nor a specific power with regard to the interest of the nation. The cultural interests of the nation have to be pursued not by the state but by the nation itself.

The Concept of Self-determination
If we look at history we can see that the notion of self-determination has been used very differently. After 1989 Germany has been given the right to unite under the auspices of self-determination. This right has not been granted to the Tibetans, to the Abchasians and the Ossetiens in Georgia. On the other hand it has been given to the Croats, the Bosniakes, the Slovenes and the Macedonians. But it has been denied to the Albanians in Macedonia, the Serbs in Croatia and in Bosnia. The Indian tribes in USA have no right of self-determination, neither has the Irish Republic with regard to the north of the Island. This north is under the right of self-determination of the British, who also by their self-determination claimed the right to go to war to the Falkland Islands.

If we look at the way the international community treated the problem

200

of self-determination, there are no clear criteria for cases, where self-determination is granted and where not. It seems more or less, that this depends largely on the question which nation does claim self-determination and in which cases the acceptance of the right does fit to the national interests of the big powers. However as long as self-determination is only a political issue, it will remain one of the key reasons for international conflicts and struggles.

Is self-determination a right, is it a collective right or is it an individual right? I will not dig into the philosophical question of rights. I just will assume, that self-determination is at least a moral and a political but not a legal right which can be implemented by an international court.

As far as the question of collective and individual rights is concerned, we can see, that those who strongly oppose the concept of collective rights do apply it themselves, when their interests are affected. When American citizens are in danger, the American state invokes its state interests in order to protect its citizens even militarily if it is necessary. This right to intervene with military or diplomatic power can only be understood as a right derived out of a collective right of the American nation. Germany has just turned down a proposal for a minority protection in its constitution, but it claims to protect the interests of the German nation, that is of its nationals (not citizens) in eastern countries and it gives them even a privilege for coming to Germany and becoming citizens. And it even protects them diplomatically, although they have no formal citizenship.

Whoever claims self-determination has to determine what are his understandings of the notion of self-determination. If we consider the conflicting notion of nations we have to reconsider the notion of self-determination. Self-determination has to be distinguished between different objectives: political (justice, police, protection of environment, self-defense) economy, social welfare and culture, education and organization. I do not perceive *"political"* in the sense of Carl Schmitt who identifies political with "friend-enemy" relationship.[13] This concept in fact is detrimental for the creation of a real political union. It is the basis of an identity of nation and state excluding all other nationals from the political community, that is from the fundamental state-rights.

As far as political issues are concerned the concept of self-determination is bound to a specific territory. This means that from this point of view the concept of self-determination has to respect actual boundaries. It is a concept which recognizes the existing state boundaries.

For political purposes the existing states must have self-determination. State boundaries may not be changed unilaterally as it has been done by the unilateral recognition of Slovenia, Croatia, Bosnia and Macedonia. If nations would have in general the right to political self-determination, the next century would be in full turmoil. The concept of political self-determination is finally in contradiction to the basic right of equality. It excludes residents of a specific territory from active participation although they are as well targets of the police-power as the members of the nation are. They may however be discriminated because of their different nationhood.

The limits of state sovereignty have as consequence, that also states using their right to self-determination in political issues should let all people living and working in the territory participate in the democratic decision-making process. Residents, taxpayers, workers, soldiers, citizens, they all are direct or indirect targets of state decisions, they all are affected directly or indirectly by those decisions, thus none of them should be excluded from the participation process.

There is no reason to discriminate non-nationals or even non-citizens from decisions which focus on the protection of all human beings within the state territory.

The Justification of the State

Why do we need states? If we should need states for our own feeling of identity, then states should be identical with nations. If we would not need any state at all, then we could live in the totally open universal world market system. In fact one of the strongest advocates

202

of liberalism, F.A. Hayek, has proposed that one does owe loyalty only to the great society, the world market. "All our obligations to particular communities, or to political units, whether to state or to nation or both, must give way before this higher moral duty to universal exchange processes".[14] Both concepts do not fit the actual reality. The very reason why human beings need some state authority is the interdependence of society. And this interdependence of society has been developed by human nature which seeks greater community and which also seeks welfare, an objective which after a certain state of development can only be achieved in greater and organized societies.

The existing social interdependence creates power. If this power is not controlled by the people it will be abused and people who have become more dependent will be more and more exploited. So it is not the friend-enemy principle of Carl Schmitt which makes states, but it is much more the necessity to manage freedom in an interdependent society.[15]

Under these circumstances it is very well conceivable that states have limited sovereignty, that they are not agencies in the sense of Max Weber which are holding the monopoly of violence. Neither states nor individuals are in possession of a legitimate monopoly of violence. State agencies must – just as individuals – justify the use of violence. As for individuals violence is possible in self-defense and in emergency situations, also the state authority can only use violence, when it is the ultimate possibility to defend basic interests of the society but not of the nation.

Under those circumstances it is also conceivable that states have special mandates to implement freedom and equal rights within their given powers and competencies. State-authority can thus be split between municipal, regional, state and international authorities.

4. Summary

The nation-state based on friend-enemy concepts cannot be the state concept of the future. State-authority must be linked to political objectives and to political issues such as police protection, defense and maybe social security, all linked to territorial boundaries. The nation has to be an entity separate from the state, pursuing cultural and educational objectives.

The nation is a reality which cannot be denied. It has to be recognized. Nonetheless nations should never be builders of state authority, but they should be recognized as communities which seek to pursue cultural objectives necessary for the identity of individuals and families living within the political society: the state.

State-agencies have not the authority of a full sovereign. Each of the different agencies acts on different levels of the society with the responsibility to the territory it has the mandate of, executes a specific mandate conveyed upon it by the only real sovereign: mankind. According to this mandate state-agencies have the obligation and authority to protect all individuals living within their territories and to promote in collaboration with the national communities social welfare and economical development.

The right to self-determination has to be reconsidered within this frame of limited sovereignty of state agencies. Self-determination for political purposes is given to state agencies and not to nations. State agencies may according to their self-determination peacefully and in common consensus change political power and territorial boundaries.

Nations, on the other hand, have a right to self-determination with regard to their culture, language, religion and historical feelings. They may participate as communities in decision-making with regard to economic developments with the state agencies and they can claim a right to self-determination in the sense of autonomy with regard to their cultural identity. However their autonomy can not be abused in order to destroy the basis of the political community they are living in.

Notes

1. Comp. FLEINER-GERSTER, THOMAS, *Allgemeine Staatslehre*, Berlin, 1980, p. 146ff
2. See FORSYTH, MURRAY, *Towards Reconciliation of Nationalism and Liberalism*, p. 16
3. See CHAMISSO, ADALBERT VON, *Peter Schlemihls wundersame Geschichte*, Berlin, 1813, see also BAUMGARTNER, U., *Chamissos Peter Schlemihl*
4. GELLNER, ERNEST, *Nations and Nationalism*, Oxford, 1983, p. 6
5. POPPER, K.R., *The Open Society and its Enemies vol. 2*, London, 1966, pp. 49, 51, quote by FORSYTH, MURRAY, *Towards Reconciliation of Nationalism and Liberalism*, in: *Integration and Fragmentation the Paradox of the Late Twentieth Century*, Queens University, 1994, p. 13
6. BERLIN, ISAIAH, *Against the Current: Essays in the History of Ideas*, Oxford, 1981, P. 355, quote from MURRAY FORSYTH, p. 14
7. Comp. SCHIEDER, THEODORE, *Typologie und Erscheinungsformen des Nationalstaates*, in: *Nationalismus und Nationalstaat*, Hrg. O. Dann und Wehler, Göttingen, 1991, p. 69
8. Comp. SCHIEDER, THEODORE, a.a.O., p. 69
9. Article 2 of the Spanish Constitution: "The Constitution is based on the indissoluble unity of the Spanish Nation, the common and indivisible country of all Spaniards; it recognizes and guarantees the right to autonomy of the nationalities and regions of which it is composed, and solidarity among them all."
10. See DAVIES, CHARLOTTE AULL, *Welsh Nationalism in the Twentieth Century. The Ethnic Option and the Modern State*, London, 1989
11. MANCINI, P., *Della Nazionalità come fondamento del diritto delle genti: "Uno stato in cui molte rigogliose nazionalità vadana a soffogarsi in un'unione forzata, non è un corpo politico, ma un mostro incapace di vita"*, quote from SCHIEDER, THEODOR, *Typologie und Erscheinungsformen des Nationalstaates*, in: *Nationalismus und Nationalstaat*, Hrg. O. Dann und Wehler, Göttignen, 1991, p. 67
12. GELLNER, ERNEST, *Nations and Nationalism*, Oxford, 1983, p. 3
13. Comp. SCHMITT, CARL, *Der Begriff des Politischen*, Berlin, 1932 bzw. 1963, pp. 38-39
14. FORSYTH, MURRAY, *Hayek's Bizarre Liberalism: A Critique*, in: *Political Studies*, XXXVI (1988), pp. 235-250
15. FLEINER-GERSTER, THOMAS, *Théorie Générale de l'Etat*, Paris (PUF), 1986, p. 42ff

Reflections on Identity and Belonging

Theo van Willigenburg

1. Introduction: the Dialogical View on Identity Formation

Though, in modernity, the identity of a person is understood predominantly as individualized identity – not identity as determined by one's social role, but as the expression of the authentical self –, no one will deny that a person's identity is formed by attachments and involvements, and, therefore, by the communities to which one belongs and the cultures in which one is embedded. The self is necessarily encumbered, necessarily infected with its social, cultural and historical context. Everybody is born into a community which – to a certain degree – is constitutive for one's identity, even if one comes to resist one's origins and develop other attachments.

The communitarian conception of the social self stresses the importance of the family, neighborhood or tribe, but, if one opposes to this rather parochial and perhaps conservative idea of what counts as a constitutive community, one may as well point at a huge variety of other communities which may have identity-defining influences of different sort and strength. One may identify with the lifestyle that is associated with a type of popmusic (jazz, disco, reggae, funk, symphonic, heavy metal, gabberhouse, mellowhouse etc. etc). Or one may identify with a particular occupational community (workman or white collar) or a community of people who share a serious conviction (vegetarianism, anthroposofism). If one loosely defines a 'community' as "a body with some common values, norms and goals in which each member regards the common goals as her own"[1], than it becomes clear that one may belong to a variety of communities in which one lives parts of one's life, e.g. the community of scholars, a religious community, a large network of close friends, the gay-movement, a political party etc.

Whatever the nature of the communities that are constitutive for the self, and whatever the strength of their identity-defining influence, it is undeniable that personal identity and communal belonging have much to do with each other. The self is formed in interaction with the social environment to which it is attached. In the words of Charles Taylor[2]: human identity is created and constituted "dialogically", that is, in response to one's relations (including actual dialogues) with others. A person's identity is shaped in a process of continuing interchange with "significant others". This interchange is characterized by Taylor as a continuing dialogue, because it presupposes the acquisition of languages of communication and is, therefore, dependent on communities of communication. "We become full human agents, capable of understanding ourselves, and hence of defining our identity, through our acquisition of rich human languages of expression."[3] These modes of expression include the languages of art, gesture, love (and the like), and are acquired through interaction with others who are member of our community of communication. In dialogue, and sometimes struggle, with what our significant others want to see in us, we define our identity. It is the recognition, nonrecognition or misrecognition of others which determines the self. My identity is constituted by my reaction to the confirming, or demeaning or even contemptible picture of myself which significant others mirror back to me.[4]

The dialogical view on the formation of identity and the self contrasts to a monological view according to which "it is true that we can never liberate ourselves completely from those whose love and care shaped us early in life, but we should strive to define ourselves on our own to the fullest extent possible (...) We need relationships to fulfill, but not to define ourselves."[5]

According to Taylor, such a monological view seriously underestimates the place of the dialogical in human life. Though the modern ideal of authenticity involves the idea that being true to oneself means being true to one's own originality, which is something only a person himself can articulate and discover, this discovery is not something which I can work out in isolation, but only in negotiation "through dialogue, partly overt, partly internal to others."[6] Inwardly derived, personal, original identity has to win recognition through exchange, that is, in dialogue with and struggle against what significant others want to see in us.

With this article, I hope to contribute to a more profound understanding of the dialogical process described by Taylor, by proposing a more specific analysis of personal identity and elaborating on the identity-defining influence of the dialectical interchange with one's social environment. In section 2, I will focus especially on the social influence upon those aspects of individual identity which are usually regarded as being 'objectively' characteristic of an individual (like body type and temperamental traits), and I will stress, more generally, the importance and inescapability of 'social channeling' mechanisms. The possibility for an individual to resist social channelling and to develop an identity in contrast to social expectations, will be addressed in terms of the appropriation of 'ideal identities'.

In section 3, I will give a short comment on the meaning of 'belonging to a community of significant others'. I will address the cosmopolitan argument that belonging to a community may be enjoyable, but is not something individuals *need* in order to constitute their personal identity. In the final section, I will go into the question, where the significant others, whose recognition or nonrecognition may be constitutive for personal identity, are to be found. In the intimate sphere (family, life-style groups), in the occupational sphere, and in the sphere of ethnic, religious and/or cultural groups, personal identity may be closely connected to belonging. For it is in these spheres that we continuously interact with significant others whose recognition may be important to us. The question is in what sense this picture can be enlarged to include our belonging to a national group. Why would our co-nationals be counted among our significant others? Can nationality be an important part of our identity?

2. Identity

The analysis of personal identity which I propose is based upon the work of Amélie Rorty and David Wong who define personal identity in terms of a structure of central traits.[7] A person's identity is constituted by a specific configuration of central traits, that is, by a specific configuration of core dispositions to desires, beliefs, habits, attitudes and actions. A central trait or core disposition does not gain centrality or importance because it would individuate a person, or because it develops as a constant factor throughout an individual life time. It is not a single trait, but always a complex configuration of traits which individuates a person, and core dispositions may be constant to various degrees throughout an individual's lifetime, dependent upon the relation to other traits. A disposition is regarded as a core disposition if it makes a systematic ("lawlike") difference to the way a persons acts, reacts and interacts, or, more generally, if it makes a difference to a person's course of life (e.g. because it makes a systematic difference "to the habit-forming and action-guiding social categories in which she is placed").[8] Though a disposition does not need to be life-long constant, it should, of course, exert its influence at least more than momentary in order to make a systematic difference to a person's course of life.

Starting from this definition of personal identity, Taylor's dialogical view on identity formation can now be understood as follows: the core dispositions which build the configuration of traits that constitute one's identity are neither fully subjectively expressed and appropriated, nor fully contextually and socially determined. Both subjective appropriation and social determination are involved, though Taylor does not really make clear how 'subjective' and 'social' relate to each other (in spite of his phrasing in terms of dialogue). Taylor mainly emphasizes that identity formation is *neither* fully subjective, *neither* fully social. He pictures identity formation in contrast both to socially defined identity (role-identity, or identity fixed by one's social position), and to unencumbered identity which would be the result of authentic, individual self-definition. Just as identity is not formed in a monological dependence upon prefigured social roles, it cannot be true that identity is the sole result of individual creativity and expression of authenticity. One's identity is not fully determined by the family, social niche, culture, time and place in which a child, adolescent and adult is embedded, but it is neither formed from scratch.

210

The necessity to stress both individual uniqueness and social determination, can be shown by focusing on those aspects of identity which are usually placed on either the subjective/ individual side or the social side of the scale. Take the dispositions which are usually thought to pick out one's individuality. Even the features which may be regarded as objectively characteristic for an individual, like one's body-type (slender, heavy, small, tall, muscular, limber, stiff or plump) may only become part of one's self-conception and individual identity as a result of a dialogical interchange with one's social environment. Not only are there social norms about 'ideal' body-types, but various somatic qualities are socially associated with specific traits.[9] Limberness is often associated with gracefulness, tallness (and a deep voice!) with authority, and corpulence with sluggishness (though plumpness and even serious corpulence may also be associated with compagniability, good-naturedness or jocularity).

Also central temperamental traits like measure of aggression, friendliness, trust, distrust, lightheartedness or gloominess, which are to a high degree individually determined, may find their place as part of our personal identity, determining our action and life-plan, in a process of interaction with the cultural narratives that picture the standard set of typical action routines associated with paradigmatic temperaments and characters.

It may be that in modernity one's identity is only to a limited extent determined by one's social position, class or role, but that does not mean that certain socially defined institutional roles (especially family-roles like the role of the father or mother, and occupational roles) may not be of great influence in identity formation. It has been shown, furthermore, that from early age on children may be cast to play a certain kind of role in the social narrative[10], like the 'cornerstone' elder child, the 'eternal' outsider, the sissy boy, the tommy girl, the protester, the conformist. In a process of 'social-role channeling', a child "tends to develop habits of perceptual salience, emotion, and motivation that are appropriate to the role in which he has been cast. When they are strongly socialized, reinforced, or rewarded, such habits can become central traits."[11] This is especially the case, if there is a good match between social role casting and a person's somatic and temperamental traits. Social role casting may even cause the development of traits that would otherwise have remained relatively recessive in the individual.

It seems, then, that, in the dialogue with one's social environment, the social expectations, norms, roles and narratives, play a dominant role. Is there any chance for the individual to take the initiative in this interaction, to become the dominant conversation partner? The modern idea of personal identity-formation as an expression of one's authenticity can best be understood in terms of the influence of so called 'ideal' identities on the ongoing process of identity formation.[12] Ideal identities set directions for the development of central individual dispositions characterizing an individual. Many ideals are culturally specific, and it is clear that children, youngsters and adults constantly take example from the heroes of their kind (teenagers even imitate the gestures of a popstar, managers may try to imitate the style of a famous captain of industry). Still, a person's ideal conception of herself may develop in strong *contrast* to social expectations and norms. Instead of appropriating the gender-bound image of a hard-core macho, a boy may subjectively appropriate the ideal of a sensitive and responsive friend (thereby risking to be cast into the role of a softy pansy-boy or the role of the sensitive budding artist). Instead of appropriating the gender-bound image of a caring, self-effacing person, a girl may subjectively appropriate the ideal of becoming a modern Calamity Jane.

As Taylor has argued, the desire to distinguish oneself from others may be as much a driving force in identity formation as the appropriation of socially defined roles and ideals. Denial and rejection are as much part of the interaction between individual and environment as are confirmation and appropriation. The dialogue between individual and significant others not only consists of agreement, but certainly also of dissent, objection and even protest. A person may take his or her freedom to form, reform and revise dispositions which build up one's identity. A person is strongly influenced, but not fully determined by the social expectations and the cultural narratives in which he or she is born. The amount of freedom one has in subjectively forming one's identity depends on the psychological force of the social channeling mechanisms and of the centrality and force of the somatic and temperamental traits which accord with the social roles in which one is cast.

It should be clear by now, that there is no strong opposition between sociocentric and pure individualistic conceptions of identity. Both subjective expression and appropriation ànd social channeling play a role in identity formation. At some times, and in some places, high value may be attached to 'authentic' identity-formation independent of social role and ideal. At other times, and in other societies accommodation to and internalization of social expectation and norms may be highly valued. But any corporative society will meet its individual members who refuse to accommodate. And any liberated individual who claims that he will choose his own identity, free of social influence, will have to admit that one's identity not only consists of what is subjectively appropriated, but also of characteristics which are *there*, independently of their acceptance or even acknowledgment by a person.

3. Belonging

Stressing the core role of social channeling in identity-formation is another way of stressing the importance of one's social environment or 'community'. Jeremy Waldron notices that the term 'community' is often used in absence of "any settled sense about the scope and scale of the social entity" that the user of the term has in mind.[13] I do not think that this is a problem (given Avineri's loose definition of a 'community' as "a body with some common values, norms and goals in which each member regards the common goals as her own"[14], as long as this looseness does not result in a one-sided picture of what could count as a community. In the introduction I stressed, in accordance with Waldron, the identity-forming importance of communities, like the pop-culture or the gay-movement, which are usually avoided as examples by communitarian writers.

That belonging to communities in this varied sense is important to identity formation is not in question. What is much more debated is the character of the belonging. Cosmopolitanism, as defended by Waldron in his article in this volume, denies that there is a human yearning or *need* to belong. According to a weak cosmopolitan view, people may like and enjoy belonging and immersion in the culture of a particular community, but it is not something that they *need*.[15] Strong cosmopolitanism even contends that belonging to a particular community may inhibit the flourishing of individuals in a mobile, multicultural world: "(...) the hybrid life-style of the true cosmopolitan is in fact the only appropriate response to the modern world in which we live."[16]

It could be argued that strong cosmopolitanism is self-defeating, because the abandonment of a commitment to local particularities will result in a process of cultural homogenization or globalization (the 'coca cola' culture), which – as a result of the alienation and anomalies it causes – will evoke the resurgence of cultural particularity. However, as Maris notices, "[M]ulticultural interaction does not necessarily lead to homogeneous culture without any character, it is just as likely to generate a new cultural diversity as has happened in Latin America."[17] It may well be that the cosmopolitan finds himself at home on a world-wide cultural marketplace, which not only provides free access for all, but also covers enough cultural differences to stimulate worthwhile individual flourishing. Would it then be true that 'belonging' to a particular community is no longer a *need*?

Michael Sandel argues that we *need* communal belonging, because belonging confers character and depth on our choices and our actions, as the communities to which we belong communicate important and determinate conceptions of the good.[18] I think Sandel is right, up to a certain point. A cosmopolitan may have access to a world-wide marketplace of cultural materials (including specific 'conceptions of the good'), and therefore the cosmopolitan life need not be shallow and abstracted. However, shopping on a worldwide cultural market-place as such, will not lead to the formation of personal identity. According to the dialogical view on identity-formation, an individual needs to communicate with others who are significant to this individual. Significance is only assigned if one's relationship to these others is *intrinsically* worthwhile. The fact that the recognition, nonrecognition and misrecognition of others in a group count to me shows that I consider my membership of this group as intrinsically valuable. Identity-formation through dialogue with the social environment presupposes some measure of identification with the environment. Membership as such has to be valued in order to make the identity-forming dialogue between members in a community possible. Of course, this does not presuppose allegiance to a homogeneous group or a single cultural frame-work, nor does belonging to a community presuppose that one has one's roots in that community. The cosmopolitan may very well refuse "to think of himself as defined by his location or his ancestry, or his citizenship or his language"[19], but some form of social determination, some personal commitment to a community, some investment in intrinsically worthwhile memberships will be unavoidable.

Perhaps we should not take Waldron's picture of the cosmopolitan life in which "[B]its of culture come into our lives from different sources" and in which "we draw our allegiances from here and there and everywhere" as a denial of the importance of attachment and belonging for identity-formation, but as a way to stress that "each person has or can have a variety, a multiplicity of different and perhaps disparate communal allegiances."[20] The emphasis on this variety and multiplicity is one of the strong points of cosmopolitanism, especially as Waldron has a very interesting solution to the problem of the *management* of all these different cultural allegiances and involvements in identity-conferring communities. Does the idea of multiple attachments and involvements not suppose some managerial entity, an agent existing in distinction from each of the disparate elements that together constitute the person? And is this managerial self, as Sandel has argued[21], not a pure fiction because it is an ethereal entity not to be identified with any of its choices, with any attachment or substance? Walzer suggest that we should not think of the management of identity-formation in terms of some essential 'I' which manages the process of interaction between individual and significant others, but in terms of the democratic self-government of a pluralistic population. "Maybe the person is nothing but a set of commitments and involvements, and maybe the governance of the self is just the more or less comfortable (or at times more or less chaotic) coexistence of these elements."[22]

This image is stimulating. We can imagine personal identity formation as a shifting sequence of coalitions of characteristics. There may be occasions of inner conflict and imbalance. There may be a tension between the allegiances to various communities. Various aspects of identity may be conflicting. This may lead to further evolution of personal identity. But there will always be a coalition of mutually reinforcing and constraining identity-aspects which build the core of one's identity. A shifting core, though. One could compare the development of one's personal identity with the journey of a ship on sea. The ship may change its materials, forms and load, but, in order to keep the ship floating, any change or repair is only possible if one keeps the rest of the craft, temporarily, intact. In time, the whole ship may be renewed, but still it could be regarded as the same ship (in spite of its changed character), not because it possesses some unaltered core or essence, but because of its continuing history, its unique route over the seas, its unique history which has become part of its identity as *that* ship.

4. National Identity

If belonging is important to identity-formation, would belonging to a nation be important in this respect too? May one's nationality be an important determinant of one's personal identity? Could our co-nationals and other foreign nationals be counted among our significant others, in dialogue with whom we form our identities? Can the nation be an identity-conferring community, in spite of its highly *imagined*, even mythical nature? (Much of what 'makes' a nation is invented or manufactured, national symbolism often rests on debatable historical myths.)

This depends on whether one's nationality gains sufficient centrality among the set of social and individual characteristics that build up one's personal identity. Just as in some places and times the social-role aspect may have more centrality in identity-formation than the

216

subjective aspect, and vice versa, the awareness of belonging to a nation may vary in centrality for personal identity. The political situation or the absence of sufficient opportunities for identification may result in a rise of national feelings causing persons to stress their national identity. One could suspect that in societies that tend to give more centrality to role and group identity individuals would count national belonging as more important than in societies that tend to give more subjective centrality to role-independent temperamental and ideal traits. However, it could also be argued that in more individuality-oriented societies only the nation can function as an object of sometimes strong, but mostly vague and hardly reflected feelings of belonging. Other constitutive communities may be opposed to as providing bonds which are too galling, while the nation is sufficiently abstract to identify with in a more detached way.

In order to distinguish the variety of ways by which a personal characteristic can be central to one's disposition, Rorty and Wong introduce the concept of 'ramification'.[23] The extent to which other dispositions are dependent on a certain trait determines its degree of *objective ramification*. Its degree of *contextual ramification* is determined by the extent to which the trait is exemplified across distinctive spheres (e.g. public and private domains, work and leisure) and across different types of relationships. The degree of *social ramification* is the extent to which a trait affects the way a person is categorized and treated by others. Gender and age are socially strongly ramified, because they are associated with stereotypes that set directions for role casting. Also race, ethnicity, sexual orientation and occupation may be characteristics which can profoundly affect individual action and social expectation and reaction. A person's group identity may generate specific sorts of strongly identity-forming interactions ('dialogues'). One's nationality may in some societies be a strongly ramified characteristic, which means that in social interaction it seriously counts whether one is a co-national or not.

As with all sorts of group identity which are strongly socially ramified, nationality may involve a strong 'in-group' and 'out-group' feeling, which may result in negative reactions to members of the 'out-group'. As Richard Roberts argues, identity as belonging inevitably involves difference and not belonging: "(...) inclusion of the one in recognition and thus belonging" involves the "inevitable exclusion of the other".[24] In the continuing and renewed stories or narratives of national identity, the *antagonism* towards other nations is a core theme, *opposition* is an embedded attitude, and *conflict* a readily available result. The invention of a national tradition involves the emphasis on cultural difference and the construction of a specific, diverging ethnic or historical identity.

Social ramification of national identity may thus involve an emphasis on otherness and difference (which actually may be completely fictional). Furthermore, strong social ramification of nationality may result in strong objective and contextual ramification, positively or negatively: one strongly identifies in various contexts as a national, or one gains personal identity by resisting to the social expectations of one's co-nationals in this respect – risking to be branded as a traitor!

I do not think that there is any reason to allege nationality any more 'objectivity' as a group characteristic than other group-related identities. Some groups may be more suited as identity building communities (negative as well as positive), because with some groups there is a clearer sense and awareness of belonging and not belonging. Nationality may be a more or less important social aspect of one's identity. But there are so many identity forming factors (subjective and social) which interact, reinforcing or counterbalancing each other – social channelling mechanisms reinforcing or counterbalancing the relative centrality of somatic and temperamental traits and vice versa –, that no general hypothesis about the psychological importance of national belonging could stand empirical scrutiny. The importance for identity of national belonging depends on the degree of social ramification of nationality as an identifying characteristic in comparison to the ramification in the individual of other person-related and social traits.

218

Notes

1. AVINERI, S., DE-SHALIT, A. (eds), *Communitarianism and Individualism*, Oxford: Oxford University Press, 1992, Introduction, p. 6
2. TAYLOR, C., *Multiculturalism and "The Politics of Recognition"*, Princeton: Princeton University Press, 1992, p. 25-37. See also Ch. TAYLOR, *The Ethics of Authenticity*, Cambridge, Mass.: Harvard University Press, 1991, pp. 31-53
3. TAYLOR, o.c., 1992, p. 32
4. TAYLOR, o.c., 1992, p. 25
5. TAYLOR, o.c., 1992, p. 33
6. TAYLOR, o.c., 1992, p. 34
7. RORTY, A., WONG, D., *Aspects of Identity and Agency*, in: FLANAGAN, O., RORTY, A., (eds), *Identity, Character and Morality. Essays in Moral Psychology*, Cambridge, Mass.: MIT Press, 1990 (1993), pp. 19-36
8. RORTY & WONG, o.c., 1993, p. 19
9. RORTY & WONG, o.c., 1993, p. 21
10. RORTY & WONG, o.c., 1993, p. 22
11. RORTY & WONG, o.c., 1993, p. 23
12. RORTY & WONG, o.c., 1993, pp. 23-26
13. WALDRON, J., *Minority Cultures and the Cosmopolitan Alternative*, in: *University of Michigan Journal of Law Reform*, 24: 3&4, 1992, pp. 751-793, reprinted in this volume
14. See note 1
15. WALDRON, o.c., 1992, Ch. 4 (this volume)
16. WALDRON, o.c., 1992, Ch. 4 (this volume)
17. MARIS, C.W., *FRANGLAIS. On liberalism, nationalism, and multiculturalism*, Section 5. (this volume)
18. SANDEL, M., *The Procedural Republic and the Unencumbered Self*, in: AVINERI, S., DE-SHALIT, A., (eds), *Communitarianism and Individualism*, Oxford: Oxford University Press, 1992, pp. 12-28
19. WALDRON, o.c., 1992, Ch. 1 (this volume)
20. WALDRON, o.c., 1992, Ch. 9 (this volume)
21. See note 18
22. WALDRON, o.c., 1992, Ch. 9 (this volume).
23. RORTY & WONG, o.c., 1993, p. 20
24. ROBERTS, R.H., *Identity and Belonging*, Section 1 (this volume)

Reflections on Collective Rights and State Sovereignty

Wibren van der Burg

1. Introduction

In the modern world, there are not many states that are not multicultural. Most states incorporate more than one ethnic or national community.[1] It need not be argued that this gives rise to many practical problems and conflicts up to the level of civil wars or even world wars: Sarajevo is a sad symbol of both. On the other hand, the multicultural character of a society may be a source to draw from for a rich and dynamic cultural framework. How should political theory deal with the fact of multiculturalism? This was one of the central questions of this conference; in this article some of the suggestions that have been presented in the various articles in this volume will be discussed. It should be stated from the outset that I will focus only on political theory, i.e. on theory concerning (the actions of) the state, and not on moral theory concerning (the actions of) the individual – which is the topic of Theo van Willigenburg's article.

We may distinguish two steps in an analysis of the political implications of multiculturalism. Both steps may be distinguished, but they are connected. The first step is to answer the question of why the coexistence of national or ethnic communities within the boundaries of one state should be politically relevant (section 2). There are obvious pragmatic reasons, but also arguments of a more philosophical nature. The second step in such an analysis would be to develop elements of a political theory that suggests ways of coping with the problems of multiculturalism that are theoretically sound and practically feasible. According to Türk and Fleiner in this volume, the central position of the concept of the nation-state in political theory seems to be one of

221

the main obstacles for an adequate theoretical approach of multiculturalism. There are two obvious strategies to counter this: one strategy is to go to the level below the state and to see whether individual and collective rights offer minority groups an adequate protection against the state (section 3); the second strategy chooses the opposite direction and focuses on the global level, not considering the national state as the basic unit of political theory, but the world community as such (section 4).

2. The Political Relevance of Multiculturalism

A fundamental question that has to be tackled before we can address other questions is why national and ethnic cultures are politically relevant. A cosmopolitan liberal may argue that ethnic and national cultures belong to a private sphere in which the state has no business. Thomas Fleiner suggests that – though clearly in the current international situation we cannot ignore national identity – a situation is desirable in which state and nation are no longer linked and in which culture and education are outside the state's sphere. In the last section I will return to his suggestion, but first we must analyse the positive arguments for considering culture a politically relevant issue. We may distinguish four main types of reasoning dealing with the question of why cultural pluralism should be seen as a relevant fact and why culture is the state's business. One is of a more pragmatic character; the other three have a more theoretical nature.[2]

A. Avoiding Conflict

The first line of argument is a very practical one and therefore in actual politics the most important one: the clash of ethnic and national identities is one of the most pervasive factors in political conflict, both within and between states. In Yugoslavia and the Russian Federation it led to civil wars, in Spain (the Basques) to a more limited form of organised violent conflict. In some countries cultural pluralism is a major obstacle to a smooth functioning of the political system: Belgium and Canada are good examples here. And even in those countries where the minority groups are now rather peacefully integrated, completely

222

ignoring the existing cultural pluralism would probably result in the resurgence of latent tensions: the situations of the Frisians in the Netherlands and Germany and of the Sorbs in Germany may be good examples. With respect to immigrant minorities, it seems that almost every Western country is confronted with problems like violent attacks on immigrants and their property. As a general conclusion we may therefore say that the state will ignore cultural pluralism only at its own peril.

This line of argument suggests an approach of compromise and mutual accommodation. Important as this may be in practical politics, theoretically it is not very satisfying. In the long run it may not be adequate in practice either. If political recognition of minority cultures is regarded only as a compromise, this compromise will be inherently unstable and vulnerable to shifting power constellations. The underlying conflict will always remain latent. Only if we can find a sound theoretical basis for practical compromise, we may hope that in the end the recognition of the minorities will be accepted as legitimate by both minority and majority. Moreover, this practical argument offers no suggestions about the contents or even the direction of state policies. It merely suggests that the state should take cultures seriously only in so far as this is necessary to avoid conflicts. As long as minorities do not complain, or if they are too weak to cause any serious trouble, there need not even be a reason for the state to recognise their interests. In some situations, it might even seem wise to suppress ethnic identities. For all these reasons, the practical argument needs to be supplemented by a sound theoretical one.

B. Culture As a Public Good
The first principled line of argument remains within the liberal-individualist framework.[3] A generally accepted fundamental principle of modern political philosophy is that the state should treat its citizens with equal concern and respect.[4] This principle has often been interpreted in a very abstract, neutral way so that all contingent differences between individual citizens are ignored as much as possible. In this interpretation, liberalism clearly cannot recognise the importance

223

of particular cultural identities, because it abstracts from this contingent characteristic.

Will Kymlicka (whose theory is discussed in this volume by Walter Lesch) has suggested a different interpretation of equal respect, in which both universal and contingent characteristics of the personal identity of citizens are taken into account. Equal respect for all citizens means respecting their full personality, including contingent characteristics as cultural identity. The individual remains the primary focus of Kymlicka's political philosophy, but he fully recognises the fact that the identity of this individual is partly socially and culturally determined. If belonging to a national or ethnic culture is partly constitutive of someone's identity and if a continuing cultural framework is necessary for the flourishing of the individual, then cultural membership and the cultural framework must be considered primary goods for him. The cultural framework is not a private good like food: it is a good that the individual shares with others. To be more precise, it is a public good: it is indivisible and can only be provided through a co-operative effort of the community.[5] Cultural membership has a somewhat mixed character: it is a private good that presupposes the public good of a common cultural framework.

This line of argument is, in my opinion, a very convincing one, and it is the most promising approach in political theory to deal with the claims of cultural minorities. It suffices to demonstrate that culture is politically relevant. Still, it is far from complete. The thesis that *a* rich cultural framework is a public good, is uncontroversial – we will deal with this in subsection D. We have to make an additional argument: that it is *this* specific minority culture that is relevant to a citizen's flourishing and that it is his membership of *this* cultural group that is a primary good, and that this is a good worthy of state protection.

Jeremy Waldron offers three strong arguments against Kymlicka's position; I think, however, that these arguments result in a better understanding of what Kymlicka holds and what he does not hold rather than refute him. The fact that I was raised within a certain

224

culture, does not imply that this specific culture is necessary for my flourishing; perhaps a different cultural framework may do as well, or even better (Waldron ch. 8 (this volume): 'We need culture, but we do not need cultural integrity.'). This counter-argument is, in my opinion, only partly relevant. It is a strong argument against those extreme conservatives who hold that the state should preserve minority cultures exactly in the way they are now. Clearly, this is not Kymlicka's position. To uphold his position, we need only assume that, at least for some people, being member of one's own cultural group is partly constitutive of a personal identity, and that therefore the continual flourishing of the cultural framework of this group (open as it may be to the dynamics of change) is a very important good for them. For most of us, it is not a matter of choice to which culture we belong. One does not choose to be a member of a culture; one is born into it. Even if, later in my life, I should adopt a cosmopolitan perspective, I cannot completely detach myself from my own national or ethnic origins. 'Someone's upbringing isn't something that can just be erased; it is, and will remain a constitutive part of who that person is.' (Kymlicka 1989, 175) Though, theoretically, I may recognise the value of other cultures, and though I may enrich my own cultural identity with elements of those other cultures, it is my own culture to which I have grown accustomed and which is therefore of special value to me. It is not strictly essential to me, but neither is education. I could live without my own culture, but my life would be greatly impoverished. This is all that is needed to show that membership of a flourishing culture may be considered an important or primary good.

Waldron (ch. 4 (this volume)) gives a second argument against considering cultural membership a primary good: the fact that a cosmopolitan personality is possible. Again I think this is only a counter-argument against a more extreme position than the one Kymlicka holds. Indeed, cultural membership is not a universal primary good: some people can do without it. But for most of us it is a very important good. The fact that not all women (let alone men) get pregnant and bear children, is a valid argument to show that child-bearing is not a universal good for all women, but it is not a valid argument against those who hold that having the opportunity to bear and raise children is a major good for many women, and that government policies protecting that good (like paid pregnancy and maternal leave) are therefore justified, even if the good is not universal. We may even hold that this good is so important that it should be protected by special rights. For Maris and Waldron cultural membership is not a good, but that does not mean that, if it is a good for some, it may be so important for them that it is worthy of state protection.

A third point made by Waldron is that even if cultural membership were a good, it would not be the state's business, just like religion is a major good for many citizens but should not be protected by the state. Why should the state protect or even actively support this culture instead of leaving it to the private sphere? The state does not take care of every primary good; a religious identity may be as important as a cultural one, but surely the state has no obligation to support the Amish in order to preserve their church. We still need to establish whether the state has any active obligations towards this specific primary good of cultural membership. A first remark on this point is that states in fact often protect and support religions. Not only is religious freedom protected; conscientious objections against military service and social security are recognised. In many countries, churches and religious institutions even get financial support from the state. In my view, this is often justified, on the ground that they offer important public goods, like mental support to those in the army, in universities or in hospitals. A second remark is that the answer to this question depends on one's general political outlook. If one prefers a minimal state like Nozick's, then the state presumably has no business in the sphere of culture. If, on the other hand, one is committed to something like a Western European ('Rhinelandic') welfare state, then the state has a more active role in supporting various types of public goods. If it is accepted that the state should support art, education, science and so on, then it seems to me that consistency yields the conclusion that the state should support those minority cultures that are an important public good for their members.

C. Culture as a Non-Reducible Collective Good

The second principled line of argument transcends the liberal-individualist framework. It considers culture to be a non-reducible collective good. It is this claim which may be found in Taylor and, in this book, in Türk. A non-reducible collective good pertains to a collectivity as such. A good is a non-reducible collective good, in so far as it is more than the aggregate of the goods which arise out of the individual membership of the collectivity.[6] This claim gives rise to many important theoretical questions, such as how we can adequately conceptualise such goods and how we can establish that something is a non-reducible collective good. But I will leave these considerations aside and, for the sake of argument, simply assume that a culture is such a non-reducible collective good.

Even so, this is not yet a complete political argument for the proposition that states should take care of minority cultures, and especially not why they should prefer the continued existence of a minority culture over a gradual immersion of the minority in the majority culture. Politics should be oriented towards goods, but in a pluralist society confronted with scarce means not all goods can be equally realised or protected, and some goods, like religious salvation, are even regarded as belonging to the private sphere.[7] Politics is about choices, and we need a good argument to defend why the state should protect one good rather than another. The majority culture is a good as well, and it would certainly be enriched if those now devoting their energy to preserving the minority culture, would in future direct their endeavours towards enriching the majority culture with elements from the minority culture. Moreover, why should it be a non-reducible collective good that in two hundred years time French is still alive in Quebec rather than everyone speaking English? Having only one language certainly facilitates communication and probably leads to fewer cultural conflicts. If we leave aside the interests of the members of a culture, we should rather hope for a diminishing cultural plurality, so it seems.

Political argument is comparative: a policy or a general political structure should promote good X rather than good Y. What arguments would we have to say that minority culture A should be considered so valuable that the state must preserve it for future generations rather than let it submerge in (and hopefully enrich) majority culture B? To make political decisions we often have to compare the value of beautiful nature with the value of good roads, but the value of two cultures is a different issue. The reason is that a culture is partly constitutive of a person, and therefore the value of a culture cannot be judged from a neutral perspective. The value of different cultures is largely incommensurable. In some respects, however, they may not be fully incommensurable, and we can make more neutral judgements, e.g. whether a culture is richer, more varied or is better adapted to its context.

One may try to argue that this specific minority culture A is somehow better than culture B. Of course, this is what members of a culture often believe, because it is *better for them*, being the persons they are, partly constituted by that culture. Perhaps they think their culture is richer, has an older tradition, and offers them words to express their feelings more precisely than would be possible in other languages and cultures. But when, from an external perspective, we compare two cultures, usually most of the criteria would rather point towards a greater value of the majority culture. Simply because of the numbers, there will be a greater variety of books and theatres, the majority language will be better adapted to modern culture, and so on. At the most, we may consider the cultures to be of equal value or incommensurable, as may be the case with the French and the English in Quebec, as they both belong to a larger cultural community. But even this falls short of arguing that the French Canadian culture might be considered better than the English, and therefore this line of argument will fail to establish the good of a culture in such a way that minority protection can be based on it. If two cultures are equally good or incommensurable, the value of the culture can be no legitimate reason to give one of them special protection. An analogy may clarify this point: if the state is asked to interfere with the pollution of a small lake by a major industry, while the value of an unspoilt lake equals the value of the jobs that the company provides, it has no legitimate reason for interfering; it would only have so if one of the two clearly is more valuable than the other.

My conclusion is that, although a minority culture may be a non-reducible collective good, I do not see how this can be a good reason for state action to protect the culture against merging in the majority culture, or even against simply disappearing. To avoid misunderstandings: I do not deny that a culture is valuable for its members and that it is valuable for its future members; but this dimension can be adequately expressed when we regard culture as a public good. What I try to analyse here is the dimension that transcends those individualistic terms.

I may illustrate this with a more personal experience. I was raised bilingually, in Frisian (an old language spoken by about 600,000 persons in the north of the Netherlands) and in Dutch. There are, in my opinion, valid arguments for special measures to protect the Frisian language as a public good – arguments that may be based on the individual needs and goods of Frisians that are alive now or that will live in the future. Personally, I would regret it if I knew that this minority culture would no longer exist in the year 2100, simply because this language is valuable to me and it would imply that a living cultural tradition of which I am part, will cease to exist. All this can be adequately expressed by regarding Frisian culture as a public good. But I do not see how I can make a good argument based on the value of Frisian language and culture as such, that would establish it as a non-reducible collective good that merits state action for its preservation. It may perhaps be argued that Frisian is a more beautiful and poetic language than Dutch, because it has a much richer variety of sounds, and that it has a longer history than the Dutch language. Yet, by most 'objective' criteria, Frisian clearly is not a 'better' language or culture: Dutch has a much larger literature and is better adapted to modern society. If we look at it, detached from the interests and the good of those who live now and enjoy it, the existence of a Frisian culture is not better than the existence of a Dutch culture enriched by the incorporation of Frisian culture.

D. Cultural Pluralism as a Good

The last reason for the political relevance of cultural pluralism is well known. We should value cultural pluralism as such because it enriches the cultural framework. This argument does not hold that a specific minority culture is valuable as a public or a collective good, but that a broad variety of cultures is valuable as a public good.[8] Most liberal thinkers incorporate some variety of this general argument in their theory: pluralism is valuable because it offers choice and makes experimentation possible, and because it is an important source of cultural materials.[9] The state should aim at a great variety of cultures on its territory, because it offers us and future generations a greater choice. Our grandchildren need not necessarily value Van Gogh, but at least we should offer them the possibility to decide for themselves whether they enjoy his work or not. Perhaps our grandchildren do not value the Quebec culture any more, but we should offer them the free choice, and therefore preserve the culture.

One should doubt, however, whether this really is a good argument for protecting minority cultures in the way they should be protected according to their more communitarian defenders. A pluralist culture offers us a choice; but does a plurality of cultures offer us the same choice? As a culture is partly constitutive of my identity, I cannot pick cultures in the same way I pick books. I can pick elements of cultures, but this is only possible if cultures are open to change and external influences, and if outsiders are allowed to enter and insiders allowed to leave.

There are degrees of freedom and openness here. Some cultures are more open than others, and therefore allow more choice to pick elements of other cultures in recreating a personal identity. If what is at stake in the value of cultural pluralism are the ideals of freedom of choice and of experimentation, then we should protect minority cultures only in so far as is necessary to guarantee these freedoms, and the protective measures should be consistent with these freedoms. Free exit from and access to minority groups should be guaranteed, just like the freedom to combine elements of various cultures. Both the majority culture and the minority culture should be open cultures to which everyone has equal access. This means that Frenchmen may experiment with English words if they want, and that a Québecois may freely choose whether to send her children to a French or an English school. It means that the Inuit and other native Americans would have no possibilities to limit membership of the group, and so on. In sum, it would correct the free market of cultures in giving the various cultures more equal access to the market, e.g. by giving subsidies to minority cultures, but it would not permit any protectionist measures that shield off the minority from the outside world. And it is exactly this type of protectionist measure that forms the core of the criticism by communitarians like Taylor, who claim that individualist liberalism cannot do justice to minority cultures.

The argument from the value of pluralism is an important argument for state support of minority cultures. But, in my opinion, it only adds strength to the argument from culture as a public good, and has the same individualist limits. These limits may even be stricter, because the argument from pluralism explicitly condemns certain protectionist measures (such as limited access to membership) that might be justified on the basis of a culture as a public good argument.

The analysis of the various arguments for state support and protection of minority cultures leads to a simple conclusion. In political theory, the justification of protection for minority cultures should be founded on an individualistic basis. Cultures are a public good for their members; that is why they matter for the state. That they are a collective good as well, may be a ground for an active cultural policy in general, but not for an active policy to protect specific minority cultures. That a pluralist culture has independent value may give additional force to arguments for protective measures, but does not add anything substantive; it may even be an argument against certain illiberal forms of protectionist measures.

3. Collective Rights to Preserve a Cultural Identity

One of the central issues in the debate on cultural pluralism is whether we should protect (members of) cultural minorities by recognising collective rights.[10] This issue is connected with the question of why the state should support minority cultures. Regarding culture as a collective good tends to lead to the recognition of collective rights rather than individual rights. When culture is regarded as a public good, however, it is still open whether individual or collective rights are the best method to protect this good.

We can leave aside the question, whether collective rights are recognised in current national or international law. In her dissertation, Galenkamp concluded that 'the question whether collectivities may have a legal status as bearers of some legal rights, has nowadays remained rather uncontested'; groups, in fact, have status and rights at the international level (Galenkamp 1993, 51). Current international law is nevertheless still very reluctant to name groups as holders of rights, preferring the attribution of rights to individual members of the group.

Our central question here is not an empirical one but a normative one: do we have good philosophical grounds to justify collective rights, and, more specifically, collective rights to preserve a cultural identity? In this volume two opposite positions are defended. Türk, basing his argument on the proposition that (in the terminology used above) ethnic and national cultures are both a public and a collective good, argues that we should recognise them; Galenkamp states bluntly that they are neither feasible, nor desirable, nor needed.

Türk's argument in favour of collective rights is in line with Taylor's attempt to construe a synthesis between liberalism and communitarianism. He argues that we should not choose between the universal and the particular, but that we should combine them. We need individual rights to protect universal values, but we should also recognise the 'ethical claim to cultural, social and administrative group rights' or 'special rights to ethnic groups'. Both types of rights follow from the principle of respect for the individual. Universal rights may be based on more individualistic dimensions of his personality, like autonomy; collective rights are a recognition of the fact that the individual is partly formed in and belongs to a community. Collective rights may be necessary for the cultural survival of a community.

In her dissertation, Galenkamp defended a position that was quite similar to that of Türk's. The paradigms of 'Gemeinschaft,' communitarianism and collective rights on the one hand, and of 'Gesellschaft', liberalism and individual rights on the other hand are both legitimate but not easily compatible (Galenkamp 1993, 154). In her article in this volume, she seems to have abandoned this position in favour of a straightforward liberalism that tries to do justice to the collective dimension of personal identity within an individual rights framework. Her argument now is that we can and should do without collective rights. I think her case is put forward in a very clear way; at least her article shows that the problems linked to collective rights constitute a serious warning not to recognise them unless we really have no alternative. Rather than critically discussing each of her arguments and confronting them with Türk's, I will go one step beyond her analysis and see whether, indeed, a liberal scheme of individual rights can be developed that makes collective rights superfluous, at least with respect to the protection of minority cultures.

In the literature (in this volume, e.g. by Galenkamp), the concepts of 'collective rights' and 'special rights' are often seen as equivalents; I think, however, that there is an important difference. In the standard distinction between collective (or group) rights and individual rights, the question of who is the subject or right-holder is the crucial criterion: the individual or the collective. Another distinction is the one between universal and special rights, where the criterion is whether everyone has these rights, or only specific groups or persons. The right to speak one's language is formulated as a universal right because everyone is entitled to it (though it may give rise to special rights for members of minorities); the right to special aid for (members of) minority groups is a special right, because members of the majority are not entitled to it. The debate between Galenkamp and Türk seems to be one between individual, universal rights on the one hand, and collective special rights on the other. I think the middle ground may largely be covered by recognising individual special rights, rights that individuals have as members of a special cultural community.[11]

How far can a liberal-individualist political theory go in protecting minority cultures? To answer this question, I will start with a standard individualist approach to rights, and then progressively introduce more social dimensions.

1. Most traditional rights are primarily oriented towards private goods: life, liberty and property. Some rights have a strong social dimension: freedom of religion and association, though vested in the individual, are usually or even by definition exercised in a social setting. Protection of goods with a social character through individual rights is therefore perfectly well possible within a traditional rights framework (cf. Raz 1986, 251). Goods that arise from belonging to a cultural community need not be an exception to this. Just as we recognise freedom of religion, so we may recognise freedom of language: the right to speak one's own language whenever one wants to, be it in a private sphere or in an official setting like a courtroom. Of course, this right cannot be unlimited; we need not expect an English judge to understand Polish. In some cases a system of translation facilities may be adequate, but in other cases we could specify the universal right to speak one's own language in court by saying that there is a right to use a specific language on a certain territory. The best way to formulate this specification is by constructing a special right, e.g. the right to speak Frisian in court in the Frisian-speaking part of the Netherlands.[12]

Individual special rights to private goods with a social character fit perfectly well into a liberal rights framework. This category of special rights will mainly be liberty rights that guarantee freedom from state interference with enjoying one's own culture. Even if state action is required, it will usually only be minimal. Examples are permitting the use of Breton first names (a right that until recently was denied by the

French government) or allowing the use of minority languages in official settings (a right which in many Western countries is not fully recognised). However, for the continued existence of a minority culture more is needed, even if in many cases of ethnic conflict the recognition of these minimal rights would already be a major advance.

2. The next step is to formulate special rights to a public good. Most universal rights to a public good have only recently been recognised; an example is the right to a clean environment. They are more like standards of aspiration than strict claim-rights; still, they can be useful and sometimes they have direct legal implications. A flourishing culture can be seen as such a public good as well; a wide variety of books, plays, films, television, et cetera, in one's own culture is a public good.[13] Analogous to the right to a clean environment, we may construe the right to a rich cultural environment.

For members of a majority culture, this right is usually reasonably provided for by the free cultural market. Some additional state support for 'high culture' like the arts, or for a public broadcasting service is nevertheless necessary, as well as some regulation to ensure that the market remains free rather than being dominated by a small number of media tycoons and large publishing and broadcasting companies. For members of minority groups, however, the situation is different.[14] The commercial prospects for a book are usually much worse, simply because there is a smaller number of readers. As a result, without additional state funding books would be much more expensive and the variety of books would be very small. With other arts, like drama, it may even mean that no quality products are available at all, simply because it is impossible to earn a living through the theatre in a minority culture. Not every cultural group is equally affected by this problem of unequal access to the cultural market-place. The French culture in Canada and France, on which Maris focuses, is clearly more viable under market conditions than the Inuit culture. Perhaps his thesis that empirically speaking, 'it is implausible to argue that national cultures could not survive without state encouragement and enforcement,' it is empirically implausible that national cultures cannot survive without state enforcement' holds for large cultures like the French,[15] but for small minority cultures like the Inuit I think there are good reasons for rejecting it.

For small minorities, the universal right to a rich cultural environment may be the basis for a special right for their members, namely that the state supports and protects the minority culture. Only if we do this, the members of minority and majority will be treated more or less as equals, though clearly even with state support the minority culture will have a weaker position. There are various legitimate ways to implement this right. Just as the state may restrict commercial signage for environmental reasons, so it could do for cultural reasons: a billboard on the Big Ben might be prohibited. I fail to see why this should be different for other aspects of the cultural environment, and why the state should not be allowed to demand that all advertisements on a minority's territory are either bilingual or are stated in the minority language.

A cosmopolitan may now argue that it is unclear why the right to a rich cultural environment should be the ground for a right to support a specific culture.[16] Could we not say that members of the minority culture have an adequate cultural environment, because they can enjoy the majority culture as well? Why then should the state support this culture instead of culture in general? Some support for the minority culture might be warranted, just as the state supports opera and public libraries. But special additional support is not warranted, so the argument may be. I think this argument is faulty, because it suggests that the choice of a culture is completely free. But, as I have argued above, it is not. I cannot choose languages and cultures in the same way I choose my food.[17] Having access only to a culture which is not my own, not merely means that I get fewer cultural goods than others or at a higher price (reading literature in a foreign language is always more difficult than reading it in one's own) but may also affect my sense of personal identity and capacity. Therefore, if a rich cultural infrastructure is essential for my personal identity and welfare, it must include the culture that I belong to and the language that I am used to. Other cultures and elements from other cultures should be optional, even to the extent that I may reverse my preferences as a real cosmopolitan. The possibility of a cosmopolitan lifestyle may be a good argument against a general right to support for specific cultures, but cannot be an argument against a special right to such support for those persons who feel more strongly connected to their own minority culture.

3. Instead of formulating an individual special right to freedom of language or to active support for a minority culture, one may also construe these as the collective rights of a minority culture. Even if they are formulated as the rights of individuals, reference to the group culture is usually necessary. Often it will be simpler to formulate these as the rights of groups rather than as the rights of the members of groups. I do not see any major arguments against this construction, and sometimes it may be a more effective and fruitful approach. Such collective rights are justifiable; yet, they do not add anything to the individual rights framework and are completely derivative rights, both in contents and in justification. We may call them reducible collective rights, because they can ultimately be reduced to rights of individuals acting as members of a collective group.[18]

A collective right may be considered non-reducible in so far as it is more than the aggregate of the rights which arise out of the individual membership of the collectively. When Galenkamp states so provocatively that special rights are neither feasible, nor desirable, nor needed, she seems to refer only to those non-reducible collective rights.

Aboriginal land rights present a problem: are they reducible or not? For the survival of an aboriginal culture it may be essential that the land of the group is held in common. It would be slightly artificial to formulate this as an individual right. Nevertheless, in my opinion, the reason why we must respect collective rights to land is because it is necessary for the flourishing of the individual members of the culture as members of a cultural group. Though they are indivisible in the sense that they cannot be divided in rights to equal shares of the land, they are reducible, because their ultimate basis is the individual.[19]

237

4. Political theory consists of more elements than rights alone. We do not have a right (let alone a human right) stating that Rembrandt's paintings should be protected so that we can enjoy them. Yet, it is clearly not only a legitimate state policy to support art, but often also a duty. Not everything members of minority cultures want, can be claimed as a right, but that does not prevent a liberal state from going beyond the rights framework and support minority cultures in many ways. The state may even have a duty to do so.

The argument so far is completely consistent with an individualistic approach. Full recognition of the individual and reducible collective rights discussed so far would, in my opinion, adequately protect almost all aspects of cultural communities that should be legally protected. Realising this ambitious scheme of rights would be a real step forward. Yet, there are two elements of the case for protection of cultural groups that cannot be fully addressed in this way.

The first problem that cannot be fully addressed in this individualistic approach is mentioned by Taylor and Maris. Members of a community usually want more than only the right to enjoy their culture for themselves. They see themselves as part of a common project, a valuable common tradition that they inherited from their ancestors and that they should preserve for future generations. If free market principles of choice and experiment determine the course of the culture, and especially if members of the cultural group are free to leave the group or to introduce elements of the majority culture into the minority culture, the latter might wither away – even if actively supported by the state. Non-reducible collective rights that limit these freedoms may be necessary to preserve the culture for future generations.

A second problem for which an individualist framework is not fully adequate, occurs when a culture withers away. There will be some people left who will have to switch off the light or, in less dramatic terms, in their old age people will be confronted with the fact that their culture is not as lively as when they were young: there is hardly anyone left with whom they can share their culture, their language and enjoy so many things that were once essential to their identity. Collective rights may prevent this withering away of a culture.

For both problems, collective rights that go further than would be possible in an individualistic framework may be a solution. Collective rights should guarantee the right for minorities to ward off the dominant culture and language from their territory, to send all children belonging to their group to their own schools, to prohibit intercultural marriages, and to limit exit and entrance options. So, we may conclude that in some cases a recognition of non-reducible collective rights is necessary to protect minority cultures.

There may be a need for (non-reducible) collective rights here, but this alone does not justify them. A first remark may be that we should doubt whether this is really feasible. If a culture is already so weak that it cannot be preserved without the full protection that a sophisticated individualistic liberalism can offer, we must doubt whether it can be preserved in the long run by freedom-restricting measures. The youth revolt of the sixties and the history of the Communist countries in Eastern Europe have shown that it is extremely difficult for the state to control behaviour in the cultural sphere.

A second remark concerns the question of justification. The collective rights suggested here would give rise to serious interference with the freedom of both outsiders and members of the groups. It is very difficult to justify such freedom-limiting interventions. Though they are meant to protect the individual cultural rights of some of the members, the freedom of some other members is seriously restricted. Can we justify this? Kymlicka and Taylor are among those who argue that we sometimes can, whereas Galenkamp is strongly opposed.[20] It seems to me that this interference can rarely, if ever, be justified, and least in a liberal society in which individual cultural rights are adequately guaranteed. If there is official recognition and state support for the minority culture, if it is not simply because of poverty and lack of educational and professional chances that members want to leave their community or join the majority culture – as now often is the case with indigenous cultures – but simply the fact that they prefer the other culture, then it is hard to make the case for restriction of their freedom.[21] The arguments for protection of minority cultures that I discussed above, are based on the idea that these cultures are still valuable to their members. These arguments cannot justify the artificial preservation of an insulated 'Disneyland-culture' (as sketched by Waldron Ch. 8) when the members no longer want the culture or when they want to adapt it to modern society.

Cultures change all the time. We do not grant older people the right that their culture is preserved for their sake, e.g. that for the sake of those who still cling to the hippie culture of the sixties, this subculture should be artificially preserved. It is a fact of modernity that every generation, when old, is confronted with a culture in which they find themselves partly strangers and in which perhaps essential values that they held dear (like marriage 'till death do us part') are no longer generally accepted. Of course, the state should give the older generation the freedom to live as it was used to, and even support special cultural activities for this 'minority culture', but the state can hardly be expected to take illiberal measures that force the younger generations to sustain a culture that they no longer want. Why then should we act differently with regard to cultural minority groups?

A similar counter-argument can be made against the idea that the continued existence of the minority culture is a common project of its members and that this project should be protected by collective rights. We do not do that for other projects to which people are devoted. Many persons are devoted to their church or to their political ideals; their greatest aim in life, which may even partly constitute their identity, may be that their church will still flourish in a hundred years time or that their ideals will be realised. But that clearly is no argument for a special status for this church or for these ideals. Why then should we award a special status to my minority culture, when this is the project to which I am devoted?

To sum up the argument: genuine collective rights to protect minority cultures beyond what is possible within the individualist liberal framework, will usually seriously restrict the freedom of members or outsiders. It is difficult to see how this can be justified. An appeal to the importance of this specific culture as a collective good or to the common project of its continued existence is no ground for a special status in political theory. An appeal to the interests of the older generation cannot overrule the interests of the younger members of the culture that want change for themselves.

For a general conclusion, this sketch is not sufficient; there may be exceptional cases in which genuine collective rights are both necessary and justified. I think these exceptions mainly concern compensation for historic injustices, and especially when it is necessary to guarantee that in the transition from an illiberal society to a liberal one in which individual rights are fully respected, the minority does not wither away. But collective rights are clearly not a panacea for the problems of multiculturalism. In my opinion, we had better stick to liberalism and expand the liberal rights framework.

My tentative conclusion may be presented in the form of an amended version of Galenkamp's thesis. It can be formulated in an almost paradoxical way: When collective rights are justified (as reformulations of individual rights), they are not really necessary (just because they are merely reformulations); when they are necessary, they are usually either not feasible or not justifiable.

4. Reconsidering the State

Both Fleiner and Türk argue that the concept of a culturally homogeneous nation-state is at the core of theoretical and practical problems. The dominant position of the nation-state in political theory can be corrected at two levels: the intermediate level below the state – that of the cultural communities and their members – and the international and supranational levels beyond the state. Construing rights and other protective mechanisms for (members of) cultural minorities is one way to mitigate and counterbalance these problems.

Fleiner argues for the other approach: the fundamental level at which political theories of the state are built, should be that of the world community, without connecting this to a Utopian idea of a world-state. States should be considered to have a mandate from mankind. The state should be regarded as one functional organisation among others, with a specific, limited task; however, this restriction should be built on territory and function, not on national or ethnic lines. The link between nation and state should be relinquished.

Theoretically, this is an interesting approach, and it seems to be a fruitful starting-point for philosophical reflection on the character of the state. I would, nevertheless, like to mention two problems that may too easily be neglected in such an institutional cosmopolitan perspective.[22]

One problem is a matter of political psychology. One of the major sources of loyalty to the state is precisely the fact that it is a national state. An important part of communitarian criticism has been that liberal states that ignore this national dimension may not be able to raise adequate feelings of loyalty, and that, as a result of this, societies may disintegrate.[23] Perhaps they are legitimate in the sense that they are theoretically justified, but their legitimacy in the sense of their being able to command loyalty and obedience from the side of their citizens, may be quite problematic. Jürgen Habermas and others have tried to counter this objection by suggesting a constitutional patriotism.[24] It is doubtful, however, whether this will always be adequate. Perhaps it may be so in states such as Switzerland and the Netherlands, but what about societies like Belgium, Canada or the Russian Federation? Certainly, the non-national state held together by constitutional patriotism is an inspiring ideal, but in many countries this ideal is too far from reality to be useful in practical politics. Fleiner acknowledges the importance of national feeling, but it remains unclear how he wants to combine this with his main thesis.

A second problem is a matter of cultural politics. Fleiner (section 3 (this volume)) suggests that the state should stay out of the spheres of culture and education. The cultural interests of the nation should be pursued not by the state, but by the nation itself. This seemingly neutral position is, in my view, quite problematic. As I have argued above, if we leave culture and education completely to the free market, minority cultures will have major problems to survive. Active state support will therefore usually be justified. The state could, of course, delegate this care for culture and education to the various national and ethnic communities, and respect their cultural autonomy, as Fleiner suggests. But then a host of new problems arises. Do these cultural communities have a claim to state funding – and if so, how should the funds be divided? – or should they have the right to levy taxes themselves? If funding and taxation are simply in proportion to the numbers of their members, the smaller communities will not be able to attain the same standards of quality for the same price as the larger ones. What counts as a cultural community? If we recognise the Turkish immigrants in the Netherlands as such, then the next question is whether we should also recognise the Turkish Kurds as a separate community. And so on: what is the minimum size of a group to be recognised as an independent community which has rights to state support for their culture and education? It seems that all the problems about determining the limits of the national groups, so convincingly sketched by Fleiner, find their analogue at the level of determining the limits of the various cultural communities within a state.

These are two serious problems for a more cosmopolitan approach, but rather than being insurmountable obstacles, they are points to which further explicit attention will have to be paid. The perspective Fleiner suggests, seems worth exploring, though it seems to me that it should be combined with an active state policy towards a pluralist culture and towards a plurality of cultures rather than with abstinence. Further elaboration of individual rights to cultural collective goods may be an important element of this attempt to rethink the nation-state. The articles in this volume have made it clear that there is still much to do, not only in the field of practical politics and diplomacy, but also in the construction of better political and moral theories. Moral and political philosophers have an important contribution to make to this theoretical work.

Notes

1. For reasons of simplicity, the term cultural groups will be used here to refer to both national and ethnic groups.
2. I will not discuss a fifth type of argument, namely that special protection for minority cultures is justified as a form of compensatory justice for historic injustices. This may be an important argument, e.g. in the case of the aboriginal peoples of America, but a whole cluster of very complex problems is connected to it, which cannot be fully discussed in the context of this article.
3. When I use the term 'individualist', this has nothing to do with atomism. I try to construct a position that is strongly socialised in fully addressing the social dimension of personal identity, but still distinctly individualist in the sense that the individual ultimately is the central value of political theory. Thus, I subscribe to what Hartney 1991, p. 297 calls 'value-individualism'.
4. The principle of equal concern and respect has gained great popularity through the work of Ronald Dworkin, but I think he correctly assumes it is a principle that is acceptable to almost everyone in Western society. Dworkin 1978, 180.
5. On public goods, see Rawls 1971, p. 266 ff. and Raz 1986, p. 198 ff.
6. Galenkamp 1993, p. 132.
7. This is a variation on Waldron's third argument that was discussed in subsection 2B. While it is not valid in the case of culture as a public good, because here it can be reduced to private goods, the argument has a different standing with respect to non-reducible collective goods.
8. The cultural framework is even a very special type of public good: not only is it not diminished by consumption, but it is even reinforced by consumption: the more people speak their language and read books or magazines, the more the culture flourishes.
9. Cf. Raz 1986, Waldron, ch. 8 (this volume), Kymlicka 1989, p. 81.
10. A very interesting collection of essays on various dimensions of this topic may be found in the special issue on collective rights of the *Canadian Journal of Law and Jurisprudence*, vol. IV no. 2 (July 1992).
11. The analysis of special rights below is largely based on my dissertation, Van der Burg 1991, pp. 161-168 and on Young 1990. The fact that special rights are often treated as equivalent to collective rights, is not surprising. The most important reason for according special rights is that members of special groups need them because of their group membership. Even then, it is important to distinguish whether the group as such is the right-holder, or the individual members are the right-holders. Moreover, some

special rights are not connected with group membership: pregnancy leave may be regarded as a special right, but not as a group right.

12. The question of when the existence of a group should give rise to such special rights can only be answered by way of a detailed analysis of many relevant factors. 'Critical mass' and 'history' must be among those factors – see Brett 1992, pp. 357-358.

13. In fact, the cultural environment has a more mixed character of private and public good, because many elements (especially those of 'high culture') are not completely free. There is a limited number of theatre tickets, one has to pay for them, and so on. For my analysis this mixed character is not really relevant, because rights to private goods are less problematic than rights to purely public goods.

14. Cf. Kymlicka 1989, chapter 9.

15. See however, the interesting analysis of the French Canadians in Brett 1992.

16. Cf. Waldron, ch. 8 (this volume).

17. Cf. Kymlicka 1993, p. 175.

18. Cf. Donnelly 1990, p. 48.

19. I must admit that this conceptualisation does not do justice to the claims of many aboriginal peoples: they claim that it is a right inherent in their cultural tradition, which includes past and future generations. Whether political theory should recognise this far-reaching claim is a topic of discussion. I do not think there are convincing reasons to do so, but this point cannot be elaborated here.

20. Cf. Appiah 1994, 163, who warns for the danger that we replace one kind of tyranny by another.

21. Most societies, however, are not so liberal. Perhaps in the transition period to a more liberal society, collective rights may be justified as temporary measures for reasons of compensation of unjust circumstances, and as an extra protection against illiberal circumstances.

22. The concept of institutional cosmopolitanism is introduced by Pogge 1992, p. 50.

23. An interesting discussion of this topic can be found in a special issue of the *Boston Review* Vol. XIX (1994) 5 on 'Patriotism or Cosmopolitanism'.

24. Habermas 1994, p. 134.

References

APIAH, K. A., *Identity, Authenticiy, Survival: Multicultural Societies and Social Reproduction*, in: TAYLOR, C. et al., *Multiculturalism. Examining the Politics of Recognition*, Princeton, NJ: Princeton University Press, 1994, pp. 149-163.

BRETT, N., *Language Laws and Collective Rights*, in: *Canadian Journal of Law and Jurisprudence*, vol. IV, no. 2 (1992), pp. 347-360.

BURG, VAN DER, W., *Het Democratisch Perspectief. Een verkenning van de normatieve grondslagen der democratie*, [The Democratic Point of View. An Exploration of the Normative Basis of Democracy] (diss. Utrecht University) Arnhem: Gouda Quint, 1991.

DONELLY, J., *Human Rights, Individual Rights and Collective Rights*, in: BERTING, J. et al. (eds.), *Human Rights in a Pluralist World,* Westport: Meckler, 1990, pp. 39-62.

DWORKIN, R., *Taking Rights Seriously*, Cambridge, Mass.: Harvard University Press, 1978.

GALENKAMP, M., *Individualism versus Collectivism. The Concept of Collective Rights*, (diss. Erasmus University Rotterdam) 1993.

HABERMAS, J., *Struggles for Recognition in the Democratic Constitutional State*, in: TAYLOR, C. et al., *Multiculturalism. Examining the Politics of Recognition*, Princeton, NJ: Princeton University Press, 1994, pp. 107-148.

HARTNEY, M., *Some Confusions Concerning Collective Rights*, in: *Canadian Journal of Law and Jurisprudence*, vol. IV no. 2 (1992), pp. 293-314.

KYMLICKA, W., *Liberalism, Community and Culture*, Oxford: Clarendon, 1989.

POGGE, T.W., *Cosmopolitanism and Sovereignty*, in: *Ethics* 103, 1992, pp. 48-85.

RAWLS, J., *A Theory of Justice*, Oxford: University Press, 1971.

RAZ, J., *The Morality of Freedom*, Oxford: Clarendon Press, 1986.

TAYLOR, C., *The Politics of Recognition*, in: C. Taylor et al. (1994), *Multiculturalism. Examining the Politics of Recognition*, Princeton, NJ: Princeton University Press, 1994, pp. 25-73.

YOUNG, I.M., *Justice and the Politics of Difference*, Princeton, NJ: Princeton University Press, 1990.

Contributors

Wibren van der Burg is Senior Researcher in Jurisprudence at Tilburg University, The Netherlands. He is treasurer 1991-1995 of the Societas Ethica, the European Society for Research in Ethics.

Thomas Fleiner is Professor of Law at Fribourg University, Switzerland.

Marlies Galenkamp is Lecturer in Jurisprudence at the Erasmus University, Rotterdam, The Netherlands.

Robert Heeger is Professor of Ethics at Utrecht University, The Netherlands, and is president 1991-1995 of the Societas Ethica, the European Society for Research in Ethics.

Walter Lesch is Lecturer in Moral Theology at Fribourg University, Switzerland.

Cees Maris is Professor of Jurisprudence at the University of Amsterdam, The Netherlands.

Richard H. Roberts is Professor of Divinity and Director of the Institute for Religion and the Human Sciences at the University of St. Andrews, Great Britain.

Hans Joachim Türk is Professor Emeritus in Philosophy and Social Ethics at the Fachhochschule Georg Simon Ohm, Nürnberg, Germany.

Jeremy J. Waldron is Professor of Law (Jurisprudence and Social Policy Program) at the School of Law, University of California, Berkeley, United States.

Theo van Willigenburg is Lecturer in Ethics at Utrecht University, The Netherlands, and is secretary 1991-1995 of the Societas Ethica, the European Society for Research in Ethics.

About the Societas Ethica

The Societas Ethica is the European Society for Research in Ethics. The Societas has more than 200 members from approximately 19 countries, including both moral philosophers ánd moral theologians. The Societas Ethica is a platform for the exchange of scholarly work, ideas and experiences stemming from very different intellectual and philosophical traditions.
The Societas Ethica was founded in 1964. Since its beginning, it has strongly stimulated contacts between scholars in different countries, surpassing political, ideological and religious curtains. Both research in the analytical tradition and research in the traditions of continental philosophy and theology have its esteemed place within the Societas.

Each year the Societas organizes a conference (mostly at the end of August). Members and non-members are invited to give a lecture or prepare a paper on the year-theme. The year-theme reflects an actual interest and debate in either applied ethics or fundamental ethics.

The Societas is bilingual: Engels and German are the official languages for conferences and publications. French is welcome, but cannot meet widespread understanding.

Secretariat 1991-1995
Centre for Bioethics and Health Law
Utrecht University
Heidelberglaan 2
NL-3584 CS Utrecht

Fax: (NL) 30-533241